Artificial Intelligence - Social, Ethical and Legal Issues

Edited by Elmer P. Dadios

Published in London, United Kingdom

Artificial Intelligence - Social, Ethical and Legal Issues
http://dx.doi.org/10.5772/intechopen.1002134
Edited by Elmer P. Dadios

Contributors
Abid Hussain, Adriana Antonieta Romero-Sandoval, Ahmad Alzahrani, Athanasios Simotas, Carla Pitarch, Carolina Migliorelli, Dimitrios Kardamakis, Elina Kontio, Gloriana J. Monko, Golnaz Sahebi, Ishrat Fatima, Jussi Salmi, Luís Marte, Mar Galofré, Mohamedi M. Mjahidi, Paula Subías-Beltrán, Paul Libbrecht, Pertti Ranttila, Roberto Nai, Rosa Meo, Sandra Rebholz, Silvia Orte, Wolfgang Müller, Ying Zheng

First published in London, United Kingdom, 2025 by IntechOpen
IntechOpen is the global imprint of INTECHOPEN LIMITED, registered in England and Wales, registration number: 11086078, 167-169 Great Portland Street, London, W1W 5PF, United Kingdom

For EU product safety concerns: IN TECH d.o.o., Prolaz Marije Krucifikse Kozulić 3, 51000 Rijeka, Croatia, info@intechopen.com or visit our website at intechopen.com.

British Library Cataloguing-in-Publication Data
A catalogue record for this book is available from the British Library

Artificial Intelligence - Social, Ethical and Legal Issues
Edited by Elmer P. Dadios
p. cm.

This title is part of the Artificial Intelligence Book Series, Volume 34
Topic: Applied Intelligence
Series Editor: Andries Engelbrecht
Topic Editor: Vladimir Robles-Bykbaev

Print ISBN 978-0-85466-497-9
Online ISBN 978-0-85466-496-2
eBook (PDF) ISBN 978-0-85466-498-6
ISSN 2633-1403

IntechOpen Book Series
Artificial Intelligence
Volume 34

Aims and Scope of the Series

Artificial Intelligence (AI) is a rapidly developing multidisciplinary research area that aims to solve increasingly complex problems. In today's highly integrated world, AI promises to become a robust and powerful means for obtaining solutions to previously unsolvable problems. This Series is intended for researchers and students alike interested in this fascinating field and its many applications.

Meet the Series Editor

Andries Engelbrecht received the Masters and Ph.D. degrees in Computer Science from the University of Stellenbosch, South Africa, in 1994 and 1999 respectively. He is currently appointed as the Voigt Chair in Data Science in the Department of Industrial Engineering, with a joint appointment as Professor in the Computer Science Division, Stellenbosch University. Prior to his appointment at Stellenbosch University, he has been at the University of Pretoria, Department of Computer Science (1998-2018), where he was appointed as South Africa Research Chair in Artifical Intelligence (2007-2018), the head of the Department of Computer Science (2008-2017), and Director of the Institute for Big Data and Data Science (2017-2018). In addition to a number of research articles, he has written two books, Computational Intelligence: An Introduction and Fundamentals of Computational Swarm Intelligence.

Meet the Volume Editor

Elmer P. Dadios earned his Ph.D. in Manufacturing Engineering from Loughborough University in the United Kingdom in Robotics and Intelligent Systems. He edited and published five books on fuzzy logic systems and a book on control and automation. He published over 600 Scopus-indexed technical papers in highly reputable journals and IEEE Xplore. He received the 2023 Philippines National Academy of Science and Technology (NAST) Academician award. In 2022, he received the Severino & Paz Koh Lectureship Award in Engineering from the Philippine American Academy of Science and Engineering and was honored with the Lifetime Achievement Award by the National Research Council of the Philippines. He currently holds the rank of Distinguished Professor and a University Fellow of the De La Salle University Manila in the Philippines. He is one of the founders and the Chairman of the Intelligent Systems Innovation Corporation Board. He was the past Chair of the IEEE Philippines Section, past EXCOM member of the IEEE Region 10, past Chair of the IEEE Region 10 Awards and Recognition Committee, the Founder and Chair of the IEEE Computational Intelligence Society Philippines Chapter, and IEEE Robotics and Automation Society Philippines Chapter.

Contents

Preface

The main motivation for developing Artificial Intelligence (AI) since the term was coined in the 1950s has been studying how to enable computers to perform tasks that humans do more effectively. Artificial Intelligence is one of the best and most significant discoveries of the 20th century. This book presents the impact of Artificial Intelligence on the progress of humanity. It aims to define the scope of Artificial Intelligence evolution by analyzing its history, current benefits and challenges, and further implications for social, ethical and legal issues. The impact of Artificial Intelligence on innovation will be examined, particularly in relation to human coexistence. The integration of economic and ethical values will be explored to drive progress in Artificial Intelligence. This book also discusses the pros and cons of Artificial Intelligence and its potential future applications, considering public concerns about global safety.

This book comprises nine chapters, carefully selected and arranged into three sections.

The first chapter, "Medical Ethics in the Era of Artificial Intelligence: A New Landscape in Medical Practice?", examines how Artificial Intelligence contributes to medical practice by enhancing the rules and standards of medical ethics. It was found that, under extreme conditions, doctors often face many ethical dilemmas and legal challenges that prevent them from making the best possible decisions with minimal side effects. Accurate medical diagnosis requires comprehensive knowledge of a patient's family history and psychological information, which is why Artificial Intelligence is crucial in executing precise decisions. In this way, AI is one of the pillars of medical ethics in modern medical practice.

The second chapter, "Medical AI in the EU: Regulatory Considerations and Future Outlook", discusses the potential and applications of Artificial Intelligence, which have already become a reality in many fields. However, challenges remain in the medical sector. The healthcare industry worldwide faces significant issues, including an aging population that requires more care, a stagnant workforce, rising treatment costs, and the increasing complexity of medical products that challenge the expertise of healthcare professionals. Artificial Intelligence has made significant progress in addressing these problems. This chapter examines some of the ethical and legal challenges AI faces in healthcare.

The third chapter, "The Role of Transparency in AI-Driven Technologies: Targeting Healthcare", delves into the pivotal role of transparency within AI-based applications, emphasizing its importance for reliability, accountability, and ensuring the ethical usage of AI targeting healthcare contexts. It examines multiple transparency characteristics and identifies its problems and limitations based on digital health real-world use cases. Current efforts and recommended strategies aiming at boosting transparency are discussed. It also examines ethical considerations like privacy, fairness, and security, which are crucial for developing transparent and reliable AI solutions.

The fourth chapter, "Designing Trustworthy AI in Higher Education", reviews available design approaches for building trustworthy Artificial Intelligence systems and evaluates their applicability in the context of higher education. Beyond the legal obligations, the trustworthy use of AI systems is not well publicized. Applying Artificial Intelligence systems and tools in the context of higher education imposes many challenges with respect to data privacy and ethics.

The fifth chapter, "Unlocking the Potential of Artificial Intelligence in Academic Libraries", discusses the best features of Artificial Intelligence in education and libraries, its barriers and the challenges that hinder libraries from adopting it. Emerging technology has brought a tremendous revolution in our activities, making our work easy and efficient. Artificial Intelligence in education and libraries is commendable, and it has made library operations more sophisticated and faster.

The sixth chapter, "Exploring AI Applications in Essay-Based Assignments: Affordances and Risks", examines the feasibility of using AI to provide feedback on essay-based assignments. It investigates AI applications in essay evaluation, utilizing data from four AI-generated essays and their corresponding feedback. Results indicate that assessors could detect characteristics consistent with AI generation and noted ethical concerns regarding deviations from academic standards.

The seventh chapter, "Competencies Replaceable by Artificial Intelligence in the Tuning Project for Latin America", explores the collaboration between AI technologies and human professionals, emphasizing the potential to uphold values such as trust, empathy, and ethical practice. This chapter investigates which generic competencies within the Tuning Project in Latin America can be taken over by AI and which ones still require human intervention.

The eighth chapter, "From Bias to Balance: Navigating Gender Inclusion in AI", presents current methodologies for embedding inclusivity into AI development and provides a blueprint for developers, researchers, and policymakers committed to closing the gender gap. It serves as a critical resource for anyone seeking to understand and implement gender-inclusive practices in AI, pushing the boundaries of what it means to achieve fairness in the digital age.

The ninth and final chapter, "Machine Learning in Procurement with a View to Equity", explores the use of machine learning in analyzing big data from tenders. It discusses how this technology can benefit public administrators and economic operators by enhancing the procurement process and providing exploratory and cognitive tools to extract valuable insights from available big data.

Elmer P. Dadios
Department of Manufacturing Engineering and Management,
De La Salle University,
Manila, Philippines

Section 1

Challenges and Opportunities of AI in Medical Healthcare Technologies

Chapter 1

Medical Ethics in the Era of Artificial Intelligence: A New Landscape in Medical Practice?

Athanasios Simotas and Dimitrios Kardamakis

Abstract

Purpose of this study is to examine how AI interferes with medical practice by enhancing medical ethics rules and standards. Also, this research examines how AI contributes to medical confidentiality which stands as a key role of medical ethics to its mandate for beneficence. Another matter is a complete medical diagnosis that demands accurate family history and psychological information about the patients. Qualitative research has been conducted from August 2020 through December 2021 with the use of a closed type of questionnaire including both questions and case studies. The type and form of the questionnaire have been determined by the nature of the medical profession and the very limited free time of physicians. The questionnaire was distributed only to medical doctors and physicians in Greece who were registered as active members of medical associations. Within the context of Medical Ethics, AI can be used to minimize the human error and help the doctor decide according to the best interest of the patient. In the future AI will be even more capable so further research must be under way to recreate boundaries and keep AI accountable for actions or mistakes that have been made under its control.

Keywords: artificial intelligence, medical ethics, legal challenges, medical practice, best interest of the patient, autonomy, beneficence, justice, ethical challenges, clinical practice

1. Introduction

Artificial intelligence (AI) is the simulation of human intelligence processes by machines, especially computer systems. AI requires specialized hardware and software for writing and training machine learning algorithms. Examples of AI applications include expert systems, natural language processing (NLP), speech recognition and machine vision. In general, AI systems work by ingesting large amounts of labeled training data, analyzing that data for correlations and patterns, and using these patterns to make predictions about future states. Programming AI systems focus on cognitive skills such as Learning, Reasoning, Self-correction, and Creativity. Especially AI applications in Medicine are classified either as virtual (from electronic health record systems to neural network-based treatment decisions) or as physical (robotic surgery, care for the elderly) [1]. Artificial intelligence (AI) and machine learning (ML) technologies are revolutionizing health care by offering unprecedented opportunities to enhance patient care, optimize clinical workflows and advance medical research. AI applications have transformed healthcare. While the cognitive component of AI is superior to that of human intelligence, it lacks consciousness, intuition and adaptation to unexpected situations. Furthermore, fundamental questions arise regarding data security, the impact on healthcare professionals and the distribution of roles between physicians and AI especially concerning consent to medical care and liability in the event of a therapeutic harm.

Legal practitioners are increasingly utilizing various types of AI and data analytics tools and smart virtual assistants to enhance their work efficiency, streamline tasks, and improve client services. The goal of those tools is to assist lawyers in managing their workload more efficiently, improving client services, and enabling them to focus on higher-level legal tasks that require human expertise, resulting in the transformation of legal tasks – from legal research and review to contract management and the prediction of litigation outcomes Smart virtual assistant tools based on Machine learning (ML) and NLP are proving useful to assist lawyers in legal research and e-discovery, predictive legal analysis, case management and legal advice.

The use of AI in legal practice, however, brings about various legal and ethical issues. These include accuracy and accountability, transparency, trust, communication, and duty of competent representation, bias and fairness, privacy, data protection, conflict of interests, and duty of confidentiality, lack of human judgment and interpretation, and job displacement and loss of domain expertise. There is clearly great promise in what AI tools can and will do to support legal professionals in their work but beyond the hype, there is still a need to fully understand how and when to use this technology and what are the inherent risks [2].

Medical Ethics are general regulations which act as a guidance for good clinical practice according to doctor's free consciousness and the respect to human autonomy and dignity. There are four pillars that constitute the concept and spectrum of medical ethics: Justice, autonomy, beneficence, and non-maleficence, which hold health care professionals accountable for keeping up with both medical legislation and empirical ethics in medicine. The term "Medical Deontology" refers to confidentiality, the limits of physician's responsibility for the best interest of the patients, relationships among physicians and health care professionals as well as the physician's ethical boundaries. According to Medical Deontology, the physician must evince maximum attention and apply all his experience to restore patient's health or bring relief from distressing symptoms.

Medical practice consists of all medical actions and options of physicians, surgeons and every medical or clinical specialty that intervenes with patients, handling crucial and sensitive cases. AI rises as a limitless source of potential by enhancing doctors' knowledge. Physicians deal with very difficult situations at hospitals such as emergencies and surgeries, so every physician needs to adopt and operate according to the unspoken habits of the medical system, while controlling AI options under the rules of Medical Ethics and current legislation.

The aim of this study is to examine how AI can affect medical practice in the context of medical ethics rules and standards. This is the first time that AI is being put under analysis of its contribution to medical ethics and deontology standards in medicine. In extreme conditions like the recent Covid-19 pandemic, health personnel were struggling to handle mass life failure and at the same time to confront with ethical dilemmas and legal challenges. Also, this research examines how AI contributes to medical confidentiality which stands as a key role of medical ethics to its mandate for beneficence. Another matter is a complete medical diagnosis that demands accurate family history and psychological information about the patients. AI can execute precisely, evolving as a fifth pillar of medical ethics in medical practice.

2. Materials and methods

Under this perspective, qualitative research has been conducted from August 2020 through December 2021 with the use of a closed type of questionnaire including both questions and case studies. The type and form of the questionnaire have been determined by the nature of the medical profession and the very limited free time of physicians. The questionnaire was distributed only to medical doctors and physicians in Greece who were registered as active members of medical associations. Answers have been collected by 452 physicians across all ranks, ages, genders, different specialties and clinical expertise. About 71% of the physicians worked in NHS Hospitals, 16% in Private Hospitals and 13% in Private Practices. The research findings have been severely affected by the pandemic – Covid-19 and the mass life failure. Moreover, all hospitals and clinics dealt with the fact that they have had too few staff members to operate effectively. These two key factors have shaped the collected answers (**Table 1**).

3. Results and Discussion

3.1 Medical ethics in the era of AI

In recent years, there has been an increasing debate about the application of new methods of data analysis in clinical practice, with unknown long-term consequences and questionable results for the medical profession [3]. In the period of the Covid-19 pandemic, computerized AI information systems helped the medical profession

Phases of the study	
P1	**References and scientific studies examination for the development of the research**
P2	Design of questionnaire and sample determination
P3	Questionnaires to participants
P4	Statistical analysis and qualitative findings
P5	Writing process of discussion and conclusions

Timeline analysis of individual phase

Phases of study	**May 2020**	**Aug 2020**	**March 2021**	**until**	**Dec. 2021**	**Jan. 2022 to Sept 2022**	**Oct 2022**	**Dec 2023**
P-1								
P-2								
P-3								
P-4								
P-5								

Table 1.
The demographic data of the participants are shown in **Table 2**. **Table 3** *shows the questions and the answers.*

Type of questionnaire			
Google Forms	69		15,26%
E-mails	188		41,59%
Paper copy	195		43,15%
Gender			
Men		62,3%	
Women		37,7%	
Other			
Specialties			
Oncologists			54.9%
Internists			7.9%
Cardiologist			5,8%
Pediatricians			4,3%
Surgeons			4,3%
Other specialties			22.8%
Place of work			
NHS Hospital			71%
Private Hospital			16%
Private practice			13%
Age of participants			
20–35			9,7%
36–55			57,5%
56–80			24,1%
No answer			8,7%
Residency			
Athens			27,53%
Piraeus			5.79%
Thessaloniki			11,59%
Patras			46,37%
Rest of Greece			8,72%

Table 2.
Demographic data of participants.

enormously by suggesting ways to better utilize the available medical resources (e.g., oxygen masks and emergency beds) when the human mind, in the chaos of the clinical effort to save as many lives as possible, was not in the mental clarity of utilizing all available information and opportunities. In the context of protecting both doctors and patients in all aspects of the medical profession, the World Health Organization has issued guidelines and requirements for the use of this new technology, with a view to defending human rights and medical ethical values in the face of a revolutionary scientific method that can make a major contribution to public health [4].

Questions	Answers		
	Yes	No	Do not know/ no answer
1. Do you think that there is breach of medical ethics rules at clinical practice?	70%	15%	15%
1. Are you aware of any medical ethics database or a handbook at your clinic?	13%	57%	30%
1. Have you even been registered at a conference about medical ethics?	43%	55%	2%
1. Have you ever supported the dignity of the patient even against the rules of medical ethics?	60%	22%	18%
1. Do you think that a very important illegal medical action is ethical if it is made without patient's consent?	36%	46%	18%
Case studies	**Right**	**Wrong**	
1. A 16-year-old mother left the clinic with the newborn baby avoiding the obstetrician without the presence of the biological father.	36%	64%	
1. The gynecologist did not inform the husband for the genetically transmitted disease of the of the pregnant mother	34%	66%	
1. The surgeon ordered for surgery the 60-year-old patient over the 17-year-old one despite both having been transferred there at the same time from the same severe car accident.	79%	21%	
1. The physician vaccinated the patient against his will because he was religiously opposed to any relevant action.	48%	52%	
1. The physician informs over the telephone a relative of a pregnant woman for her will to proceed to abortion due to psychological problems.	21%	79%	
Do you think that the rules of medical ethics affect medical decision about:			
	Yes		No
1. Abortion	87%		13%
1. Organ transplantation	95,7%		4,3%
1. Personal information disclosure (GDPR)	94,2%		5,8%
1. The use of stem cells on human surgery	88,4%		11,6%
1. The use of participants in clinical studies	91,3%		8,7%
1. The reproductive cloning	86%		14%
1. The postmortem fertilization	73,9%		26,1%
Education on medical ethics			
Questions	**Yes**	**No**	**Do not know/no answer**
1. Has your professional institution any medical ethics rules database or a handbook?	13%	56,5%	30,5%
1. Have you ever participated in a conference or a seminar about medical ethics?	43,5%	55,1%	1,4%
1. Do the rules of medical ethics affect the creation of DNA database?	87,4%	11,6%	1%

Table 3.
Questionnaires.

Many scientific communities are applying AI, driven by the extraction of quality workloads with minimal errors, combined with data mining and big data analytics. The horizons opened for their constructive application in healthcare are limitless, as are the possible combinations of drugs and treatments for patients. Particularly worthy of mention in medicine is the method of bio-statistical informatics, which is called upon to make full and efficient use of the new capital of AI. As new technological clinical applications and possibilities emerge, it seems inconceivable today that AI should not be exploited to maximize the benefits for both the doctor and the patient.

However, the manner and conditions of such an undertaking in the light of the good clinical practice are placed under the fear of the heresy of judgment. It is humanly impossible for the physician to include in the exercise of his medical profession the processing of the extensively increasing volume of medical data of patients within the framework of his already burdened duties. AI has already shown great examples in many aspects of medicine such as efficient analysis of patient medical data on a large scale, finding potential risks to patients, and therapy regimens.

In addition, AI capabilities include advanced diagnostic and monitoring techniques in the field of patient health, data mining for optimal patient care through the comparative study and analysis of medical literature and clinical reports (patient risk stratification), evaluation of the effectiveness of patient health diagnosis and monitoring methods, and adaptation of AI to different disease situations through appropriate computational tools.

At this point, the major challenge that AI poses to medical ethics and good practice becomes immediately apparent. Diagnostic methods cannot constitute diagnosis as such because they substitute medical judgment [5]. The AI can suggest many possible answers to the doctor, but the doctor must judge which one best fits the patient's symptoms. Once again, the most appropriate methods of treatment are left to the doctor's discretion, since he is now only required to choose one of the suggestions made by the AI. In a sense, the judgment is removed because, in the circumstances, only the medical board could resolve the disagreement between the doctor and the AI. Every doctor has certain qualitative characteristics that cannot currently quantify with the help of technology. The empathy, compassion, understanding and differential thinking that evolves from these qualities of human character make AI incomplete and incapable of putting such qualitative variables into the mathematical equations which is required to solve in a short time.

3.2 AI and medical ethics: Searching for the missing link

The effectiveness of AI is based on the mining of big data, where research, analyses, comparisons, and inferences are made to stage clinical cases and propose treatment options. More specifically, the software can extract massive data from electronic records of existing patients, such as genetic modifications, symptoms, treatments, and outcomes of treatment regimens. Then, the AI software applies the data of these patients to similar clinical cases of new patients, thus managing to predict the most appropriate combination of treatment options. In the same way, AI can predict the correct diagnosis by evaluating, using complex software tools, thousands of parameters, and details that may escape medical attention [6].

However, achieving this function requires clearly expressed and written informed consent from patients. Since this is in question, the health system is called upon to rigorously examine whether the rules are being complied with personal data protection regulations because otherwise, the right to the free development of the individual's personality, as enshrined in constitutional amendments, is suspended. On a practical level, the good clinical practice is seriously affected because the doctor relying on AI for the safety of the diagnostic process may not have very important data at his disposal, due to the barrier to data mining by the European General Data Protection Regulation, which would otherwise help the physician make the best decision for the patient. In cases where there is an error in the electronic assessment systems, the physician is in an extremely difficult position because he is affected by a lack of ability to form a correct judgment, whereby the medical judgment is consequently removed.

3.3 The necessity to adjust the rules of good clinical practice in the era of AI

One of the most basic parameters in good clinical practice is the confidentiality of communication between doctor and patient, as reflected in the rules of medical ethics. The doctor will be able to act correctly, after listening to the patient, regarding all the factual and psychological elements that make up the difficult mosaic of correct diagnosis. AI can only help in clinical practice if it is full of information. The programmer should have at his disposal the set of data that will help him to introduce into the software the appropriate research and analysis parameters. If a patient, due to religious beliefs, does not wish to provide blood for the appropriate tests or for transfusion in the case of a hematological disease, then he/she will report this to the physician so that he/she can adapt the method of treatment or the appropriate procedure with respect to the patient's right to autonomy. In case the AI data has not defined religion as a data parameter, then the physician who will rely only on the software, fails in practice, even if in the reality of computers, he/she seems correct. In that spectrum, good clinical practice should always monitor the proposing outcome of an electronic system no matter how accurate it may seem [7].

This becomes even more evident in the cases of medical boards, where the human interaction of fellow physicians and doctors and discussion of patient issues bring about the best possible outcome for the patient. In an oncology board where more specialties are involved, due to the critical condition of a patient, AI can help by making available to doctors all those possible options that are most appropriate, so that the board can make the best decision for the patient. Such a case introduces into medical practice the notion of collective good deed, since the decision on the legitimate and beneficial action comes through the co-decision of the collective body called the medical council. Therefore, it is immediately clear that AI cannot participate as a complete entity in collective bodies and therefore cannot co-decide. However, a skilled programmer could integrate the rules of medical ethics into the parameters considered by the software to draw qualitative conclusions that respect the patient's personality and right to information and autonomy.

Another concrete example that demonstrates the great potential of artificial intelligence is the assistance in prenatal diagnosis, with indications of serious fetal malformations that lead to the birth of an abnormal newborn or there is an unavoidable risk to the life of the pregnant woman or a risk of serious and lasting damage to her physical or mental health. In the context of the confidentiality of the doctor-patient relationship and communication, AI could consider multiple factors of sensitive data of the pregnant woman to extract appropriate information about the development of a fetus that was produced in a way that falls under the provisions of termination of pregnancy [8]. The rules of good clinical practice must be adjusted to meet the new era. In the near future, informed consent will have to include the intervention of AI as far as upcoming results is concerned.

3.4 Legally binding actions and medical ethics through AI

There have been many cases where a physician under his care two or more patients in critical condition who need treatment at the same time in such a way that there is no possible option to cover the best interest of all patients. The doctor must choose under the pressure of limited time and resources. The beneficence of one patient may be in contrast with the maleficence of the other patient. Nowadays, legal systems around the world enforce strict penalties to doctors who discriminate between patients, even under difficult situations. AI may create important safety nets to physicians who must deal with such crucial operational tactics. A strong date base with proper programming will be able to extract much more accurate outcome possibilities than a single physician or an old predictive algorithm. Setting many symptoms in a multitasking electronic board may result in a quick guide to heal the most severely wounded patient who otherwise would have passed away. This could be a fine way to respect medical ethics even if the legal system would rule against such judgment.

A good example would be the situation where the AI system guides the doctors to treat a young patient with allergic reaction of unknown cause who has been transferred second to the emergency room than an old patient who came in first with a different diagnosis. Both have been injured, and now they are still alive, but if the doctor respected the rule of law, then his action would be legal and lethal at the same time. Moreover, there have been situations where medical ethics respecting patient's autonomy may cause a critical failure. When blood transfusion is not permitted by the patient or the caregiver for religious reasons, then artificial intelligence would be able to step up and find a way to support a life worth living without disrespecting autonomy of the patient. The balance of law and medical ethics could put in good use the AI systems in a way that conflicts between actions would not be either illegal or causing maleficence to patients.

A key element of medical ethics is the beneficence of the patient, and it is very crucial in patients in critical conditions such as comatose state. A legal action is to pull the plug when doctors can confirm that there will be no coming back but the surrogate or the next of kin may act otherwise. AI may be used to manage sensitive health information of the patient. Doctors could use this data to execute brain stimulation in a way that a patient may come back from a trauma due to a severe car accident or soldiers who have been wounded at war [9]. Such technological advances could really affect many legal binding actions that prevent the best interest of a patient according to medical ethics. In that way AI will be able to bridge any gap between justice and beneficence which are two of the founding pillars of medical ethics.

3.5 AI and medical practice: Opportunities and restraints

One of the greatest enemies of medical ethics is violence in health care institutions which is a social problem that hides in the shadows of almost every Hospital and Medical Practice. There is either psychological (vis compulsiva) and verbal abuse or physical abuse (vis absoluta). Physicians are constantly victims of violence coming from patients or their relatives. Sometimes a doctor can be a victim of verbal abuse even at clinic by a superior officer. The same situation applies to nurses and administrative officers. AI could be the key to unlock a new way of protecting victims in the hospitals and clinics [10]. The system could create a special registry of violence reports with categories about the person who offended and the victim, separating the type of abuse and the outcome. A fine example would be the administrative officers who are always in the front line, dealing with many difficult cases of relative and surrogates who can be offensive. Medical ethics guidelines apply to all medical staff and paramedical administration, but the patients and their relatives are those who will lose their patience at different extreme circumstances.

Another restraint at the medical practice is the law itself. Usually, medical ethics have guidelines that obey certain laws, but the physician is not fully aware of the legal concept. AI may be a quick way to bridge that important gap between ethical decision making under proper legal mandate. In the emergency unit, time is not the best alley of the medical team and many times there can be a great difficulty to operate within legal boundaries so AI using high-speed scanning capabilities would be able to provide the physician with the proper legal background, enabling the surgeon to perform for the best interest of the patient. In some incidents, there may be more than one applicable legal action so a properly programmed electronic assistant could analyze multiple options and let the doctor propose the best possible action to the patient, leaving the final decision to the person in need. In the same concept, strong decision-making demands an accurate and full medical file. AI can extract the most detailed information about a disease using the available data and contribute to the diagnosis and treatment when there is not enough time and at the same time serving the purpose of personalized medicine according to medical ethics.

3.6 The burden of ethical decision in organ transplantation through AI

There have been many medical cases where a physician has been between two crucial options and not enough time to decide, but probably the most important choice in surgery could be the organ transplant. It is a procedure deriving from the person as an organ donor who will not survive, and he or she is offering life to patients who will not survive either without a new organ. Most of the cases, patients wait long enough to face a critical condition when any surgery will not be enough. Health law and medical ethics co-exist to help doctors and surgeons in the best interest of the patient who needs an organ transplant, but a revelation has risen to change everything for the better. AI data base will enable doctors to find a compatible organ for the patient immediately and thus making a surgery under success. This new era of technological advance will free physicians from the heavy burden of an ethical decision with unknown future consequences.

In many cases, the surgery is a success, and the patient may live some more years with a new organ, but through months of living a good life, a body may reject a donated organ and another perfect match seems impossible. There is an important ethical debate over the transplantation of animal organs to human beings. Although it is a legal action in many countries, the patients will not survive because either the organ is rejected or there are many fatal side effects. Moreover, ethicists argue that people should not kill animals for organ transplant to humans. AI may be the proper scientific way to solve this problem and make organ transplant allocation between patients accurate and quick by combining calculations over perfect compatibility and minimum side effects. A fine example of saving precious time through AI would be the daily co-ordination in national and international level of all the available organs that have been offered for transplant to patients in need [11].

3.7 Problem solving vs. decision making within medical ethics spectrum

In every day medical practice, young physicians tend to use a new program that is developed under an advanced AI platform known us generative pre-trained transformer with the commercial branded name "ChatGPT." This product is marketed as an improved problem-solving version of previous developments by programmers. This program is not only designed for questions and answers but also for image scanning and analysis, helping doctors as a highly promising scientific tool for the clinic [12].

In practice, a physician can open the application on the mobile phone and scan with the onboard camera the patient's test results images for quick and accurate analysis and treatment. Until now, there are no legal consequences upon the electronic system itself let alone the developers or the marketing company because a system can only answer so many questions as the developer makes it predict by proper programming. The potential of ChatGPT is very strong in analyzing optical coherence tomography images, magnetic resonance images, chest X-rays, and many imaging applications. Be that as it may, it becomes obvious the fact that AI is offering great details at clinical laboratories and image processing needs of doctors, especially in surgery where a detailed presentation of the due procedure may unveil important data that the surgeon must take into consideration before operating [13]. Moreover, radiation oncologists and hematologists will be benefited from the precising execution of the new intelligent tools of blood analysis and chemotherapy or immunotherapy protocols. Ethical challenges arise though, every time a physician will tragically rely on this new form of technology and a patient will be in critical condition. The hammer of justice will crash upon the human factor who makes the decision and not upon an application or a program. An experienced doctor can spot the difference between two possible options for the best interest of the patient, but the patient should be properly informed about the options available by the AI because the patient's autonomy must always be respected and be put first and foremost [14].

3.8 Accountability of AI according to medical ethics

The goal of medical ethics is always to secure the best interest of the patient, but this should be achieved without sacrificing the physician's own beliefs and well-being. Legal challenges arise when a fatal mistake may occur due to AI. For the time being, no legal foundation exists to hold AI itself accountable for privacy violations especially in concern to medical files and sensitive information. There is yet a legal foundation to accuse AI of negligence upon a patient in critical condition. Uncontrollable self-aware AI programs are not in accord with medical ethics because they lack the human factor of empathy and there may be no legal foundation for penalties because there is no human presence to be connected to. Ethical challenges are under debate when a double-blind clinical study becomes a victim of algorithmic bias caused by bad data [15]. If a self-aware artificial program malfunctions and there is no human factor to put the blame on, then soon enough science may find itself without practical protection either by law or by practice. Future amendments should be reconsidered when it comes to self-aware computer dynamic and its potential impact to the world of actions and consequences.

3.9 The elements of empathy and sympathy of medical ethics in AI reality

Empathy is the ability to emotionally understand what other people feel, see things from their point of view and imagine oneself in their place. Sympathy is the feeling of pity for another human being and the relief for not having the same problems [16].

Both have the elements of emotion and understanding on a human manner. A physician should always weight every option according to rule of beneficence for the best interest of the patient. Thus, comes to the surface the healing method of personalized medicine which means that a medical protocol or a surgical procedure is tailored exactly to the patient's needs. AI is capable of meticulously analyzing every step of the process within a personalized medical care plan with speed and accuracy but without any empathy or emotion. This is a great example of the assistant role of AI to the physician since it may cover every possible fact and data, leaving the final call to the human factor [17].

In this way, the doctor will be kept accountable for any mistakes or critical side effects to the patient without expecting a computerized network to substitute medical staff in decision making. A crucial case may shine light to this serious matter. A very close relative of an emergency doctor is in critical condition with only a few days left. The doctor is devastated and not capable of making any decision at this stage for the beloved person. AI system reports that due to lack of beds at the clinic the doctor should act to remedy the issue as soon as possible. Medical ethics guide the doctor in treating the patient within the directives of palliative care to let the patient pass away with dignity. For the time being there is no way to hold this doctor accountable for not complying with the report of the electronic system [18]. To the contrary, every medical professional should practice medicine with empathy for the best interest of the patient according to the rule of non-maleficence. Dignity is a constitutionally guaranteed right in many nations, deriving from the protection of personality according to medical ethics tables [3, 4]. **Tables 4** and **5** offer a consistent description of key elements regarding the role of AI in medical practice and medical ethics.

1. Patient privacy and data security	i. Ensuring the confidentiality of patient information in AI systems. ii. Addressing potential breaches and misuse of data. iii. 60% of the patients lack trust of AI in healthcare.
1. Informed consent	i. How to properly inform patients about the use of AI in their care. ii. Ensuring patients understand how their data will be used by AI systems.
1. Bias and fairness	i. Identifying and mitigating biases in AI algorithms to ensure equitable treatment across different populations. ii. Ensuring AI systems do not perpetuate existing health disparities.
1. Transparency and accountability	i. Ensuring AI systems are transparent in their decision-making processes. ii. Establishing clear lines of accountability when AI systems are used in medical decisions.
1. AI in diagnosis and treatment	i. Ethical considerations of AI assisting or replacing human judgment in diagnosis and treatment plans. ii. Ensuring that AI recommendations are evidence-based and reliable.
1. Autonomy and human oversight	i. Balancing the use of AI with maintaining human oversight and control in medical decisions. ii. Ensuring that AI aids rather than overrides human expertise and patient autonomy.
1. Regulation and governance	i. Developing appropriate regulatory frameworks to oversee the use of AI in healthcare. ii. Establishing guidelines and standards for the development and implementation of AI technologies.

1. Impact on healthcare professionals	i. Addressing the impact of AI on the roles and responsibilities of healthcare professionals. ii. Ensuring that AI enhances rather than diminishes the value of human skills and expertise.

Table 4.
Ethical considerations about interception of AI technology in medical practice.

Covering matters	Ways of contribution
Education	Create an international platform of guidelines in many languages to help doctors learn medical ethics and artificial intelligence potential.
Imaging analysis	Detailed presentation of all available electronic files of patients on every specialty either pathology or surgery.
Problem solving	Special registry of fast and accurate possibilities of resolving an issue between the programmed spectrum of medical ethics.
Decision making	Help the doctor decide according to the best interest of the patient and not just substitute the human judgment with information and data.
Accountability	Set an electronic platform including all the medical legislation which is very important to the physician on clinical practice.

Table 5.
Contribution of AI on medical ethics.

4. Conclusions

Within the context of Medical Ethics, AI can be used to minimize human error and help the doctor decide according to the best interest of the patient. Having taken everything into consideration, an advanced algorithm will be able to become the devoted servant of the physician by selecting one out of many key options for the best interest of the patient. Medical ethics guide the physician to concentrate on the patient according to legal standards, and accurate information is available through the most promising and advanced technology available to date. A modern physician will be the key person for communicating every option available to the patient. AI contributes in different ways across many specialties. Surgery takes advantage of accurate imaging analysis while emergency doctors rely on fast problem-solving. In pathology, decision-making can minimize mistakes due to AI contribution. Even in cases where AI may be the last resort, every medical professional can always balance the technological guidance with human empathy. AI enhances patient privacy and data security wile mitigating biases and ensuring that informed consent will be made properly. AI can hold physicians accountable for their actions according to medical ethics and enforce transparency in co-decision-making process between doctor and patient. The principles of justice, autonomy, beneficence, and non-maleficence have been the four pillars of medical ethics for millennia. AI is rising as the fifth pillar of medical ethics cementing its endurance in future challenges. It will ensure that the best interest of the patient is taken into consideration regardless of personal opinions of medical professionals engaged in a healthcare plan. In the future, AI will be even more capable so further research must be underway to recreate boundaries and keep AI accountable for actions or mistakes that have been made under its possible controlled contribution or side effects [19, 20]. The emergence of ethical concerns surrounding Artificial intelligence has led to an explosion of high-level ethical principles being published by several public and private organizations. However, there is a need to consider how AI developers can be practically assisted to anticipate, identify, and address ethical issues regarding AI technologies, particularly for the development of AI intended for healthcare settings, where applications will often interact directly with patients in various states of vulnerability. Despite the mammoth advantages of AI in the medical field, there exists inconsistency in the ethical and legal framework for the application of AI in healthcare. Although research has been conducted by various medical disciplines investigating the ethical implications of AI in the healthcare setting, the literature lacks a solid and holistic approach.

Acknowledgements

This effort has been made possible because of the vision of emeritus professor Dimitrios Kardamakis.

Conflict of interest

The authors declare no conflict of interest.

Author details

Athanasios Simotas* and Dimitrios Kardamakis
Medical School, University of Patras, Patras, Greece

*Address all correspondence to: up1058520@upatras.gr

References

[1] Amisha Malik P, Pathania M, Rathaur VK. Overview of artificial intelligence in medicine. Journal of Family Medicine and Primary Care. 2019;**8**(7):2328-2331. DOI: 10.4103/jfmpc.jfmpc_440_19. Available from: https://www.techtarget.com/searchenterpriseai/definition/AI-Artificial-Intelligence [Accessed: June 18, 2024]

[2] Gauci J-P, MacAlpine H. Use of Artificial Intelligence in Legal Practice, Authored by Irene Pietropaoli, with the Support of Iris Anastasiadou. London: British Institute of International and Comparative Law Report; 2023

[3] IBM. What Is Artificial Intelligence in Medicine? [Internet]. Armonk, NY: IBM; 2024. Available from: https://www.ibm.com/topics/artificial-intelligence-medicine

[4] Robert R, Kentish-Barnes N, Boyer A, et al. Ethical dilemmas due to the covid-19 pandemic. Annals of Intensive Care. 2020;**10**:84

[5] James TA. How Artificial Intelligence Is Disputing Medicine and What it Means for Physicians. Boston, MA: Harvard Medical School; 13 Apr 2023. Available from: https://postgraduateeducation.hms.harvard.edu/trends-medicine/how-artificial-intelligence-disrupting-medicine-what-means-physicians

[6] Alowais SA, Alghamdi SS, et al. Revolutionizing healthcare: The role of artificial intelligence in clinical practice. BMC Medical Education. 2023;**23**:289

[7] World Health Organization. Ethics and Governance of Artificial Intelligence for Health. Geneva: World Health Organization; 2021. Available from: https://www.who.int/publications/i/item/9789240029200

[8] Oprescu MA, Miro-amarante G, et al. Artificial intelligence in pregnancy: A scoping review. IEEE Access. 2020;**8**:181450-181484

[9] Lee EJ, Kim YH, et al. Deep into the brain: Artificial intelligence in stroke imaging. Journal of Stroke. 2017;**19**(3):277-285

[10] Critical Condition: Violence Against Health Care in Conflict. 2023. Available from: https://reliefweb.int/report/occupied-palestinian-territory/critical-condition-violence-against-health-care-conflict-2023

[11] Tourani R, Dennis H, et al. Consensus modeling: Safer transfer learning for small health systems. Artificial Intelligence in Medicine. 2024;**154**:102899

[12] Ethan W, Joshua O, et al. GPT-4 and medical image analysis: Strengths, weaknesses and future directions. Journal of Medical Artificial Intelligence. 30 Dec 2024;**6**:6-29

[13] Sarofim M. Devil's advocate: Exploring the potential negative impacts of artificial intelligence on the field of surgery. Journal of Medical Artificial Intelligence. 30 Mar 2024;**7**:23-158

[14] Ahmed L, Constantinidou A, Chatzittofis A. Patients' perspectives related to ethical issues and risks in precision medicine: A systematic review. Frontiers in Medicine. 2023;**10**:1215663. DOI: 10.3389/fmed.2023.1215663

[15] Mike T. 12 Risks and Dangers of Artificial Intelligence. Builtin.

2024. Available from: https://builtin.com/artificial-intelligence/risks-of-artificial-intelligence

[16] Oxford University Press. Oxford Dictionary, Revised Edition. Oxford, UK: Oxford University Press; 2011

[17] Uymaz P, Uymaz AO, Akgül Y. Assessing the behavioral intention of individuals to use an AI doctor at the primary, secondary, and tertiary care levels. International Journal of Human–Computer Interaction. 2023;**40**:1-18

[18] Becker A. Artificial intelligence in medicine: What is it doing for us today? Health Policy and Technology. 2019;**8**(2):198-205

[19] Rajeev R et al. Ethical AI in Healthcare: A Focus on Responsibility, Trust and Safety. Jersey City, NJ: Forbes; Jan 2024. Available from: https://www.forbes.com/sites/forbesbooksauthors/2024/01/04/ethical-ai-in-healthcare-a-focus-on-responsibility-trust-and-safety/ [Accessed: January 5, 2024]

[20] McLennan S et al. Embedded ethics: A proposal for integrating ethics into the development of AI. BMC Medical Ethics. 2022;**23**:6

Chapter 2

Medical AI in the EU: Regulatory Considerations and Future Outlook

Pertti Ranttila, Golnaz Sahebi, Elina Kontio and Jussi Salmi

Abstract

In many countries around the world, the healthcare sector is facing difficult problems: the aging population needs more care at the same time as the workforce is not growing, the cost of treatments is going up, and the more and more technical medical products are placing serious challenges to the expertise of the healthcare professionals. At the same time, the field of artificial intelligence (AI) is making big leaps, and naturally, AI is also suggested as a remedy to these problems. In this article, we discuss some of the ethical and legal problems facing AI in the healthcare field, with case study of European Union (EU) regulations and the local laws in one EU member state, Finland. We also look at some of the directions that the AI research in medicine will develop in the next 3–10 years. Especially, Large Language Models (LLMs) and image analysis are used as examples. The potential of AI is huge and the potential has already become a reality in many fields, but in medicine, there remain obstacles. We discuss both technical and regulatory questions related to the expansion of AI techniques used in the clinical environment.

Keywords: artificial intelligence, image analysis, large language models, health care, medical AI, ethics

1. Introduction

Artificial Intelligence has a very promising future in the healthcare sector. The medical environment constantly produces a lot of structured and unstructured data about the patients. There exist in many diseases millions of patients with the same symptoms, treatments, laboratory tests, etc. From early days, the medical field has been of special interest to the AI researcher community [1, 2]. The early researchers were quite optimistic about the prospects of AI in this field, but soon it was discovered that the number of details was too much for the AI systems of the 1980s. During recent years, the AI technologies have advanced both in terms of methods and hardware so much that quite many promises of the 1980s can be realized [3]. The neural network approaches can model complex diseases effectively and they are already in use in many fields. Also, the Large Language Models could be used to mine information from free-form patient texts, and they could be used in communication with the patients. However, a big hurdle to developing AI in the medical field is the tight data security. The data are highly sensitive, because they contain very intimate details about recognizable individuals. Also, the consequences of errors in AI devices are much greater in treatment processes than e.g. in interactive gameplay. Therefore, the medical field is strictly regulated, which makes it difficult to realize all the benefits of modern AI systems. There is a trade-off between the efficacy of medical devices and the risk level, and wisely, the health sector regulators are quite conservative with new technologies.

Scientific articles exist on the use of AI in the clinical work, but not that many systems are in daily routine use. Some works have been published on AI systems that are actually in use in hospitals. The well-known Mayo Clinic Cancer Center has developed a method using hypothesis-driven AI, where conventional knowledge about cancer treatment is combined with traditional data-driven data science [4]. Many research groups have developed LLMs that are tested on real-life data, but reports of their use are scarce.

Our interest in this chapter is to discuss both the technical and regulatory aspects of advancing the use of AI in the clinic. Often, the technical questions are more easily answered than the regulatory ones. An engineer can develop a model for performing an AI task independently but showing that it works and is safe is usually a more difficult and costly task. In this chapter, we will discuss more closely the regulatory and ethical aspects of AI in healthcare sector (Section 2), and we will look at some possible uses of AI in this sector (Sections 3 and 4). The sections in this chapter have been written by experts as introductions to the recent advancements in those fields.

1.1 Methodology

The EU regulation texts were collected from the EU website. The Finnish law texts were collected from the website of the Ministry of Health and Welfare of Finland and other government sources. The articles regarding the AI Act and medical device regulation (MDR) were searched with PubMed with the following keywords (**Table 1**). The articles were analyzed on the relevancy regarding the issues. To determine whether a paper is relevant, the paper needs to match all search components. The number of articles was too large to be covered in this review, so the most relevant and high-quality articles on this subject were selected by the authors. The literature review for Section 3 was conducted using various sources and databases including PubMed and IEEE (The Institute of Electrical and Electronics Engineers). The goal was to explore the role of AI in medical image analysis, particularly research

Section	Keywords	Since	Number of hits
2	"Synthetic data" + "healthcare"	2023	101
2	"Federated learning" + "healthcare"	2023	154
3	"Radiography research" + "Finland"	2021	3
3	"Error in Radiology"	1992	26
3	"Medical Imaging Technology" + "Applications"	1990	76
3	"Motion artifact reduction" + "magnetic resonance imaging"	1988	52
4	(Healthcare) AND (LLM OR ("large language model"))	2023	334

Table 1.
Search keywords for articles.

for diagnosing common diseases. The reference articles were chosen by matching. The literature review for Section 4 was conducted using PubMed. The goal was to explore the role of LLMs in medical image analysis. The reference articles were chosen by matching.

2. Medical device and AI regulation in EU and Finland

2.1 EU-level regulation

The European Union has several laws regulating the use of medical devices and artificial intelligence. The MDR [5] defines several levels of regulation for medical devices depending on their risk to the patient. Separate regulations exist for *in vitro* diagnostic medical devices (*In vitro* Diagnostics Regulation (IVDR)) and other medical devices (MDR). The devices may contain artificial intelligence algorithms, and the new EU Artificial Intelligence Act (EU AI Act) [6] defines another set of regulations for AI applications. Further regulation in the use of personal information was introduced in the General Data Protection Regulation (GDPR) [7]. When developing medical devices with AI capabilities, all of these must be followed and the device must be audited for both the MDR and AI act. The auditing is performed by specialized companies, notified bodies, which do not currently have enough experience in the AI auditions [8].

The purpose of the regulation is to ensure the safety and efficacy of the systems. The companies producing the devices must present evidence on these to the notified body when the system is brought to the market and they must set up a monitoring procedure to ensure that the use of the devices stays safe as long as they are in use. The reporting and monitoring requirements are higher when the risk level of the system is higher, see **Table 1** for the risk levels. If the users of the device report problems with the device, the producer must also have a process for correcting possible errors in the product. This places high costs on the companies. The exact guidelines on how the medical AI devices should be audited are not clear yet.

The AI act defines four levels of risk in MDR, see **Table 2**. Devices with unacceptable risk are not allowed. These include e.g. social scoring systems and systems, which manipulate children to do dangerous things. High-risk devices are allowed but they require conformity assessment to ensure that they follow the principles of trustworthy AI, which have been defined here [9]. The principles include lawfulness, adherence to ethical principles, and robustness and reliability of the system. According to the trustworthiness guidelines, the AI system must be transparent, so that it can explain why it takes certain decisions. It must be inclusive, so that it works equally well with minorities. This is mostly a question of training data, which must be non-biased. Furthermore, the systems must be robust, they must be safe with regard

Class I	**Low risk**
Class IIa	Medium risk
Class IIb	Medium risk
Class III	High risk

Table 2.
Risk levels in MDR [5].

to data security, and they must enhance the capabilities of human doctors, nurses, and patients. Most medical AI systems presumably fall in the high-risk category, and so they need conformity assessment.

The AI Act is several hundred pages long. Understanding all the requirements combined with the requirements of the MDR, the process of developing AI systems for high-risk clinical use is a daunting task, especially for small- and medium-sized enterprises (SMEs). Already the regulation in medical applications in both the USA and Europe is so difficult that it hinders innovation. On the other hand, the regulation encourages companies to make better products and it helps in financing the research and development (R&D) because once the product is certified and in the market, it will not have cheap and simple competitors (**Table 3**).

2.2 Case study of Finland

To develop AI systems for medical use, clinical data are required. In each EU country, there can also be national laws that must be followed. EU directives override local legislation, but they can be complemented locally. In Finland, there are several laws that govern the use of medical data, which have been collected in hospitals in normal treatment processes for research and development purposes [10]. The Secondary Use Act [11] dictates that clinical data can be used for research and development purposes by applying for them from a national authority, Findata. Findata gives permission to use the data and collects the requested data from hospitals, harmonizes them, and releases them for the researchers in a specially audited secure computing environment. Findata is needed only if data were collected for normal treatment processes, and it is combined from more than one register keeper's registries. Currently, there are about 10 audited environments in Finland. Individual-level data cannot be downloaded from the environment. Only aggregate results, AI models, and statistical analysis results can be downloaded. Normal tools for statistics and also AI applications can be provided by the owner of the secure computing environment.

In Finland, there exist plenty of clinical data [10]. The healthcare system is publicly funded and mostly also publicly organized. There exist five university central hospitals where tertiary care is provided. These hospitals have good coverage of the population because private hospitals have a very small market share of tertiary care. The data have been recorded digitally for 15–20 years and they include everything from laboratory results to visits in the ward. In principle, the possibilities for developing AI systems in Finland are good, but there are some caveats. First, the public authority, which oversees the use of clinical data, Findata, has been struggling to complete data requests in a reasonable time. The waiting times have been 6–14 months. Second, the secure computing systems are not optimal places to develop proprietary complex AI systems. They may lack the capacity for training deep neural

Minimal risk
Limited risk
High risk
Unacceptable risk

Table 3.
Risk levels in AI Act regulation [6].

networks and the environment may not be customizable enough so that the routine development processes of companies can be transferred to the secure environments.

However, even though there are practical problems, the way that data with good coverage from all over Finland can be acquired through a single application is very interesting for researchers and pharmaceutical companies. In the traditional way of getting access to retrospective patient data, the researchers have had to contact quite many registers directly and apply for access. This can be very time-consuming and for a foreign company, it may mean the necessity to start research cooperation with local doctors in the country because in many cases this is required as part of the application process. There are still uncertainties on how this applies to image data or genomic data.

Furthermore, data from several countries are difficult to combine [10]. Hospitals and health organizations are, in general, reluctant to grant access to their data. Yet, if one wants to produce an AI medical device for the European or global market, it is necessary to train it and test it with several datasets preferably from several countries. The patient population is different, and the treatment and e.g. laboratory analysis methods are different, and therefore the usefulness of the system cannot be guaranteed with patient data from just one source.

A possible solution to the problem combining data from several sources is to use synthetic data [12]. Synthetic data are similar to the original data, but they have synthetic patients who cannot be identified in the original dataset. Synthetic data generating algorithms work in the way that they develop a mathematical model of the original patients and the data collected from them. Then synthetic data can be generated by drawing samples from the model. The relationships between the features are preserved, so that if a patient has e.g. diabetes, his blood glucose laboratory tests will be such that they match a diabetes patient. Special care must be paid to the quality control of the data: it must be similar to the original data, so that it can be used in the place of original data and get the same results and it must be private enough so that the original patients' data are not revealed. After synthesizing the data, the synthetic data must be checked for quality and privacy. Quality means whether the synthetic data have the same essential statistical features as the original data, and privacy test means testing whether the original patients' identities can be revealed from the synthetic data [13].

Another solution is to use federated learning [14]. In federated learning, an AI model is developed in a distributed fashion. All the data providers keep the data safely within their firewalls, but they allow a local training process to run, which then sends the model parameters to a server that combines the parameters from different locations to a global model. The advantage is that the data do not move, but the data providers must allow the running of the training algorithm.

2.3 Regulation and effectiveness

In the medical field, safety precautions are more meaningful than cutting-edge technology. Any technology must be proven safe before it can be used. Also, because in many countries the healthcare sector is financed from taxpayers' money, a certain cost-benefit analysis is also done. It is quite obvious that the AI systems would have very good cost-benefit ratio in many cases. Certain image-based AI devices have already been adapted, e.g. in digital pathology, it is accepted that a computer can pre-analyze the images and help the human doctor find the interesting areas in the images. This is much less accepted in the decision-making process. An AI system could select the treatment line for a patient based on a multitude of data, including laboratory values, pathology statements, previous treatments, etc. But this is an area where the acceptance of AI algorithms is less strong. The transparency of the most effective machine learning (ML) methods, like neural networks, is not perfect. No doctor would accept in his work an AI expert system, which does not give any grounds for its decisions. The regulations demand a very comprehensive study of the medical devices, and it is currently almost impossible to perform this on an AI system. Yet, they could be useful in many cases, and they are trusted in other fields. It remains to be seen, when will there be enough trust to bring medical AI products to the market.

3. Image analysis

3.1 Introduction to image analysis

Medical imaging is an old method in health care. The oldest methods like X-rays and ultrasound have become important diagnostic methods for healthcare professionals. Non-invasive methods have benefits, as they can show internal organs and tissues without physical contact or surgery. Later, more advanced methods like CT, MRI, fMRI, PET, and SPECT have also become important medical imaging tools for the diagnosis and treatment of diseases.

Despite sophisticated technology for generating medical images, image analysis is a challenging process, as it requires special expertise and a considerable amount of time. The task is tedious, especially when analyzing three-dimensional (3D) images like CT, MRI, and PET. Unavoidably, there is a risk of perceptual or cognitive error when analyzing medical images. It is obvious that errors in radiology are severe, and based on studies the interpretation error rate can be 3–5% or even higher [15].

The amount of medical imaging is increasing, as it has become a useful method for diagnosing diseases. Another need for medical imaging services is in rendering first aid to diagnose patients. In Finland, the annual amount of all taken medical images is millions [16]. The increasing amount of medical imaging indicates the importance of the method. On the other hand, medical imaging service entails a significant cost for the taxpayers. The availability and cost of the healthcare system are already challenges in Finland. The lack of radiologists is also a challenge for the Finnish healthcare system [17]. Additionally, the population in Finland is aging, which typically increases diseases and demand for medical imaging services.

3.2 AI-based image analysis

AI-based image analysis is a process for interpreting medical images by AI. Many AI-based image analysis systems utilize Convolutional Neural Networks (CNNs) [18]. These are typically deep-learning models that utilize supervised learning. The models can be trained with various annotated medical datasets. The training data can contain ordinary two-dimensional (2D) images. Using a proper model architecture, the model can also learn spatial information from 3D images, which makes it useful with scanners that produce layered medical image data.

There are important factors that need to be considered when AI is applied to image data. In practice, these models require a considerable amount of annotated training data, which can be a challenge to gather, also bias, on the datasets is a challenge to overcome. Neural networks are universal approximators, so the accuracy of the system is dependent on the accuracy of the approximation. Training and validation of the model are always based on a limited dataset, which cannot represent all the possible inputs. Image data are high dimensional, and it requires a large and complex model to extract patterns from them. The complexity of the model and the number of training parameters make it a sort of "black box," which prevents humans from understanding how the model makes decisions. Research on explainable AI (XAI) aims to mitigate this issue. Additionally, computational and memory requirements are noteworthy. Adapting new technologies like AI requires trust and acceptance from the clinical personnel as well as from the patients. Non-transparency and the challenge of validating the model are significant issues, especially in clinical use. Employing AI in clinical use raises questions about ethics and accountability.

Despite the technical and ethical challenges, AI-based applications are promising. AI-based image analyzing systems can automatically recognize abnormalities like tumors or lesions in the medical image [19]. Even though the AI model can already make predictions itself, patients in the Finnish healthcare system have the right to receive decisions from a real person. However, current AI-based systems can speed up medical image analysis by assisting radiologists. Another use case for AI is improving the quality of data. AI-based systems can improve the quality of the imaging process, i.e., reducing motion artifacts on MRI scanning [20].

Medical image analysis by AI can be a feasible solution in countries where medical image data for training are available. Typically, the AI model for medical imaging is based on sensitive training data. Availability, quality, and quantity of data are critical parts of developing AI solutions. In Finland, digitalization is carried out at a high level [21], and medical data have been collected for decades. National digital medical records contain unstructured data, like medical imaging data. However, current legislation does not allow utilizing the full potential of health records [22]. Allowing better access to national health records could be beneficial also for innovations and patients.

3.3 Anonymous synthetic medical image data

Anonymized synthetic medical image data are under active research also in Finland [23]. Synthetic data might provide a solution for producing privacy-protected data for scientists and companies. The technology is based on generative models like GAN (Generative Adversarial Network) models [24]. There are also some other generative methods for image generation like diffusion models. The main idea is to train a generative model to create anonymous but realistic-looking image data. One interesting possibility is medical image modality transformation. The idea of medical image modality transformation is to generate an artificial image based on one or more input modalities. For example, MRI images can be transformed into CT images by using a trained neural network. The method could save time and resources in the healthcare system, and it would also be more convenient and safer for the patient [25].

However, training generative models requires some real image data, unfortunately, the real data are strongly regulated, which cause a "chicken and egg" problem for developing AI models. A possible solution is an audited, secure platform that complies with regulations and allows companies to develop their own AI models using anonymized real data. However, some trained models have the risk of leaking sensitive training information [26]. To tackle this problem, it requires that the AI model be proven to be anonymous, which is a challenging task, especially with deep-learning models.

3.4 Medical image research and development in Finland

The research of AI-based image analysis is active in Finland. Several Finnish research organizations, institutions, individual researchers, and companies are doing research and applications on image analysis. Naturally, a lot of research is done together with international partners. Open science has an important role, especially in medical AI where the availability of data is crucial for research. It is also obvious that medical issues are global, and cooperation and collaboration are beneficial for everyone.

This chapter introduces examples of impactful research projects conducted in medical imaging. The list contains a summary of selected research projects that are related to common diseases in Finland. These research projects are also conducted in national and international collaboration with Finnish researchers and research organizations.

Helsinki University Hospital (HUS) has been developing AI-based methods for detecting subarachnoid hemorrhage (SAH) from CT scans. SAH is a potentially life-threatening condition and early detection is crucial. About 75% of patients with SAH will die within a year if it is not detected early. The accuracy of the developed algorithm is promising, as it was able to detect correctly 136 out of 137 cases from a total of 1300 CT scans [27].

Researchers from Aalto University, Digifundus Ltd., and Central Finland Central Hospital have developed AI-based methods for detecting diabetic eye diseases. Retinopathy is a leading cause of vision loss for diabetic patients. The developed model can detect accurately diabetic retinopathy and macular edema from medical images [28]. Diabetes is a common disease, and an estimated 500,000 people have diabetes in Finland.

Researchers from the University of Tampere and Karolinska Institutet in Sweden have developed an AI model that can accurately diagnose and grade prostate cancer from the medical image. Researchers trained the AI model with data containing more than 8000 scanned samples from prostate biopsies [29]. The accuracy of the model was the same as the world-leading specialist. In Finland, prostate cancer is the most common cancer among men. The mortality rate in Finland is also above the average European level.

Researchers from the University of Tampere along with other international collaborators have researched the saliency of breast lesions in breast cancer using an AI model [30]. Deep-learning model decision-making is typically a complex process. However, with medical image data, saliency maps can be used to analyze this process. Saliency maps are visual representations of how the model makes decisions based on different areas on the input image.

3.5 Conclusion

Medical imaging and the need for medical imaging analysis are increasing in Finland. Currently, medical image analysis is mostly based on human labor that cannot be upscaled easily. Resources for providing medical imaging are limited; keeping up an adequate level will be harder in the future.

Current research results of AI-based systems are promising. The scalability of AI-based systems is also an advantage, as it enables cheaper and more accessible medical AI. Research is active in the scientific community and research results are widely available. Open science can be seen as important for smaller countries like Finland.

Our national datasets cannot provide a large coverage, especially for rare diseases. However, sharing and using medical data requires that legislation support it, at the same time ethical questions also need to be considered.

4. Large language models (LLMs) in health care

4.1 AI in Finnish and global health care

Artificial Intelligence (AI) systems, particularly machine learning (ML) and a subset of it, Large Language Models (LLMs), are pivotal in translating data into actionable insights that inform decision-making processes. Large language models, such as ChatGPT, are powerful generative systems capable of rapidly synthesizing natural language responses. Research on LLMs has highlighted both their potential and their pitfalls, particularly in clinical settings. [y]. Recent breakthroughs in LLMs like Generative Pretrained Transformer 4 (GPT-4) and Llama 2 have demonstrated their potential across a wide array of sectors, with notable advancements in the health industry [31, 32].

The health industry is experiencing a significant increase in the application of LLMs. These models are employed in various applications, from disease prediction and diagnosis to personalized treatment plans and healthcare management. One of the primary applications of LLMs in the healthcare sector is to augment the tasks of medical professionals in documenting patient health records post consultations. By comprehending and generating human-like text, LLMs can assist medical professionals in recording patient interactions, thereby enhancing the accuracy of the work and reducing the time spent on administrative tasks. This not only minimizes the time and cost associated with record-keeping but also enables medical professionals to devote more attention to patient care. Furthermore, LLMs function as AI assistants for healthcare staff, offering support in various tasks, such as scheduling, patient communication, and data analysis [32, 33].

The escalating adoption of these technologies underscores the transformative role of ML and LLMs in revolutionizing healthcare delivery and outcomes. The overarching objective is to improve patient care while reducing costs and enhancing accuracy and efficiency. This narrative aligns with the broader goal of leveraging AI to address complex challenges and drive progress in various sectors [34].

Numerous studies underscore the significance of Artificial Intelligence (AI) in revolutionizing the healthcare sector in Finland [32, 35–40]. HUS Helsinki University Hospital, a global leader in healthcare AI, has been utilizing AI for data analysis and diagnostic support since 2015. Miikka Korja, the Chief Innovation Officer at HUS Helsinki University Hospital, posits that health-related AI could be Finland's next major breakthrough, comparable to Nokia. AI is particularly effective in analyzing large volumes of data, including text and images, swiftly and efficiently. However, the actual data analysis is still performed by human professionals. In 2017, HUS initiated a development project, AI Head Analysis, under the CleverHealth Network ecosystem. The project's objective is to enhance the treatment of brain diseases by developing diagnostic support tools with the aid of AI. The fundamental principle of the CleverHealth Network ecosystem is a collaboration between HUS's doctors and nurses, who contribute their clinical expertise, and Finnish and international technology companies, which provide various software, hardware, marketing, and business expertise [41, 42].

Silo AI, a company based in Finland, is leveraging the power of Generative Pretrained Transformers (GPTs) for health applications. The company's AI assistant is built upon an open Finnish GPT language model. In the initial phase, the language model is fine-tuned for conversation and taught Finnish healthcare vocabulary using the technology of SiloGen, a subsidiary of Silo AI specializing in language models. The suitability of the language model for the Lifecare patient information system is also confirmed [43]. The AI assistant operates based on the semantic similarities between the user's own searches and the data from the language model. Testing of the AI assistant is conducted on Tietoevry's own platform, ensuring secure processing and privacy of the data.

Private companies in Finland and in the Nordic countries emphasize the importance of European technology companies developing their own AI and language models tailored to their specific needs. They see Generative AI (GenAI) as the next widely impacting evolution cycle and is actively working to discover and concretize the benefits of GenAI. This is done by running efficient use cases across industries together with customers and an expanding network of partners, with ethical AI as a key design principle.

4.2 Introduction to LLMs

Large Language Models (LLMs), a subset of generative AI, represent a significant breakthrough in the field of artificial intelligence, particularly in Natural Language Processing (NLP). They have revolutionized NLP and found applications in a variety of domains. The evolution of LLMs, trained using deep neural networks on extensive text datasets, has significantly advanced NLP. The development of these models has been propelled by the need to comprehend and generate human-like text, the increasing availability of large text corpora, and advancements in machine learning algorithms and computational power [44].

The first generation of LLMs, such as Word2Vec and GloVe, focused on word embeddings but struggled to capture the context of words within a sentence. The advent of transformer-based models marked a significant advancement in the field. In 2017, Google pioneered the "Transformer" architecture, initially designed for machine translation, which later proved highly effective, achieving state-of-the-art results in numerous Natural Language Processing (NLP) tasks. Following this breakthrough, a series of LLMs utilizing the "Transformer" architecture were developed, including Bidirectional Encoder Representations from Transformers (BERT), Generative Pretrained Transformer 2 (GPT-2), and Generative Pretrained Transformer 3 (GPT-3). These models can understand the context of words in a sentence, generating human-like text and answering complex questions. Among these, GPT-3, developed by OpenAI, is particularly notable. It boasts of 175 billion machine learning parameters and was trained on a diverse range of internet texts. Other models in this series include the Pathways Language Model (PaLM), LLM Meta AI (LLaMA), and GPT-4 [45, 46].

4.3 The impact of LLMs on healthcare and medical research

In the healthcare and medicine sector, Large Language Models are emerging as a powerful tool, providing substantial improvements in both clinical and research areas. They can automate the generation and summarization of medical documentation, thereby enhancing the creation of detailed and precise medical reports. This automation not only facilitates healthcare professionals in efficiently handling patient data but also improves the monitoring of patient history and treatment protocols [31, 47].

The integration of this advanced language processing technology is revolutionizing the management of medical information and the conduct of research, paving the way for more innovative and effective healthcare solutions. Particularly in digitally advanced regions like Finland, where health data are readily available, LLMs are proving to be invaluable. They assist in documenting patient medical reports, analyzing patient data, predicting disease progression, personalizing treatment plans, and even extending their utility to areas, such as medical imaging analysis, drug discovery, and genomics. This amalgamation of AI and health care is not only enhancing the efficiency of medical practices but also opening new avenues for personalized patient care and advanced research [35].

However, the use of LLMs in medicine also brings with it challenges. These challenges include data privacy issues, the need for large, annotated datasets for training, and the risk of model biases. Moreover, both the MDR and the AI act of EU must be followed when using LLMs in medicine. The potential of LLMs in medicine is vast, but realizing this potential requires overcoming these challenges. With the right approach and regulatory framework, LLMs can play a significant role in improving healthcare outcomes [35].

4.4 A high-level description of LLMs

Introduction: LLMs are a type of artificial intelligence model designed to understand and generate human-like text. They are “large” in terms of the size of the neural network they use and the amount of data they are trained on. They are trained on a large corpus of text data and learn to predict the next word in a sentence. This enables them to generate coherent and contextually relevant sentences [35, 48].

Architecture and training: Initially, sequence modeling tasks were performed by Recurrent Neural Networks (RNNs) and Long Short-Term Memory (LSTM). However, the introduction of the Transformer model has revolutionized this field, and it is now widely used for these tasks. LLMs are typically built on Transformer architectures, known for their ability to handle long-range dependencies in text. The Transformer model, a cornerstone of modern sequence modeling, is characterized by its unique architecture. This architecture is composed of multiple layers of feed-forward networks and attention blocks stacked together [49].

The attention mechanism, a key component of the architecture, operates as follows:

Given the inputs

$$Q, K, V \in R^{N \times d} \tag{1}$$

It calculates the outputs.

$$\mathrm{O} \tag{2}$$

According to the formula

$$O = soft\max\left(QK^{T}\right)V \tag{3}$$

Where:

- Q represents the set of queries in the attention mechanism,
- K denotes the set of keys in the attention mechanism,
- V signifies the set of values in the attention mechanism,
- N is the number of queries, keys, and values,
- O is the output of the attention mechanism, and
- a normalization factor is disregarded for simplicity.

The softmax function is a mathematical function that converts a vector of numbers into a vector of probabilities, where the probabilities of each value are proportional to the relative scale of each value in the vector. QK^T can be interpreted as a matrix of similarity scores between the queries and keys. These scores are then used to weight the values in the attention mechanism, reflecting the relevance of each value to each query.

d represents the length of the input sequences and retrieves a weighted sum of the values corresponding to those keys, based on the computed similarity scores. The transformer architecture can be categorized into three primary variants: encoder models, decoder models, and encoder-decoder models. The encoder models process input sequences in parallel, while the decoder models generate sequences sequentially. The encoder-decoder model accepts a sequence of inputs and generates a new sequence of outputs. Each variant serves a distinct purpose and is chosen based on the specific requirements of the task at hand [48, 50].

The training of LLMs involves feeding them a large amount of text data, including text from the internet, books, websites, and other written materials. This learning process is unsupervised, implying that the model learns statistical patterns in the data, such as the probability of a word following another word or a sequence of words, without any explicit labels or targets. In essence, LLMs primarily employ self-supervised learning, a variant of unsupervised learning where the system learns to predict a part of its input from other parts. This approach leverages large amounts of unlabeled data by creating pseudo-labels from the data itself, thus not requiring manual annotation. This is particularly useful in scenarios where obtaining labeled data for every possible class is impractical. The model leverages its learned knowledge to infer about the unseen classes, thus demonstrating a form of artificial generalization [31, 37, 48, 51, 52].

4.5 Challenges associated with the use of large language models (LLMs) in health care

The deployment of Large Language Models (LLMs) in the healthcare and medicine sector is a promising development, with potential to revolutionize patient care and treatment outcomes. However, this advancement is not without its challenges. These challenges, which are critical to address for the responsible and ethical application of these technologies, are as follows.

Data privacy: LLMs in health care often interact with sensitive patient data. The challenge lies in ensuring the privacy and confidentiality of these data, as there is a risk of inadvertent disclosure of private health information during the generation of responses.

Bias in training data: The quality of LLMs' outputs is heavily dependent on the data they were trained on. If these training data contain biases, the models may inadvertently perpetuate these biases, leading to potentially unfair or discriminatory outcomes in healthcare decisions.

Regulatory compliance: The healthcare sector is subject to stringent regulations, such as the General Data Protection Regulation (GDPR) in the European Union and Health Insurance Portability and Accountability Act (HIPAA) in the United States. Ensuring that the application of LLMs complies with these regulations is a significant challenge.

In conclusion, while the integration of LLMs into the healthcare and medicine sector holds immense potential, it is crucial to address these challenges to ensure their responsible and ethical application. Future research and development efforts must focus on devising strategies and mechanisms to mitigate these issues [35, 36, 53, 54].

4.6 Future direction of LLMs in Finland's health care

The future of LLMs in medicine, particularly in Finland, looks promising. Finland's robust healthcare system and extensive health data provide a promising landscape for the application of Large Language Models (LLMs) in medicine. The country's digital infrastructure, combined with a strong commitment to research and development, paves the way for LLMs to revolutionize various aspects of health care [49, 55–60].

Personalized treatment plans: LLMs can analyze vast amounts of patient data to develop personalized treatment plans. By understanding the nuances of medical text, these models can identify patterns and correlations that may not be immediately apparent to human practitioners. This could lead to more targeted and effective treatments, improving patient outcomes.

Health records documentation: The task of documenting patient health records can be time-consuming for healthcare professionals. LLMs can automate this process, ensuring accurate and efficient record-keeping. This not only reduces the administrative burden on healthcare staff but also minimizes errors that can occur in manual documentation.

Improved patient engagement: LLMs can be used to enhance communication between healthcare providers and patients. For instance, they can generate patient-friendly explanations of medical conditions and treatments or provide reminders for medication and appointments. This can lead to improved patient engagement and adherence to treatment plans.

Recording patient interactions: LLMs can assist in recording patient interactions during consultations. These records can be valuable for reference in future consultations, ensuring continuity of care.

Enhanced healthcare delivery: By automating various administrative tasks and providing decision support, LLMs can enhance the efficiency of healthcare delivery. This allows healthcare professionals to focus more on patient care, leading to improved healthcare outcomes.

Research and development: Finland's strong focus on research and development provides ample opportunities for the application of LLMs in medical research. These models can assist in analyzing research data, generating hypotheses, and even enhancing the writing of research papers.

Regulatory compliance: With the stringent healthcare regulations in Finland and the European Union, LLMs can be trained to ensure compliance in healthcare practices. They can be used to monitor and flag potential regulatory issues, helping healthcare providers to maintain compliance.

In conclusion, the future of LLMs in medicine in Finland looks promising. However, it's crucial to address the challenges associated with their use, such as data privacy and bias in training data. Researchers are actively striving to augment the ethical and responsible use of LLMs, concentrating on reducing instances of bias and misinformation. As advancements in AI and machine learning persist, we anticipate witnessing an increase in innovative applications of LLMs within Finland's healthcare sector [57, 59, 61].

5. Conclusion

In this article, we have discussed both the regulatory and technical issues regarding the use of AI in health care with Finland as an example. We have shown that the technology exists to use AI in the clinical field in many tasks. It is used in other fields successfully for other tasks, and they could be incorporated in the clinic through normal R&D processes. Maybe the most straightforward products would be in the field of digital pathology image analysis and communication with patient using LLMs.

We have used as a case study the regulation in the EU and specifically Finland, an EU member state. The healthcare AI sector is regulated by legislation both on the Finnish and on the EU levels. Most of the innovations and products are made in private companies, and for SMEs, the cost of certifying the products may be prohibitive. For this reason, many companies decide to market their products not as medical devices but as less regulated wellbeing or consumer devices. On the other hand, there is an obvious need also from the companies' side to guarantee that their products are safe and efficient. Failures in critical devices would be a business nightmare, even to larger companies.

We have looked at the use of imaging AI in e.g. pathology and cancer care, where AI-based solutions can replace radiologists in detecting abnormalities in certain types of images. Convolutional neural networks have revolutionized this field, and they can achieve better results than expert radiologists. Synthetic data are also a promising approach, which can even reduce the number of images taken about a patient.

The AI applications that are used in clinical settings today are restricted mostly to closed imaging systems, which do not use the electronic health record (EHR) systems or send information outside the closed system. These systems apply normal imaging AI algorithms to perform the imaging better, so they have not changed the treatment processes, which would be the most important benefit of AI systems, if they would be fully used in the future.

The integration of Large Language Models (LLMs) into health care is a transformative development, with the potential to revolutionize patient care and treatment outcomes. The application of LLMs in health care is expanding, from disease prediction and diagnosis to personalized treatment plans and healthcare management. In particular, Finland, with its robust healthcare system and extensive health data, is poised to leverage LLMs to enhance healthcare delivery significantly.

However, the deployment of LLMs in health care is not without its challenges. These include ensuring data privacy, addressing bias in training data, and complying with stringent healthcare regulations. Overcoming these challenges is crucial for the responsible and ethical application of LLMs in health care.

Looking ahead, the future of LLMs in medicine, particularly in Finland, is promising. With continued research and development, and with strategies in place to mitigate the associated challenges, LLMs can play a significant role in improving healthcare outcomes. As we continue to explore and understand the capabilities of LLMs, we can anticipate a future where AI and health care are even more intertwined, driving progress and innovation in the sector.

All of these fields of AI require careful research in a challenging regulatory environment, where the normal level of scientific accuracy is not enough. The products must be proven in practical clinical work, and they must be constantly monitored. Yet, they can provide big advancements in the quality of health care and simultaneously reduce the amount of human labor in the treatment process.

In the future, a crucial question is making the regulatory steps faster, more predictable, and better known by the actors in the field. Experienced notified bodies should be widely available and passing the regulatory hurdles should be routine for the companies in the field. This requires dialog between the lawmakers and the companies in the commercial field. The regulation is not likely to change, but the standard interpretations of the laws are not established yet. Both the healthcare officials and the companies have incentives to accomplish this.

Author details

Pertti Ranttila*†, Golnaz Sahebi†, Elina Kontio and Jussi Salmi
Turku University of Applied Sciences, Turku, Finland

*Address all correspondence to: pertti.ranttila@turkuamk.fi

† These two authors contributed equally

References

[1] Holman JG, Cookson MJ. Expert systems for medical applications. Journal of Medical Engineering and Technology. 1987;**11**(4):151-159. DOI: 10.3109/03091908709008986

[2] Maleki Varnosfaderani S, Forouzanfar M. The role of AI in hospitals and clinics: Transforming healthcare in the 21st century. Bioengineering (Basel). 2024;**11**(4):337. DOI: 10.3390/bioengineering11040337

[3] Jassar S, Adams SJ, Zarzeczny A, Burbridge BE. The future of artificial intelligence in medicine: Medical-legal considerations for health leaders. Healthcare Management Forum. 2022;**35**(3):185-189. DOI: 10.1177/08404704221082069. Epub 2022 Mar 31

[4] Xianyu Z, Correia C, Ung CY, Zhu S, Billadeau DD, Li H. The rise of hypothesis-driven artificial intelligence in oncology. Cancers. 2024;**16**:822. DOI: 10.3390/cancers16040822

[5] Regulation (EU) 2017/745 of the European Parliament and of the council of 5 April 2017 on medical devices, amending directive 2001/83/EC, regulation (EC) No 178/2002 and regulation (EC) No 1223/2009 and repealing council directives 90/385/EEC and 93/42/EEC (text with EEA relevance). Official Journal L. 2017;**117**:1-175. Available from: http://data.europa.eu/eli/reg/2017/745/oj [Accessed: July 19, 2024]

[6] Proposal for a Regulation of the European Parliament and of the Council Laying Down Harmonised Rules on Artificial Intelligence (Artificial Intelligence Act) and Amending Certain Union Legislative Acts. Com/2021/206 Final. Available from: https://eur-lex.europa.eu/legal-content/EN/TXT/?uri=celex%3A52021PC0206 [Accessed: June 19, 2024]

[7] Regulation (EU) 2016/679 of the European Parliament and of the Council of 27 April 2016 on the Protection of Natural Persons with Regard to the Processing of Personal Data and on the Free Movement of Such Data, and Repealing Directive 95/46/EC (General Data Protection Regulation). Available from: https://eur-lex.europa.eu/eli/reg/2016/679/oj [Accessed: June 19, 2024]

[8] Johnson HR. The EU AI Act: How Will it Impact Medical Device Manufacturers? MDDI online. 27.2.2024. Available from: https://www.mddionline.com/artificial-intelligence/the-eu-ai-act-how-will-it-impact-medical-device-manufacturers- [Accessed: April 25, 2024]

[9] European Commission, Directorate-General for Communications Networks, Content and Technology, Ethics Guidelines for Trustworthy AI, Publications Office. 2019. Available from: https://data.europa.eu/doi/10.2759/346720 [Accessed: June 19, 2024]

[10] Salmi J, Hermansson L-L. Centralized or de centralized data and algorithms in the Finnish health care infrastructure. In: eHealth 2022 Conference, July19 21, Lisbon, Portugal.

[11] Ministry of Social Affairs and Health. Secondary Use of Health and Social Data. 2019. Available from: https://stm.fi/en/secondary-use-of-health-and-social-data [Accessed: April 25, 2024]

[12] Giuffrè M, Shung DL. Harnessing the power of synthetic data in healthcare: Innovation, application, and privacy. NPJ Digital Medicine. 2023;**6**:186. DOI: 10.1038/s41746-023-00927-3

[13] Hernandez M, Epelde G, Alberdi A, Cilla R, Rankin D. Synthetic data generation for tabular health records: A systematic review. Neurocomputing. 2022;**493**:28-45. ISSN 0925-2312. DOI: 10.1016/j.neucom.2022.04.053

[14] Guan H, Yap P-W, Bozoki A, Liu M. Federated learning for medical image analysis: A survey. Pattern Recognition. 2024;**151**:110424. ISSN 0031-3203. DOI: 10.1016/j.patcog.2024.110424

[15] Bruno MA, Walker EA, Abujudeh HH. Understanding and confronting our mistakes: The epidemiology of error in radiology and strategies for error reduction. Radiographics. 2015;**35**(6):1668-1676. DOI: 10.1148/rg.2015150023

[16] Ruonala V, editor. Number of Radiological Examinations in Finland 2019. STUK-B 242, Helsinki 2018, 34 pp + apps. 1 pp. Available from: https://www.julkari.fi/bitstream/handle/10024/138743/STUK-B242.pdf [Accessed: June 19, 2024]

[17] Bolejko A, Andersson BT, Debess J, Fridell K, Henner A, Sanderud A, et al. Facilitators for and barriers to radiography research in public healthcare in Nordic countries. Radiography (London). 2022;**28**(1):88-94. DOI: 10.1016/j.radi.2021.08.007. Epub 2021 Aug 31

[18] Lecun Y, Bottou L, Bengio Y, Haffner P. Gradient-based learning applied to document recognition. Proceedings of the IEEE. 1998;**86**(11):2278-2324. DOI: 10.1109/5.726791

[19] Pinto-Coelho L. How artificial intelligence is shaping medical imaging technology: A survey of innovations and applications. Bioengineering (Basel). 2023;**10**(12):1435. DOI: 10.3390/bioengineering10121435

[20] Cui L, Song Y, Wang Y, Wang R, Wu D, Xie H, et al. Motion artifact reduction for magnetic resonance imaging with deep learning and k-space analysis. PLoS One. 2023;**18**(1):e0278668. DOI: 10.1371/journal.pone.0278668

[21] Cordis C. Finland, the World's Most Technologically Advanced Country—UN Report. CORDIS | European Commission. Available from: https://cordis.europa.eu/article/id/17266-finland-the-worlds-most-technologically-advanced-country-un-report; n.d [Accessed: June 19, 2024]

[22] Pajula J, Viiri S, Similä H, Lähteenmäki J, Tuomi-Nikula A. Toisiolain vaikutukset tutkimukseen ja data-analytiikan sovelluksiin: Hyteairon analytiikkatyöryhmän selvitys. VTT Technical Research Centre of Finland; 2021. 31 p. (VTT Tutkimusraportti; No. VTT-R-00118-21). (in Finnish)

[23] Ammattikorkeakoulu T. Synthetic Health Data Facilitates Collaborative Medical Research and Health Technology Development. Turku University of Applied Sciences; n.d.. Available from: https://www.tuas.fi/en/articles/588/synthetic-health-data-facilitates-collaborative-medical-research-and-health-technology-development [Accessed: June 19, 2024]

[24] Goodfellow I, Pouget-Abadie J, Mirza M, Xu B, Warde-Farley D, Ozair S, et al. Generative adversarial nets. In: Proceedings of the International Conference on Neural Information Processing Systems (NIPS 2014). 2014. pp. 2672-2680

[25] Paudyal R, Shah AD, Akin O, Do RKG, Konar AS, Hatzoglou V, et al. Artificial intelligence in CT and MR imaging for oncological applications. Cancers (Basel). 2023;**15**(9):2573. DOI: 10.3390/cancers15092573

[26] Li Z, Hong J, Li B, Wang Z. Shake to Leak: Fine-Tuning Diffusion Models Can Amplify the Generative Privacy Risk. 2024. Available from: https://arxiv.org/abs/2403.09450 [Accessed: June 19, 2024]

[27] Thanellas A, Peura H, Lavinto M, Ruokola T, Vieli M, Staartjes VE, et al. Development and external validation of a deep learning algorithm to identify and localize subarachnoid hemorrhage on CT scans. Neurology. 2023;**100**(12):e1257-e1266. DOI: 10.1212/WNL.0000000000201710

[28] Sahlsten J, Jaskari J, Kivinen J. Deep learning fundus image analysis for diabetic retinopathy and macular edema grading. Scientific Reports. 2019;**9**:10750. DOI: 10.1038/s41598-019-47181-w

[29] Bulten W, Kartasalo K, Chen PHC. Artificial intelligence for diagnosis and Gleason grading of prostate cancer: The PANDA challenge. Nature Medicine. 2022;**28**:154-163. DOI: 10.1038/s41591-021-01620-2

[30] Pertuz S, Ortega D, Suarez É, Cancino W, Africano G, Rinta-Kiikka I, et al. Saliency of breast lesions in breast cancer detection using artificial intelligence. Scientific Reports. 2023;**13**(1):20545. DOI: 10.1038/s41598-023-46921-3

[31] Brown TB, Mann B, Ryder N, Subbiah M, Kaplan J, Dhariwal P, et al. Language models are few-shot learners. arXiv:2005.14165v4. 2020

[32] Clusmann J, Kolbinger FR, Muti HS, Carrero ZI, Eckardt JN, Laleh NG, et al. The future landscape of large language models in medicine. Communications Medicine. 2023. DOI: 10.1038/s43856-023-00370-1

[33] Park Y-J, Pillai A, Deng J, Guo E, Gupta M, Paget M, et al. Assessing the research landscape and clinical utility of large language models: A scoping review. BMC Medical Informatics and Decision Making. 2024. DOI: 10.1186/s12911-024-02459-6

[34] Alowais SA, Alghamdi SS, Alsuhebany N, et al. Revolutionizing healthcare: The role of artificial intelligence in clinical practice. BMC Medical Education. 2023;**23**:689. DOI: 10.1186/s12909-023-04698-z

[35] Webster P. Six ways large language models are changing healthcare. Nature Medicine. 2023;**29**:2969-2971. DOI: 10.1038/s41591-023-02700-1

[36] Liu A, Zhou H, Hua Y, Rohanian O, Clifton L, Clifton DA. Large language models in healthcare: A comprehensive benchmark. arXiv:2405.00716v1. 2024

[37] Bakhshandeh S. Benchmarking medical large language models. Nature Review Bioeng. 2023;**1**:543. DOI: 10.1038/s44222-023-00097-7

[38] Liu L, Yang X, Lei J, Liu X, Shen Y, Zhang Z, et al. A survey on medical large language models: Technology, application, trustworthiness, and future directions. arXiv:2406.03712v1. 2024

[39] Thirunavukarasu AJ, Ting DSJ, Elangovan K, et al. Large language models in medicine. Nature Medicine. 2023;**29**:1930-1940

[40] Pool J, Indulska M, Sadiq S. Large language models and generative AI in telehealth: A responsible use lens. Journal of the American Medical

Informatics Association. 2024;**ocae035**. DOI: 10.1093/jamia/ocae035

[41] Kamocki P, Witt A. Ethical Issues in Language Resources and Language Technology—New Challenges, New Perspectives. Leibniz-Institut für Deutsche Sprache R5 6-13, 68161, ELRA Language Resource Association: CC BY-NC 4.0; 2024

[42] Meskó B, Topol EJ. The imperative for regulatory oversight of large language models (or generative AI) in healthcare. NPJ Digital Medicine. 2023;**6**:120. DOI: 10.1038/s41746-023-00873-0

[43] Deep Tech. AI Model Poro Sets New Milestones for Multilingual LLMs in Europe. 2024. Available from: https://thenextweb.com/news/ai-model-poro-low-resource-language-multilingual-llms [Accessed: June 19, 2024]

[44] Naveed H, Khan AU, Qiu S, Saqib M, Anwar S, Usman M, et al. A comprehensive overview of large language models. arXiv:2307.06435v9, 10.48550/arXiv.2307.06435. 2023

[45] Pickard T. Comparing word2vec and GloVe for automatic measurement of MWE compositionality. In: Proceedings of the Joint Workshop on Multiword Expressions and Electronic Lexicons, Association for Computational Linguistics. 2020

[46] Chowdhery A et al. PaLM: Scaling language modeling with pathways. arXiv:2204.02311v5. 2022

[47] Naveed H, Khan AU, Qiu S, Saqib M, Anwar S, Usman M, et al. A comprehensive overview of large language models. arXiv preprint arXiv:2307.06435. 2023

[48] Culver CC, Hicks P, Milenkovic M, Shanmugavelu S. Scientific computing with large language models. arXiv:2406.07259v1. 2024

[49] Min B, Ross H, Sulem E, et al. Recent advances in natural language processing via large pre-trained language models: A survey. ACM Computing Surveys. 2023;**56**:1-40

[50] Li S, Song Z, Xia Y, Yu T, Zhou T. The closeness of in-context learning and weight shifting for softmax regression. arXiv:2304.13276. 2023

[51] Zhao WX, Zhou K, Li J, Tang T, Wang X, Hou Y, et al. A survey of large language models. arXiv:2303.18223v13. 2023

[52] OpenAI. Gpt-4 technical report. ArXiv, abs/2303.08774. 2023

[53] Nazi ZA, Peng W. Large language models in healthcare and medical domain: A review. arXiv:2401.06775v1. 2023

[54] Gallegos IO, Rossi RA, Barrow J, Tanjim M, Kim S, Dernoncourt F, et al. Bias and fairness in large language models: A survey. arXiv:2309.00770v2. 2023. DOI: 10.48550/arXiv.2309.00770

[55] Halton R. A Comprehensive Perspective on Large Language Models (LLMs) for Drug Discovery Scientists. 2024. Available from: https://www.sapiosciences.com/blog/a-comprehensive-perspective-on-large-language-models-llms-life-sciences-drug-discovery-scientists/ [Accessed: June 19, 2024]

[56] Pitkäranta T, Pitkäranta L. Bridging human and AI decision-making with LLMs: The RAGADA approach. In: Proceedings of the 26th International Conference on Enterprise Information Systems. Vol. 1. ICEIS; 2024. pp. 812-819

[57] Zhou H, Liu F, Gu B, Zou X, Huang J, Wu J, et al. A survey of large language models in medicine: Progress, application, and challenge. arXiv:2311.05112v5. 2024. DOI: 10.48550/arXiv.2311.05112

[58] Parsons F, Gill R, Hayes B. How Can Generative AI, Specifically LLMs Aid in Documentation. Digital Health, HIMSS; 2023. Available from: https://www.himss.org/resources/section-3-how-can-generative-ai-specifically-llms-aid-documentation

[59] Hämäläinen M. Legal and ethical considerations that hinder the use of LLMs in a Finnish institution of higher education. LREC-COLING-2024. 2024:24-27. Available from: https://aclanthology.org/2024.legal-1.5.pdf [Accessed: June 19, 2024]

[60] Yang R, Tan TF, Lu W, Thirunavukarasu AJ, Ting DSW, Liu N. Large language models in health care: Development, applications, and challenges. Healthcare Science. 2023. DOI: 10.1002/hcs2.61

[61] Karttunen P. Large language models in healthcare decision support [thesis]. Faculty of Medicine and Health Technology, Tampere University. Available from: https://trepo.tuni.fi/bitstream/handle/10024/150003/KarttunenPinja.pdf;jsessionid=C9B9D93FAB9896B3D1795AD8682CE048?sequence=2; 2023 [Accessed: June 19, 2024]

Chapter 3

The Role of Transparency in AI-Driven Technologies: Targeting Healthcare

Paula Subías-Beltrán, Carla Pitarch, Carolina Migliorelli, Luís Marte, Mar Galofré and Silvia Orte

Abstract

This chapter delves into the pivotal role of transparency within artificial intelligence (AI)-based applications, emphasizing its importance for reliability, accountability, and ensuring the ethical usage of AI targeting healthcare contexts. The chapter examines four dimensions of transparency: data, algorithmic, decision-making, and AI solution, and identifies problems and limitations in achieving them based on real-world digital health use cases. Current efforts and recommended strategies aiming at boosting transparency are discussed, emphasizing the need to define the objectives of transparency, the circumstances under which it should be applied, and the rationale behind it. This chapter advocates for collaborative efforts from stakeholders throughout the healthcare ecosystem to prioritize and implement transparent AI systems for the benefit of patients and society.

Keywords: AI ethics, transparency, digital health, artificial intelligence, reliable AI

1. Introduction

The application of AI to healthcare holds great promise for revolutionizing the quality of life and advancing human progress. AI has the potential to rapidly analyze vast amounts of data, supporting early disease detection, personalized treatment plans, and predictive interventions. Such capabilities could lead to significant improvements in patient outcomes and the efficiency of health services, marking a pivotal moment in healthcare history. Nevertheless, despite the potential for transformative change, significant challenges remain.

There is a growing concern regarding the opacity of AI systems [1, 2]. The lack of transparency in how algorithms work raises ethical and practical concerns, particularly regarding accountability and trustworthiness in medical decision-making [3]. Addressing these issues is crucial to ensure that AI evolves responsibly, respecting users' privacy, maintaining data integrity, and fostering transparency in algorithmic processes. It is only through careful navigation of these complexities that the full potential of AI can be harnessed to truly benefit individuals and society as a whole.

Transparency in AI serves a critical dual role in the governance of AI-driven systems today. Firstly, it aims to bolster trust among users and stakeholders by providing visibility into how algorithms operate and make decisions [4]. This transparency is essential for mitigating concerns related to biases or errors that may arise from algorithmic processes. Secondly, transparency promotes a deeper understanding of these complex systems, enabling stakeholders to effectively manage and regulate their deployment in various domains [5]. By enhancing visibility and comprehension, transparency contributes significantly to the sustainability [6] and ethical implementation of AI systems. This ensures that they align with societal values and expectations [7].

Nevertheless, transparency remains insufficiently implemented in current AI practices [8]. In some cases, this may be attributed to a deficiency in awareness within the practice itself, which ultimately leads to a lack of appreciation for the significance of transparency among both technology implementers and recipients. For example, the exertion of productive pressure may result in the omission of transparency measures [9]. In other situations, the lack of application of transparency may be shielded by a lack of enforceability or detail in its application. This places us in the total absence of an ethical framework. Another option is when the impact of the lack of transparency on end users is omitted. This can occur when the motivation for maintaining secrecy is driven by economic considerations, as exemplified by the opacity of some algorithms, such as the ranking algorithm of Google, which confers their owners a competitive advantage [10].

However, it is of the utmost importance to maintain a clear focus and to understand AI as a tool that has the potential to improve the well-being of society. AI should be used to facilitate progress and contribute to the construction of the society we aspire to be. Consequently, it is imperative to recognize transparency as a pivotal element in innovation, advocating for the establishment of ethical and normative frameworks as the cornerstone of research and progress.

This chapter examines the concept of transparency, with a particular focus on its application in the field of healthcare. Given the sensitivity of decisions and data in this area, it is among the most safeguarded in our society. The discussion presented in this manuscript should therefore be regarded as one that offers the most comprehensive guarantees in relation to user protection and is committed to positive developments that benefit all. Thus, it offers insights that can be adapted to other domains while preserving the necessary restrictions.

The remaining part of this chapter is comprised of four additional sections. Section 2 explores the concept of transparency, provides a definition, examines the regulatory landscape, and investigates its value and potential operationalization. Section 3 then presents challenges to achieving effective transparency and proposes solutions and success stories demonstrating that these challenges can be overcome. Subsequently, in Section 4, we examine the optimal course of action to alter the prevailing paradigm and transition toward a state of effective transparency throughout the AI lifecycle. Finally, in Section 5, we conclude with our final remarks.

2. Understanding transparency in AI

Transparency is not merely an ultimate goal but an important step toward increased knowledge and clarity [5]. It facilitates a scenario where observation and knowledge become attainable, providing a sense of control. Transparency enables the scrutiny of systems by granting access to information, leading to more informed debates and decisions. Transparency can also be understood as a mechanism for the governance of systems since it can influence practices by creating levels of visibility that allow for the supervision of processes.

Precisely defining transparency is challenging because it is often invoked without a clear definition [11] and has been widely adopted by different disciplines [12], each with its own nuanced interpretation [13]. For example, in governance and public policy, transparency typically refers to openness, accountability, and the availability of information to the public [14]; in business, it often refers to clear, honest communication and disclosure of business practices and performance [15]. Each sector adapts the concept of transparency to its specific context and needs, resulting in a rich but complex tapestry of interpretations. As a result, while the underlying concept focuses on comprehensibility, its application and implications can vary widely, making a single definition tricky. The essence of its interpretation stems from the conceptual metaphor *knowing is seeing*, which Reddy [16] used to translate from the realm of physical objects to that of mental operations. In this way, the positive interpretation of transparency revolves around knowledge and understanding, while the opposite aspect of it relates to opacity and darkness [17].

In the context of AI, the concepts of accountability and openness are frequently linked to the fundamental definition of transparency [18]. Ensuring access to and inspection of code, datasets, and related systems is critical to accountability and an important part of AI transparency. Openness is frequently framed in positive terms, such as open data or open science [19–21]. On the other hand, the AI community takes a more algorithmic performance-centric approach, underscoring the significance of explainability as a conduit for fostering comprehension and trust in systems [1].

Another perspective to be considered is that presented in the normative framework, which outlines the circumstances under which transparency should be demanded and for what purpose. This manuscript will primarily focus on the European framework at the normative level, as it provides the most effective safeguards for human rights, which are the foundation of our society. In particular, we will concentrate on those normative documents that are legally binding in nature or have been acknowledged as having a substantial impact on the regulatory framework.

In this context, the initial concept of AI transparency was proposed by the publication *Ethics Guidelines for Trustworthy AI* authored by the European Commission High-Level Expert Group on AI in 2019 [22]. The guidelines identified transparency as a crucial requirement for achieving trustworthy and human-centric AI, describing it as essential for ensuring human control and oversight. This vision was further developed by UNESCO in 2022 [23], through another soft law instrument, which emphasized the need for mechanisms to ensure ethically sustainable AI. Such mechanisms should be designed with a risk-averse approach, with due consideration given to the control of the system's potential consequences.

In the spring of 2024, the Council of Europe published the *Convention on AI and Human Rights, Democracy, and the Rule of Law*, which is binding for all signatory states [24]. While the convention does not specify a particular definition of transparency, it underscores the importance of considering the application context in order to implement proportionate safety measures. Additionally, the recently approved *AI Act* [25], which is binding for all EU member states, defines AI transparency as the development and use of systems that ensure effective traceability and explainability. This encompasses clear communication during machine-human interactions and providing clarity on the system's capabilities and limitations. The AI regulation highlights that transparency is crucial for both high-risk AI systems[1] and general-purpose AI systems (GPAI). Furthermore, the necessity for transparency encompasses the identification of all artificially generated or manipulated data, as well as the specification of the intended purpose and operational methodologies of GPAI ([25], Article 50). Besides, we must not forget other existing regulations that have an implicit impact on AI solutions, such as the *General Data Protection Regulation*, which outlines the right to an explanation where automated processing is involved ([26], Article 22).

Ultimately, the present normative framework of reference positions transparency as a cornerstone for ensuring and advancing human-centered AI. It is regarded as a crucial element for fostering a comprehensive understanding of AI systems and maintaining control over their operations, thereby promoting trust and ethical use. This entails clear communication about the functioning, capabilities, and limitations of AI systems, as well as the data they utilize. Such transparency not only helps users and stakeholders comprehend and effectively interact with AI systems but also empowers them to exercise oversight and ensure these technologies are aligned with human rights, democracy, and the rule of law. In essence, the policy framework recognizes that transparency is fundamental for building AI systems that are not only technically robust but also ethically sound and socially beneficial.

2.1 The value of transparency

When transparency fails to produce meaningful results, its intended purpose may lose its effectiveness. Simply exposing facts does not necessarily imply actual comprehension. Thus, it is critical to examine the underlying motivations for pursuing transparency in the first place. Understanding the need for transparency allows us to better strategize and implement steps to achieve it [26].

Accurate, unbiased, and transparent AI systems are particularly important to guarantee respect for the fundamental rights of individuals affected by the systems' outcomes. Despite the significant optimism surrounding the use of AI technologies, they have not yet received full acceptance in healthcare [27]. Establishing a reliable development process is key to promoting the acceptance of AI systems in this field. The potential benefits of AI are numerous, yet concerns persist regarding its drawbacks and implications [28]. These include issues such as mistrust, accountability, bias, data quality, and privacy. A significant number of these concerns can be attributed to the lack of transparency surrounding AI [29].

It is of paramount importance to comprehend the functioning of AI algorithms and the data with which they have been trained, as their potential impact on, inter alia, human dignity, human rights, and fundamental freedoms, gender equality, democracy, socioeconomic, and political processes [23]. The implementation of transparency in AI systems enables individuals to comprehend how each stage of the system is executed, taking into account its contextual and sensitive nature. It may also include insight into factors that affect a specific prediction or decision, and whether or not appropriate assurances are in place [23]. For example, Manrai et al. [30] found

---

[1] As per earlier versions of the *AI Act*, systems are categorized as high-risk based on their intended purpose, which entails significant potential for harm to health, safety, or fundamental rights of individuals. This determination considers both the severity and likelihood of potential harm, applying specifically to predefined sectors outlined in the regulation.

genetic disparities in assessing the risk of hypertrophic cardiomyopathy, in which benign variants from African patients were misclassified.

The demand for transparency is often perceived as a sign of distrust [31], yet it is widely regarded as a fundamental aspect of fostering trust within society [17]. In the context of AI, trust is crucial for its acceptance. As per Durán and Jongsma [32], the main epistemic obstacle to the trustworthiness of medical AI is represented by algorithmic opacity. As a result, algorithmic opacity makes it impossible to ground the reliability of the algorithm and, consequently, on whether researchers, physicians, and patients can trust the results of such systems. Computational reliabilism states that researchers are justified in believing the results of AI systems because there is a reliable process that yields, most of the time, trustworthy results [2, 32]. In computational reliabilism, the trustworthiness of the model's outputs can be evaluated through reliable processes that are exogenous to the algorithm, without relying on the use of explainers or the need to renounce the use of opaque systems [32]. One way to judge the reliability of the AI is when a physician compares the AI's diagnostic outputs with their own decisions made without the AI's assistance. If the beliefs about the trustworthiness of the AI are justified, the beliefs of the physician that are produced by such interaction will be justified [4].

Machine learning models are designed to learn patterns in the data, and then algorithmic decision-making may unintentionally reflect existing inequalities present in society, which are inherently present in the data [33]. The unfair behavior in machine learning systems, as defined by Crawford [34], is characterized by harm or impact on individuals. An example of unfair behavior is when the model's performance is inferior for certain groups or when it disproportionately benefits specific populations. A lack of transparency in AI-driven solutions can hinder the identification of bias and unintended consequences. Furthermore, it may also act as a deterrent to the utilization of AI, thereby denying individuals the potential benefits that it offers. Transparency plays a pivotal role in the identification and reduction of biases, the establishment of trust, and the promotion of fair outcomes.

2.2 Toward effective transparency

In the realm of AI, the concept of transparency has been widely extended to include the transparency of the algorithm [18], aimed at demystifying black box models. However, transparency should encompass various dimensions across the AI lifecycle, influencing how different stakeholders engage. We propose four levels of transparency: data, algorithmic, the decision-making process, and the AI solution as the overall system. Ensuring transparency in each component of the AI lifecycle is crucial and demands evaluation by appropriate auditors at each stage. For instance, developers typically assess technical-related or domain-specific transparency, as final users do not interact directly with the system at a technical level. This is presented in **Table 1**, which outlines the suggested transparency providers and auditors for the dimensions of transparency.

2.2.1 Data transparency

As data is at the cornerstone of each AI-driven decision-making process, ensuring transparency in data-related practices is essential for building trust. Data transparency sheds light on how the data has been collected, processed, and used. It promotes responsible data governance and mitigates inherent biases. Data governance promotes

Transparency dimension	Provider	Auditor
Data	Who provides the data and prepares the model input	• Domain expert • Who prepares the model input
Algorithmic	Who builds the model	• Domain expert • Who builds the model
Decision-making	Who builds the model	• User • Who builds the model
AI solution	Who integrates all algorithmic modules into a unified solution	• User • Who integrates the modules

Table 1.
The dimensions of transparency and the proposed roles in ensuring transparency across different stages of the AI system development.

data availability, usability, integrity, and security throughout its lifecycle [35]. Making data and its processing details accessible not only boosts transparency but also enhances the reusability and reproducibility of research. It is crucial to ensure that the data reflects diverse populations, thereby reducing the risk of disproportionately affecting certain groups. However, there must be a careful balance between transparency and data privacy. While transparency is necessary for building trust, it should not compromise the confidentiality and security of sensitive information.

2.2.2 Algorithmic transparency

Algorithmic transparency refers to the openness regarding how the algorithm operates. Openness can be defined as the ability to access and scrutinize code, data, and accompanying systems, which is essential for accountability [17]. Far from being open, proprietary algorithms typically restrict access, limiting their study and evaluation. This lack of transparency can hinder efforts to understand their inner workings. Various strategies can be employed to address the lack of algorithmic transparency. Making the implementation details and processes of the model openly accessible is essential. This includes sharing information about the system's design, development process, and specific parameters used for training. The use of open-source algorithms can help identify possible biases or errors. When open access is not feasible due to intellectual property concerns, third-party audits offer a viable alternative. These audits provide an independent assessment of the AI system, ensuring transparency and accountability without compromising proprietary information.

2.2.3 Decision-making transparency

Decision-making transparency involves comprehending how algorithms produce their outputs, which has been closely linked to explainability. It involves breaking down the model's decisions into human-comprehensible terms [18]. Previous studies suggest that AI explanations tend to increase the chances of humans accepting AI suggestions [36–38]. According to Jacovi et al. [39], providing explanations enables the user to better anticipate whether a model's decision is correct for given inputs, compared to a model without any explanation. However, this ability of a user to evaluate correctness does not make the algorithm more accurate, robust, and reliable in itself; it can only, at best, make the use of AI by the user more accurate, robust, and reliable. The criticism of explainable AI (xAI) is that while AI experts may have an understanding of xAI methods, they often lack a nuanced understanding of explanations [18]. While explainability can be useful to validate outputs or detect AI errors and can contribute to the trustworthiness of AI-as-used-by-a-human, it does not directly contribute to the reliability of the AI itself, and hence to the user's trust [4]. Attention-based mechanisms are a popular choice among the explainers, which can localize predictive regions in images, but they cannot specify which features are relevant, i.e., they can explain *where* the model places its attention but not *why* [40]. There is a need for more empirical research on transparency requirements from a user perspective [18]. The current scarcity stems from a fragmented understanding of AI transparency and it emphasizes the need to expand the conceptual scope of AI transparency to not only include the AI system, but also the various stakeholders interacting with the system, the context of the use of the system, and the larger social implications of its continued use.

2.2.4 AI solution

AI-based systems are typically integrated as a comprehensive set of tools consisting of various modules, each offering different functionalities. While transparency, robustness, and reliability may be maintained in each module, this would not automatically extend these qualities across the entire tool. Ensuring the ethical utilization of AI tools necessitates a collective effort. Responsibility for the ethical behavior of these tools lies not only with the AI developers but also with those who provide or distribute them. Additionally, AI users must ensure that the tools are validated before relying on their conclusions. As warned by Dignum [41], "trust in AI needs to be derived from trust on the socio-technical system embedding of AI." This implies that the technology alone might not solve issues such as biases, discrimination, or the safety of an AI system. Addressing these concerns requires institutional arrangements, including regulatory frameworks, regular audits, and collaborative, multidisciplinary efforts. Promoting transparency of the overall system involves reporting the intended usage of the technology and the target population to users.

3. Challenges and barriers to achieving transparency

In this context, the notion of transparency is thus not limited to the algorithmic component but also encompasses the data, the system in its totality, and the decisions reached through the utilization of such a system. Transparency in AI at all levels can provide significant value and positively shape how users perceive and interact with AI. It is precisely users' experience that determines, through their opinions, beliefs, and actions, what is socially acceptable and preferable, thus establishing the prevailing ethical framework. This cycle represents the normative cascade that shapes AI governance [42] and presents three main blocks of study for the analysis of the challenges in making transparency a reality (**Figure 1**): the ethical framework, the normative framework, and users' activity. This section will examine several challenges associated with achieving transparency through the utilization of real-world examples, with a particular focus on the three primary elements previously outlined.

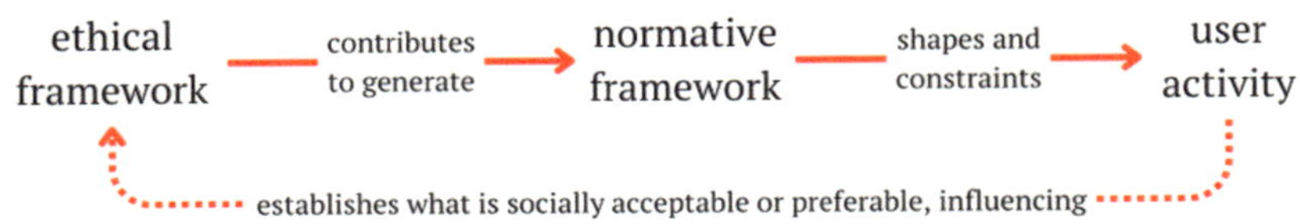

Figure 1.
The normative cascade is a concept used to illustrate how AI governance is shaped by the interdependence between ethical, normative, and user activity frameworks.

3.1 Weaknesses present in the current ethical framework

At the moment, transparency is not prioritized when it comes to developing AI. There are a number of reasons for this, such as the desire to use the latest technology simply because it is the most popular, ignoring its limitations, which contributes to the failure of many organizations to see the value of transparency in the short term as well as the long term, and the lack of demand for transparency practices, which feeds back into the weakness of the current ethical framework. Below, we explore each of these challenges in more detail.

3.1.1 Overuse of hyped AI techniques

The advent and proliferation of machine learning technologies have had a demonstrably disruptive impact on numerous aspects of our lives in recent years. This has given rise to an enthusiasm that has helped spread the mindset of technosolutionism, a term coined by Morozov that is grounded on the belief that technology can provide solutions to all society's problems [43]. The application of such trending AI-driven technologies has yielded successful results, including the advancement of diagnostic imaging methods [44, 45] and the extraction of knowledge from high-throughput data [46]. However, these hyped technologies are not adequate to solve all problems [47]. For instance, the very features that render deep learning so powerful can also prove its Achilles' heel. In some cases, such as novel biomedical omics projects that generate substantial amounts of data, deep learning may appear to be the optimal solution. However, because these projects analyze a multitude of molecular elements from only a few hundred individuals, deep learning might not be the most adequate approach. Forcing deep learning into projects where it is not the optimal solution can lead to wasted resources and potentially hinder the project's overall success [48]. Besides, it should be borne in mind that the deep learning-based breakthroughs that have fueled the high expectations have taken place in contexts where computing power and storage capacity were almost unlimited, usually unmatched by other institutions.

One of the challenges associated with the adoption of novel technologies is the tendency to prioritize the performance demonstrated in specific applications over the less visible limitations inherent to some of these technologies. For example, the black-box nature of deep learning renders this technique ill-suited to domains where a comprehensive understanding of the functionality and limitations of the tools involved in decision-making is paramount, such as healthcare. Therefore, it is crucial to avoid overhyping and blindly incorporating new technologies without careful consideration. In each application, a justification must be provided that demonstrates why the selected technique is the most appropriate method for addressing the problem. This justification should consider not only the technical requirements, such as the amount of data needed and computing power but also the usability requirements, such as the provision of information to facilitate comprehension of the solution. In other cases, alternative methodologies may be more suitable, contingent on the specific context. This is often the case with deep learning, which is inherently not interpretable [49]. The assertion is often made that "trending AI methods are better" [50]. However, it is crucial to recognize that the term "better" should not be interpreted as solely representing enhanced performance but also as a means of enhancing utilization.

3.1.2 The value of transparency is overseen

A further obstacle to achieving transparency is the perception that entities in possession of the technology perceive few immediate benefits in implementing it. This challenge is intensified by the preponderance of private initiatives in the AI sector, where financial interests frequently prevail. Scholars such as Pasquale have conducted extensive research into how algorithms employed by both corporations and governments are often shrouded in secrecy, which complicates individuals' comprehension of the decision-making processes that impact their lives [5].

In order to address this challenge, it is necessary to acknowledge that any organization offering tools or services to the public acts as a social agent with responsibilities toward society. While corporate entities may prioritize confidentiality for competitive or proprietary reasons, there is a growing recognition that embracing transparency can enhance public trust and promote societal benefits [17, 51]. By adopting transparent practices, organizations can contribute to a more educated and informed society where citizens are better equipped to engage critically with technological advancements and societal changes; this is supported by the shifts in perception observed through the utilization of the participatory Decidim platform in deliberative processes [52]. This approach not only aligns with ethical imperatives but also supports broader goals of fairness, equity, and democratic governance in the deployment of technologies that increasingly shape our daily lives.

3.1.3 Lack of demand for transparency practices

A significant challenge lies in the lack of demand and enforcement of transparency practices. This absence means that the degree of transparency of AI systems often depends on the discretion and integrity of those implementing them. This situation not only undermines efforts to ensure accountability but also perpetuates a culture within AI development that boosts rapid progress at the expense of ethical considerations. This "move fast, break things" mentality can result in the marginalization of critical concerns regarding the impact of AI technologies on society. It shifts the focus away from the prioritization of respect and empowerment of people, which should be among the central purposes of developing these technologies.

This challenge can be approached from a number of different perspectives. On one hand, in line with UNESCO's recommendations [23], enforceable transparency protocols must be established to ensure access to information, particularly information of public interest held by private entities. Such protocols would fundamentally alter the AI lifecycle by embedding transparency requirements from the initial design phase onwards. On the other hand, there is a critical need for independent organizations to oversee and enforce these protocols. The establishment of the Spanish Artificial Intelligence Oversight Agency in 2023 serves as a promising example [53]. This agency is tasked with overseeing, advising, raising awareness, and providing training to both public and private entities on the proper implementation of national and European regulations concerning the responsible use and development of AI systems, specifically algorithms. However, its effectiveness in meeting these expectations remains to be proven.

The importance of having a culture of transparency can be illustrated by reference to the audit of public systems that impact people's welfare, such as the allocation of public subsidies. In Spain, the non-profit foundation Civio conducted an analysis of a government social voucher that had erroneously denied aid to eligible individuals [54]. The decisions were made using algorithmic systems. Researchers from Civio sought information from the government to gain insight into the functioning of the tool. This inquiry revealed deficiencies in the system and led to the formulation of corrective actions. As a result, adjustments were made to ensure that subsidies were accurately distributed to those who qualified and genuinely needed them.

3.2 Weaknesses present in the current normative framework

The second area of interest concerns the established normative framework. One of the primary challenges is addressing the absence of standards to apply transparency in practice. This gap frequently hinders the implementation of transparency measures by AI practitioners, as they lack the requisite expertise to translate broad normative frameworks into practical standards. Subsequently, we will address some of the main challenges encountered, such as the difficulties of choosing the procedures to apply and the difficulty in identifying transparency requirements.

3.2.1 Absence of standards for transparency reporting

The European Union incorporated some AI transparency requirements into its *General Data Protection Regulation* [55], such as the right to explanation. However, the efficacy of these measures remains uncertain [56]. The forthcoming *AI Act* aims to strengthen those initial norms, introducing provisions such as the disclosure of AI-generated content and specific requirements for high-risk systems. These include ensuring sufficient transparency for operators to interpret system outputs and use them effectively, along with providing comprehensive instructions that detail the characteristics, capabilities, and performance limitations of high-risk AI systems.

Although various normative documents articulate the overarching goal of transparency [23, 24], there is a lack of standardized practice regarding the specific information that should be disclosed in real life. This gap has resulted in a situation where experts interpret and recommend relevant transparency measures based on individual circumstances. Consequently, the implementation of transparency practices varies considerably, depending more on the discretion and motivation of operators than on standardized procedures or agreed guidelines. This variability highlights the need for more coherent and universally applicable standards to ensure consistent and effective transparency across different sectors and contexts. For example, the need for standardized reporting is evident when comparing the information presented in different scientific publications, as the lack of consistency hinders reproducibility, comparability, and validation of results. When some machine learning-driven works fail to disclose crucial details such as the pre-processing steps applied to the data, the data splitting method, the inner workings of the model, or the hyperparameters used, it becomes challenging for other researchers to replicate the findings and compromises public trust in the system [45].

3.2.2 Transparency is not the same for everyone

Another challenge derives from understanding transparency requirements within AI-driven systems. Transparency requires tailored approaches to meet the diverse needs of various stakeholders. In the context of AI-driven healthcare solutions, it includes data scientists, healthcare professionals, patients, and legal advisors [57]. Key issues pertaining to the provision of transparency include determining who needs it, the necessary level of detail, accessibility, and timing. Addressing these issues demands multidisciplinary collaboration and an adaptive approach.

On the one hand, without the input of diverse experts early in the development process, efforts to define system transparency can fall short. Effective teams should include all stakeholders involved in the process to ensure that all perspectives are considered. Moreover, transparency requirements vary significantly depending on the application context. Some situations demand detailed algorithmic transparency to validate system reliability and fairness, while others prioritize decision-making transparency to ensure AI-generated recommendations are clear and actionable for clinicians or patients. Furthermore, the requirements for transparency vary across different stakeholders [57]. For instance, data scientists need transparency to understand data inputs and model mechanics, while patients require transparency for trust and engagement with AI recommendations.

One successful approach to this challenge is exemplified by the AI-driven patient education platform owned by DigimEvo[2] [58], which posed the necessity to enhance transparency by catering to diverse stakeholder needs. Data scientists demanded transparency to understand data inputs and decision-making processes. Consequently, the platform displays the connections between data that result in the generation of the algorithmic output. Patients also demanded transparency to assess the trustworthiness of the personalized recommendations. Consequently, recommendations are substantiated by a rationale that justifies their relevance, e.g., whether there is an alignment with the patient's clinical profile or evidence in similar pathological conditions.

3.3 Weaknesses regarding the protection of users

As highlighted above, ensuring data transparency is critical to understanding how AI systems work. It provides clarity and insight into processes and decisions that affect individuals and communities. However, achieving full data transparency is often hampered by the need to protect the rights of individuals, with privacy being a paramount concern. Balancing the need for transparency with the protection of privacy rights is a delicate task. While transparency promotes accountability and reliability, it must be managed responsibly to avoid compromising sensitive personal information. Achieving this balance requires thoughtful policies and practices that promote openness while respecting and protecting privacy rights. In this part, we delve into the intricacies of demanding transparency while preserving privacy.

3.3.1 Modeling sensitive data

In AI-driven healthcare, it is desired that patients and providers use advanced technologies with minimal restrictions, fostering innovation, transparency, and

[2] https://digimevo.com/

efficient service delivery. It enables better decision-making, reduced workloads, and improved patient outcomes. Conversely, protecting patients' personal health information is crucial. Privacy entails keeping data confidential, adhering to data protection laws, and employing strong security measures to prevent breaches and misuse. Balancing these priorities is difficult, as it requires ensuring both innovation and strict data protection simultaneously [59].

Pseudo-anonymization of patient data prevent individual identification while still allowing re-identification when necessary for accurate predictions and personalized care. This approach enhances data sharing and analysis safety without compromising patient privacy. However, it poses potential risks of re-identification if combined with other data or if the anonymization process is not robust [60]. On the other hand, federated learning emerges as a powerful approach that enables AI algorithms to be trained across a multitude of decentralized devices or servers, such as disparate hospitals, without the necessity to transfer the actual data to a central location. This approach addresses the issues of data privacy and security [61]. However, federated learning has its own challenges, such as ensuring effective learning across different datasets. By standardizing data and creating compatible protocols, federated learning can be a powerful tool for collaborative AI development in healthcare. Despite its advantages, federated learning has yet to achieve widespread clinical adoption [62].

In order to mitigate the risks associated with the loss of privacy, it is also possible to exclude variables that contain sensitive information and to investigate the primary effects that make a variable significant. It should be noted that since correlation does not imply causation, it is necessary to control for confounding variables in order to ensure that the predictions made by the model are based on relevant, non-sensitive data. The concept of explainability in machine learning plays an important role in the identification and exclusion of sensitive variables, as well as in the detection and control of confounding variables. This, in turn, helps to prevent incorrect assumptions about causality [63].

Consequently, the development of models that do not compromise privacy is a challenging endeavor, given the potential for conflict between transparency requirements and the necessity to protect sensitive information. This is illustrated in the Trustroke project,[3] which addresses challenges in stroke treatment optimization through federated learning, explainability, and pseudo-anonymization. By using a federated learning infrastructure, Trustroke develops predictive algorithms on decentralized data from multiple hospitals without transferring patient data, enhancing privacy and allowing smaller hospitals to predict stroke outcomes effectively. xAI provides transparency in decision-making, increasing trust in the models while protecting sensitive information. Additionally, pseudo-anonymization ensures data cannot be traced back to individuals, allowing necessary re-identification for accurate predictions and personalized care. These approaches collectively create high-quality, harmonized, and trustworthy datasets, addressing critical needs in stroke treatment.

3.3.2 The disclosure of sensitive data to external parties

Transparency in AI often requires disclosing details of the data used to external parties, which inevitably raises significant privacy concerns. Revealing the data used allows for a clearer understanding of how AI systems work, which is crucial for

---

[3] Funded by the European Union in the call Horizon-hlth-2022-stayhlth-01-two-stage under grant agreement No.101080564. More information at https://trustroke.eu

assessing their accuracy, biases, and decision-making processes. However, this data transparency must be carefully managed to avoid revealing sensitive personal information or proprietary data that could compromise individuals' privacy.

One approach is to disclose anonymized data, which involves the removal or alteration of personally identifiable information in order to protect individuals' privacy. However, it is crucial to conduct thorough research to determine which characteristics can be safely shared without risking re-identification. For example, it has been demonstrated that seemingly innocuous combinations of demographic characteristics can inadvertently reveal unique or nearly unique identities [64]. Another strategy is to employ differential privacy methods, which add noise or perturbations to the data to protect individual privacy while still allowing for useful statistical analysis. However, implementing differential privacy can sometimes lead to challenges in maintaining fairness, as the added noise may disproportionately affect certain demographic groups or outcomes [65].

In the field of digital health, a common challenge emerges when data utilized in the development of systems cannot be shared due to constraints imposed by initial consent agreements. They typically permit the use of data for the purpose of developing a specific system or service. However, they often do not allow for the broader dissemination or sharing of the data beyond this scope. This limitation can be attributed to concerns pertaining to patient confidentiality, data security, and legal obligations to protect sensitive health information. Consequently, while the data may be instrumental in developing innovative health technologies and improving patient care, its sensitive nature precludes its widespread dissemination. This hinders data transparency, thus preventing external audits and working on top of others' work. The resolution of this issue requires the navigation of intricate regulatory frameworks and the enhancement of consent processes in order to achieve a balance between the facilitation of data-driven advancements through the research community and the preservation of patient privacy rights. It is anticipated that the European Health Data Space, once it is fully operational, will serve as a model for other similar initiatives.

4. Future directions

In the preceding section, an examination was conducted of the complexities involved in establishing algorithmic practices that genuinely embody transparency in the various areas of AI governance, including the ethical framework, the normative framework, and user activity. To address the challenges presented, several solutions and initiatives have emerged that seek to address all dimensions of transparency: data, algorithmic, decision-making, and the AI solution as a whole. These innovations not only assist in mitigating the existing risks associated with opaque algorithms but also facilitate the advancement of transparency and ethical standards in AI applications.

Nevertheless, these innovative practices must always be complemented by a thoughtful consideration of their intended outcomes. As discussed earlier, transparency can be perceived differently depending on the perspective and context. It is therefore crucial that these methods are accompanied by clear explanations of *who* benefits from them, *what* goals they aim to achieve, *when* and under what circumstances they are applicable, *why* they are being implemented, and *how* they will be carried out. Such comprehensive considerations will ensure that transparency initiatives are not only implemented effectively but are also consistent and responsive to specific needs.

In order to carry out such an exercise, it is necessary to encourage not only multidisciplinary work, but ideally interdisciplinary work. This means that teams aiming to develop an AI-driven solution should include several profiles that can provide an ethical and normative vision, knowledge of the application domain, and technical knowledge to provide answers to the questions posed. In the case of AI-driven health-related technologies, it is essential that not only AI specialists and medical experts are involved but also bioethicists, who will contribute their knowledge on ethical and normative frameworks to the table. This will enable the development of the most appropriate solutions to meet the challenges of the particular context. Furthermore, the involvement of ethics committees in the approval of projects may extend beyond the initial stages to encompass the course of the project itself. This will reflect the fact that solutions are dynamic and problems evolve over time.

This paradigm shift would enable a transition to a new way of thinking, redefining transparency as an integrative process and promoting a proactive approach to addressing these issues. Rather than viewing transparency as a mere checkbox or compliance requirement, this new perspective would encourage an ongoing, dynamic engagement with transparency. It calls for organizations and individuals to actively seek opportunities to disclose information, clarify decision-making processes, and engage stakeholders in meaningful dialog. Embracing transparency as an integrative process fosters a culture where transparency is not just a reactive disclosure of information but an active pursuit of openness, accountability, and ethical behavior in all aspects of operations and decision-making. This proactive approach not only builds trust but also drives continuous improvement and responsiveness to societal expectations and evolving challenges.

In this vein, the proposed *AI Act* represents an important milestone in fostering trust in AI by emphasizing transparency. However, there is still room for improvement. While the legislation is commendable for its enforceable provisions, a notable limitation is the ambiguity surrounding some aspects of the requirements for transparency. This ambiguity could potentially lead to different interpretations and implementations, relying heavily on self-regulation within the industry. Consequently, there is a need for clearer guidelines and standards to ensure that transparency in the development and deployment of AI is consistently upheld across different sectors and jurisdictions. Addressing these concerns would not only strengthen the ethical and normative framework, but also increase accountability, reliability, and public trust in AI technologies as they become increasingly integrated into everyday life.

Addressing normative change will require significant effort, so it is worth exploring alternative policies that can stimulate ethical change. For example, governments could incentivize transparency and discourage unnecessary complexity through frameworks similar to social movements such as "Move Your Money," which encouraged citizens to move away from big banks [5]. By promoting transparency as a value and incentivizing organizations that adopt clear and accountable practices, governments can effectively encourage a cultural shift toward more ethical behavior. Such initiatives could not only increase public trust in institutions and companies but also create competitive pressures that encourage wider adoption of transparent practices across industries. This approach is consistent with fostering a regulatory environment that not only mandates compliance but also cultivates a proactive commitment to ethical behavior and transparency in governance and business operations.

5. Conclusions

The importance of transparency in AI for fostering sustainable development is widely acknowledged. This principle is reinforced by global initiatives such as the

United Nations' Sustainable Development Goals for 2030, which highlight the importance of transparency in institutions. These goals emphasize accountable governance and the necessity of transparent practices to enhance public trust and ensure effective service delivery. By integrating transparency into AI systems and institutional frameworks, we can advance toward a governance model that actively involves citizens and promotes confidence in democratic processes.

As the quantity of accessible data continues to expand and AI becomes increasingly prevalent, it is vital to acknowledge this growth and adopt a perspective that prioritizes transparency in AI implementation. This imperative is particularly pertinent in sectors that are vital to public well-being, such as healthcare. Transparency in AI practices ensures that decisions made by algorithms are comprehensible, accountable, and fair. In the field of healthcare, for instance, transparent AI can enhance patient trust by clarifying how medical decisions are reached, ensuring privacy protection, and promoting equitable access to health-related services.

Addressing the multifaceted challenge of understanding transparency requirements in AI-driven healthcare systems requires a cohesive approach. Key solutions include bringing together diverse teams early in the AI system development process, developing tailored transparency approaches that address stakeholder needs, and continuously refining these strategies based on feedback. In addition, increasing public awareness and education about AI technologies is critical to filling information gaps and effectively communicating transparency requirements.

The embrace of transparency in AI not only fosters public confidence but also facilitates ethical and responsible use of technology across various domains, ultimately supporting a sustainable and equitable future.

Author details

Paula Subías-Beltrán[1,2]*, Carla Pitarch[1,3], Carolina Migliorelli[1], Luís Marte[1], Mar Galofré[1] and Silvia Orte[1]

1 Eurecat, Centre Tecnològic de Catalunya, Barcelona, Spain

2 Bioethics and Law Observatory – UNESCO Chair in Bioethics, Universitat de Barcelona, Barcelona, Spain

3 Computer Science Department, Universitat Politècnica de Catalunya (UPC), Barcelona, Spain

*Address all correspondence to: psubiabe11@alumnes.ub.edu

References

[1] Ribeiro MT, Singh S, Guestrin C. "Why should I trust you?" Explaining the predictions of any classifier. In: Proceedings of the 22nd ACM SIGKDD International Conference on Knowledge Discovery and Data Mining. New York, NY, USA: Association for Computing Machinery; 2016. pp. 1135-1144

[2] Durán JM, Formanek N. Grounds for trust: Essential epistemic opacity and computational reliabilism. Minds and Machines. 2018;**28**:645-666

[3] Poon AI, Sung JJ. Opening the black box of AI-medicine. Journal of Gastroenterology and Hepatology. 2021;**36**(3):581-584

[4] Ferrario A, Loi M. How explainability contributes to trust in AI. In: Proceedings of the 2022 ACM Conference on Fairness, Accountability, and Transparency. FAccT '22. New York, NY, USA: Association for Computing Machinery; 2022. pp. 1457-1466

[5] Pasquale F. The Black Box Society: The Secret algorithms That Control Money and Information. Cambridge MA, USA: Harvard University Press; 2015

[6] Pal S. Integrating AI in sustainable supply chain management: A new paradigm for enhanced transparency and sustainability. International Journal for Research in Applied Science and Engineering Technology. 2023;**11**(6):2979-2984

[7] López Baroni MJ. Fourth generation human rights in view of the fourth industrial revolution. Philosophies. 2024;**9**(2):39. DOI: 10.3390/philosophies9020039

[8] Ehsan U, Liao QV, Muller M, Riedl MO, Weisz JD. Expanding Explainability: Towards Social Transparency in AI systems. In: Proceedings of the 2021 CHI Conference on Human Factors in Computing Systems. CHI '21. New York, NY, USA: Association for Computing Machinery; 2021. DOI: 10.1145/3411764.3445188

[9] Crawford K. The Atlas of AI: Power, Politics, and the Planetary Costs of Artificial Intelligence. New Haven, Connecticut, USA: Yale University Press; 2021

[10] Filloux F. Google News: The Secret Sauce [Article in Monday Note]. Medium. 2013

[11] Hood C, Heald D. Transparency in Historical Perspective. Vol. 135. Oxford, England: Oxford University Press; 2006

[12] Margetts H. The internet and transparency. The Political Quarterly. 2011;**82**(4):518-521

[13] Hansen HK, Christensen LT, Flyverbom M. Introduction: Logics of Transparency in Late Modernity: Paradoxes, Mediation and Governance. London, England: SAGE Publications Sage UK; 2015

[14] Christensen LT, Morsing M, Thyssen O. The polyphony of corporate social responsibility: Deconstructing accountability and ransparency in the context of identity and hypocrisy. In: The Handbook of Communication Ethics. New York, NY, USA: Routledge; 2011. pp. 457-474

[15] Pagano B, Pagano E. The Transparency edge: How Credibility can Make or Break you in Business. New York, NY, USA: McGraw Hill Professional; 2004

[16] Reddy MJ. The conduit metaphor: A case of frame conflict in our language about language. Metaphor and Thought. 1979;**2**:164-201

[17] Larsson S, Heintz F. Transparency in Artificial Intelligence. Internet Policy Review. 2020;**9**(2):1-16

[18] Haresamudram K, Larsson S, Heintz F. Three levels of AI transparency. Computer. 2023;**56**(2):93-100

[19] Larsson S. Conceptions in the code: How Metaphors Explain Legal Challenges in Digital Times. Oxford, England: Oxford University Press; 2017

[20] Fecher B, Friesike S. Open Science: One Term, Five Schools of Thought. Heidelberg, New York, Dordrecht, London: Springer International Publishing; 2014

[21] Ruijer E, Grimmelikhuijsen S, Meijer A. Open data for democracy: Developing a theoretical framework for open data use. Government Information Quarterly. 2017;**34**(1):45-52

[22] AI HLEG. Ethics Guidelines for Trustworthy AI. High-Level Expert Group on Artificial Intelligence: Brussels; 2019. Available from: https://ec.europa.eu/futurium/en/ai-alliance-consultation.1.html

[23] UNESCO. Recommendation on the Ethics of Artificial Intelligence. Paris, France: UNESCO; 2022

[24] Council of Europe. Council of Europe Framework Convention on Artificial Intelligence and Human Rights, Democracy, and the Rule of Law. Vilnius, Lithuania: Council of Europe; 2024

[25] The European Parliament. Regulation (EU) 2024 of the European Parliament and of the Council of Europe laying down harmonised rules on artificial intelligence and amending Regulations (EC) No 300/2008, (EU) No 167/2013, (EU) No 168/2013, (EU) 2018/858, (EU) 2018/1139 and (EU) 2019/2144 and Directives 2014/90/EU, (EU) 2016/797 and (EU) 2020/1828 (Artificial Intelligence Act). 2024

[26] Ananny M, Crawford K. Seeing without knowing: Limitations of the transparency ideal and its application to algorithmic accountability. New Media & Society. 2018;**20**(3):973-989

[27] Steerling E, Siira E, Nilsen P, Svedberg P, Nygren J. Implementing AI in healthcare—The relevance of trust: A scoping review. Frontiers in Health Services. 2023;**3**:1211150

[28] European Parliamentary Research Service. Artificial Intelligence in Healthcare: Applications, Risks, and Ethical and Societal Impacts; 2022. Available from: https://www.europarl.europa.eu/thinktank/en/document/EPRS_STU(2022)729512

[29] Winter PD, Carusi A. (De)troubling transparency: Artificial intelligence (AI) for clinical applications. Medical Humanities. 2023;**49**(1):17-26

[30] Manrai AK, Funke BH, Rehm HL, Olesen MS, Maron BA, Szolovits P, et al. Genetic misdiagnoses and the potential for health disparities. New England Journal of Medicine. 2016;**375**:655-665

[31] Han BC. The Transparency Society. Stanford University Press; 2015

[32] Durán JM, Jongsma KR. Who is afraid of black box algorithms? On the epistemological and ethical basis of trust in medical AI. Journal of Medical Ethics. 2021;**47**(5):329-335

[33] Barocas S, Hardt M, Narayanan A. Fairness and Machine Learning:

Limitations and Opportunities. MIT Press; 2023

[34] NeurIPS 2017 keynote by Kate Crawford. Long Beach, CA, USA: The Artificial Intelligence Channel; 2017. Available online: https://www.youtube.com/watch?v=fMym BKWQzk

[35] Cheong LK, Chang V. The Need for Data Governance: A Case Study. In: ACIS 2007 Proceedings. 100. Association for Information Systems; 2007. Available from: https://aisel.aisnet.org/acis2007/100

[36] Lakkaraju H, Bastani O. "How do I fool you?" Manipulating user trust via misleading black box explanations. In: Proceedings of the AAAI/ACM Conference on AI, Ethics, and Society. New York, NY, USA: Association for Computing Machinery; 2020. pp. 79-85

[37] Bansal G, Wu T, Zhou J, Fok R, Nushi B, Kamar E, et al. Does the whole exceed its parts? the effect of ai explanations on complementary team performance. In: Proceedings of the 2021 CHI Conference on Human Factors in Computing Systems. 2021. pp. 1-16

[38] Jin W, Fatehi M, Guo R, Hamarneh G. Evaluating the clinical utility of artificial intelligence assistance and its explanation on the glioma grading task. Artificial Intelligence in Medicine. 2024;**148**:102751

[39] Jacovi A, Marasović A, Miller T, Goldberg Y. Formalizing trust in artificial intelligence: Prerequisites, causes and goals of human trust in AI. In: Proceedings of the 2021 ACM Conference on Fairness, Accountability, and Transparency. FAccT '21. New York, NY, USA, Association for Computing Machinery; 2021. pp. 624-635

[40] Lipkova J, Chen RJ, Chen B, Lu MY, Barbieri M, Shao D, et al. Artificial intelligence for multimodal data integration in oncology. Cancer Cell. 2022;**40**:1095-1110

[41] Dignum V. On the European AI Act: Acting Is Key; 2021. Available from: https://www.linkedin.com/pulse/european-ai-act-acting-key-virginia-dignum/ [Accessed: 2 July 2024]

[42] Floridi L. Soft ethics, the governance of the digital and the General Data Protection Regulation. Philosophical Transactions of the Royal Society A: Mathematical, Physical and Engineering Sciences. 2018;**376**(2133):20180081

[43] Morozov E. La locura del solucionismo tecnológico. vol. 5010. Madrid, Spain: Katz Editores y Capital Intelectual; 2015

[44] Singh SP, Wang L, Gupta S, Goli H, Padmanabhan P, Gulya´s B. 3D Deep Learning on Medical Images: A Review. Sensors. 2020;**20**(18):1-24. Available from: https://www.mdpi.com/1424-8220/20/18/5097

[45] Pitarch C, Ungan G, Julià-Sapé M, Vellido A. Advances in the use of deep learning for the analysis of magnetic resonance image in neuro-oncology. Cancers. 2024;**16**(2)

[46] Kang M, Ko E, Mersha TB. A roadmap for multi-omics data integration using deep learning. Briefings in Bioinformatics. 2021;**23**(1):bbab454

[47] Mohiuddin Ahmed NI. Deep learning: Hope or hype. Annals of Data Science. 2020

[48] Miotto R, Wang F, Wang S, Jiang X, Dudley JT. Deep learning for healthcare: Review, opportunities and challenges. Briefings in Bioinformatics. 2018;**19**(6):1236-1246

[49] Rudin C. Stop explaining black box machine learning models for high stakes

decisions and use interpretable models instead. Nature Machine Intelligence. 2019;**1**(5):206-215

[50] Dong Y, Li J, Schnabel T. When newer is not better: Does deep learning really benefit recommendation from implicit feedback? In: SIGIR '23: Proceedings of the 46th International ACM SIGIR Conference on Research and Development in Information Retrieval. New York, NY, USA: Association for Computing Machinery; 2023. pp. 942-952. DOI: 10.1145/3539618.3591785

[51] European Commission. White Paper on Artificial Intelligence – A European Approach to Excellence and Trust. 2020

[52] Borge R, Balcells J, Padró-Solanet A. Democratic disruption or continuity? Analysis of the Decidim platform in Catalan municipalities. American Behavioral Scientist. 2023;**67**(7):926-939

[53] Ministerio de la Presidencia, Relaciones con las Cortes y Memoria Democrática. Real Decreto 729/2023, de 22 de Agosto, por el que se aprueba el Estatuto de la Agencia Española de Supervisión de Inteligencia Artificial. Spain: Boletín Oficial del Estado; 2023

[54] Belmonte E. La aplicación del bono social del Gobierno niega la ayuda a personas que tienen derecho a ella. Civio. 2019 May

[55] General Data Protection Regulation. Regulation (EU) 2016/679 of the European Parliament and of the Council of 27 April 2016 on the protection of natural persons with regard to the processing of personal data and on the free movement of such data, and repealing Directive 95/46/EC. Official Journal of the European Union. 2016

[56] Seizov O, Wulf AJ. Artificial intelligence and transparency: a blueprint for improving the regulation of AI applications in the EU. European Business Law Review. 2020;**31**(4):611-640

[57] Hogg HDJ, Al-Zubaidy M, Group TEMSSR, Talks J, Denniston AK, Kelly CJ, et al. Stakeholder perspectives of clinical artificial intelligence implementation: Systematic review of qualitative evidence. Journal of Medical Internet Research. 2023;**25**:e39742

[58] Orte S, Migliorelli C, Sistach-Bosch L, Subías-Beltrán P, Fritzsche PC, Galofré M, et al. BECOME: A modular recommender system for coaching and promoting empowerment in healthcare. In: DSP S, editor. Vol. Artificial Intelligence in Medicine and Surgery - An Exploration of Current Trends, Potential Opportunities, and Evolving Threats, 2. Rijeka: IntechOpen; 2023

[59] Williamson SM, Prybutok V. Balancing Privacy and Progress: A Review of Privacy Challenges, Systemic Oversight, and Patient Perceptions in AI-Driven Healthcare. Applied Sciences. 2024;**14**(2):1-47

[60] Kikuchi H, Yamaguchi T, Hamada K, Yamaoka Y, Oguri H, Sakuma J. Ice and Fire: Quantifying the Risk of Re-identification and Utility in Data Anonymization. IEEE; 2016. pp. 1035-1042

[61] Abhishek V, Binny S, Johan TR, Nithin R, Vishal T. Federated Learning: Collaborative Machine Learning without Centralized Training Data. International journal of engineering technology and management sciences. 2022;**6**:355-359

[62] Teo ZL, Jin L, Liu N, Li S, Miao D, Zhang X, et al. Federated machine learning in healthcare: A systematic review on clinical applications and technical architecture. Cell Reports Medicine. 2024;**5**(3):101481

[63] Strobel M, Shokri R. Data privacy and trustworthy machine learning. IEEE Security & Privacy. 2022;**20**:44-49

[64] Sweeney L. Simple demographics often identify people uniquely. Health (San Francisco). 2000;**671**(2000):1-34

[65] Pujol D, McKenna R, Kuppam S, Hay M, Machanavajjhala A, Miklau G. Fair decision making using privacy-protected data. In: Proceedings of the 2020 Conference on Fairness, Accountability, and Transparency. New York, NY, USA: Association for Computing Machinery; 2020. pp. 189-199

Section 2

Challenges and Opportunities of AI in Education

Chapter 4

Designing Trustworthy AI in Higher Education

Sandra Rebholz, Paul Libbrecht and Wolfgang Müller

Abstract

Applying Artificial Intelligence-(AI)-based systems and tools in the context of higher education imposes many challenges with respect to data privacy and ethics. For example, the EU AI Act that was adopted in March 2024 classifies many AI systems used in education as high-risk AI systems. High-risk AI systems must follow a strict set of requirements in order to be used in practice. Beyond the legal obligations, the trustworthy use of AI systems is not yet widespread. There are already approaches for assessing the trustworthiness of AI systems that shall ensure that such systems comply with existing guidelines for ethical AI. In this chapter, we review available design approaches for building trustworthy AI systems and evaluate their applicability in the context of higher education. In the real-life use case of developing an AI-based analysis system for e-portfolios from students in introductory computing courses at university, the existing design approaches are further detailed and adapted to the specific context of higher education. Furthermore, we assess the trustworthiness of the developed AI-based analysis system using the OECD Framework for the Classification of AI systems. Based on the findings, we conclude and recommend a scenario-based design process that helps build trustworthy AI-based systems in higher education.

Keywords: AI in higher education, trustworthiness, assessment, e-portfolio, natural language processing, scenarios

1. Introduction

Publicly available AI tools are rapidly emerging and finding immediate application in the educational field. This is especially true for Generative AI (GenAI) and corresponding technologies, but there is also an increasing number of initiatives in which independent AI developments are being developed for dedicated use in teaching as well as to support learners and teachers in learning processes. An example of such targeted development, which also motivates and underpins the analysis presented here, is the design and development of AI-based methodologies and tools to support teachers in the assessment of and the formulation of feedback on e-portfolios created by students as academic achievement [1]. Such an application has the potential to ease the assessment and the comparative evaluation of e-portfolios, which is typically time-consuming and elaborate due to the individual character of students' e-portfolios. However, AI-based assessment of coverage of required topics, depth of treatment of individual topics, and reflective linking of different subject areas also require trust in summarized assessments generated by AI and justifications for corresponding evaluations and reasoning. This concrete example illustrates that AI-based systems may offer much potential in the field of education but also raises questions and poses challenges related to the risks of AI and specifically to the aspect of trust that needs to be addressed. The objective of developing AI-based systems needs to be to develop systems that realize the potential benefits but at the same time make sure that the systems can also be trusted. According to the EU strategy of following a human-centric approach to developing AI systems, trust is the prerequisite for this approach.

Based on the use case of supporting the assessment of e-portfolios by AI-based methods and tools as illustrated above, our work presents an in-depth analysis of how to design trustworthy AI-based systems in higher education. Specifically, the following research questions will be addressed: What are the requirements and best practices for building trust with relevant stakeholders involved in the AI-supported analysis of complex learning artifacts such as e-portfolios? How can trust be deliberately integrated into the design and development process of such an AI-based analysis system?

In order to answer these questions, we proceed as follows. After an outline of the theoretical foundations of trust in general and trustworthiness in the context of AI-based systems, we present a detailed analysis of the specific challenges of applying AI in education. Subsequently, we review existing approaches for building trustworthy AI systems that implement the Trustworthiness-by-Design paradigm. Based on the real-life use case of developing an AI-based system for analyzing e-portfolios from students at university, we adapt and refine these approaches for the context of higher education. The derived scenario-based design and development process is described in detail, as well as the evaluation of the developed e-portfolio analysis system using the OECD assessment framework for trustworthy AI. Finally, the resulting findings are critically discussed, and the identified benefits and potential challenges of the proposed scenario-based approach are highlighted.

2. Trustworthiness of AI-based systems

In a general sense, trust is the belief *"that a person (the trustee) will act in the best interests of another (the truster) in a given situation, even when controls are unavailable and it may not be in the trustee's best interests to do so."* ([2], p. 19). According to a study conducted by Slade et al. [3], the most important element of trust is reliability and consistency of the trustee, followed by beneficence and transparency. Trust with respect to the use of a product or system can be defined as the *"degree to which a user or other stakeholder has confidence that a product or system will behave as intended"* ([4], section 3.41). Drawing on this definition, trustworthiness is the *"ability to meet stakeholders' expectations in a verifiable way"* ([4], section 3.42). Consequently, it depends on the context and type of system in order to determine the characteristics that are expected from a system and how to verify them.

In the context of AI-based systems, a variety of principles and requirements underlying trustworthy systems have been identified (e.g., see Refs. [5, 6]). Trustworthy AI-based systems comprise three components: they are lawful, ethical, and robust [5]. Based on these components, the higher-level expert group on AI (AI HLEG) of the European Commission defined a set of requirements that need to be fulfilled by a system in order to be considered trustworthy. These requirements include human agency and oversight, technical robustness and safety, privacy and data governance, transparency, diversity, non-discrimination and fairness, societal and environmental well-being, and accountability [5]. Similar principles can be found in the Recommendation on the Ethics of Artificial Intelligence adopted by the UNESCO in November 2021 [6]. Here, the need for creating awareness and literacy among the public is explicitly stated, and also the aspect of multi-stakeholders in AI governance is included in the principles.

In order to evaluate whether a given AI-based system adheres to the requirements of trustworthy AI, a standard set of criteria needs to be established and assessed for a given system. The assessment list by the AI HLEG, for instance, formulates questions for all aspects relevant to trustworthy AI [7]. The list is intended to be used as a self-assessment list for evaluating the trustworthiness of an AI system's design, development, and usage. It is important to note that not only the final system is assessed, but also the design and development process to build the AI system. Applying the assessment list in a certain domain also requires to adapt or add elements to the list to make it fit the specific requirements of the application context.

As an early pioneer in the field, the OECD AI group embraced the task of qualifying artificial intelligence systems so as to make them scrutinizable by policymakers. The working group defined in 2019 the AI principles that define the first policy directions needed to create a trustworthy AI (e.g., *shaping and enabling interoperable governance and policy environment for AI (Principle 2.3): Governments should create a policy environment that will open the way to the deployment of trustworthy AI systems)*. The OECD framework for the classification of AI systems [8] presents a series of assessment questions, each of which contributes to the principles in a documented manner. This set of mostly qualitative questions gives hints of how the principles are approached.

Going beyond the OECD framework, the NIST AI risk management framework [9] describes a process with more concrete steps to manage the risks so as to adhere to the principles and thus "guarantee" trustworthiness. The approach is even more operational with concrete indications of metrics, risks, playbooks, and processes.

The need for trusting artificial intelligence has grown explosively, with multiple other initiatives offering approaches to evaluate (e.g., the z-inspection[1]) or to certify (e.g., the 1EdTech's TrustEd apps program[2]).

With the goal of supporting the development of trustworthy AI, the European Union adopted in May 2024 the Artificial Intelligence Act (AI Act [10]), which is the first legal framework for regulating the use of AI-based systems. The framework takes a risk-based approach and applies the classification of the OECD summarizing an AI system into four levels of risk. On the top level, systems that pose a clear threat to people and businesses are categorized as systems with unacceptable risks. The development and use of such systems are forbidden. On the next level, systems are categorized as high-risk systems. They fall under the provisions of the AI Act and have to comply with strict requirements for developing, deploying, and using them. Examples of high-risk AI systems include AI-based exam scoring systems, robot-assisted surgery systems, and AI-based credit scoring systems among others. Limited-risk systems are grouped on the third level and have to adhere to certain transparency regulations. Minimal risk systems can be used without any limitations.

Despite the many guidelines, recommendations, and regulations, trustworthy AI is not the same as trusted AI [11]. Recent investigations have shown that applying

[1] The z-inspection is an evaluation process for the trust of artificial intelligence systems, it is piloted by a non-profit association of scholars. See https://z-inspection.org.

[2] The 1EdTech TrustEd Apps program offers a management solution to educational institutions https://www.1edtech.org/program/trustedapps.

up-to-date guidelines and metrics for trustworthiness does not lead to an increase in actual trust in AI systems. The authors argue that public attitudes are largely built upon the perceived trustworthiness of an AI application, which in turn is influenced by typical constructs of technology acceptance such as perceived ease of use and perceived usefulness, as well as the attitude toward AI in general.

3. Challenges of applying AI in education

From the very beginning developments in Artificial Intelligence depicted links to the field of education, and research and developments in AI were transferred to the field of education and stimulated new research approaches in the field of education [12]. Consequently, there is a long history of applications of AI technologies in education, and AI has been linked to numerous potentials and benefits in education (e.g., see Refs. [13–15]).

Educators tend to quickly adapt all types of new technologies to enrich teaching and learning, and also ones not specifically targeted to the field of education. This also applies to novel AI-related technologies. Against this background, it is not surprising that approaches to describing and classifying forms and scenarios for the use of AI in education have to be incomplete and limited. Typical approaches to classify the use of AI in education (AIED) distinguish between (a) student-focused AIED, teacher-focused AIED, and institution-focused AIED [15, 16].

Scenarios and corresponding technological approaches in the context of student-focused AIED include, in particular, personalized learning and intelligent tutoring systems, while teacher-focused AIED scenarios are often related to automatic assessment of students' learning and support in providing adequate feedback. A typical objective of institution-focused AIED is the identification of dropouts and students at risk. In addition, AI-related competencies and skills are considered an important aspect, both for students and teachers. On the students' side, these are understood as a prerequisite for the effective and reflective use of generative AI (GenAI) technologies, while they are also considered a specific learning objective of AI-enhanced learning scenarios. Similarly, corresponding competencies are considered indispensable for teachers to effectively apply AI technologies in the classroom, but also for teaching fundamental skills and fostering competencies related to AI and AI technologies. Yet, in both cases, the characteristics and the extent of such competencies are still objects of scientific discussions.

There is currently a consensus of opinion that such applications of AI technologies in the classroom and for learning and teaching also come with risks and challenges. This is based on general ethical concerns and requirements [16, 17]. The Beijing declaration [18] represents the first approach to list challenges and formulate policy recommendations specifically targeted to the field of AIED.

Recently, challenges for the application of AI in education were raised in a number of publications, in some cases on a more general level and in others on a more detailed one, and closely related to specific AI technologies, such as generative AI (e.g., see Refs. [19, 20]).

Many of the raised challenges may be related to the aspects of trustworthiness of AI technologies but also to trust in the use of humans [21]. Specific concerns may be related to aspects such as privacy and security, quality and effectiveness of AI tools, trust in presented results (e.g., with respect to possible algorithmic bias), and equity in access. For instance, in institution-focused AIED, targeted to identify possible dropouts and at-risk students, the corresponding AI system requires trust in the assessment of individual students, providing a sufficient degree of transparency on how the decision was made. At the same time, privacy must be respected.

4. Trustworthy AI by design

Despite the availability of ethical guidelines for trustworthy AI, there seems to be a gap between defining general guidelines and actually putting them into practice [22]. As the guidelines need to be applied during the whole engineering process of AI-based systems and also when deploying and using them, the design and development process of AI-based systems needs special consideration. There are various approaches on how to design and develop trustworthy AI-based systems. In the following, we present approaches that take a holistic view on developing AI-based systems and that realize a *Trustworthiness-By-Design* paradigm. All outlined approaches target and include trustworthiness as a core element of the design and development process from the beginning.

In a collection of 62 *Responsible AI Patterns*, the book [23] describes best practices in the form of solution templates for coping with the challenges associated with the design, the implementation, and the management of AI-based systems. The patterns are grouped into three categories related to product, processes, and governance considerations. Depending on the context of the application at hand, these patterns can be reused and adapted to the specific requirements of the respective domain.

In order to establish a trustworthy and responsible AI development process, [23] identifies the potential issues that can arise in the individual stages of the software development process. For each issue, the authors propose a solution to specifically address and mitigate the identified problems and risks. As an example, in the requirements phase, it is essential to collect, elicit, and document requirements with respect to trustworthy AI. As a solution, so-called *Responsible AI User Stories* can be introduced as a new type of user story. Based on predefined templates and guiding questions, the user stories are defined and worked on as part of the product backlog in an agile project. Another example of how to integrate ethical considerations in the design process is the use of envisioning cards [24] in order to strengthen awareness and reflection on how AI systems may impact human values. Envisioning cards focus on four envisioning criteria namely stakeholder, time, value, and pervasiveness. Each card describes a specific concept related to these criteria and suggests design activities to initiate discussion and engagement with possible effects and implications of AI-based systems with respect to this concept.

In addition to general best-practice guidelines, there are also company-specific approaches that are published and used in practice. Examples are the responsible AI practices recommended by Google [25], which emphasize a human-centric design approach and the importance of testing activities; the Guidelines for Human-AI Interaction [26] developed by Microsoft Research with a focus on user interface design of AI-based applications; and the IBM Design for AI [27], which explains the rationales and driving forces underlying the design of AI systems.

5. Use case: AI-based analysis of e-portfolios

In the following, we present a real-life example of how AI-based technology and tools can be applied in higher education. The application performs an AI-based analysis of e-portfolios and shows how both teachers and students can benefit from using such tools in teaching and learning.

E-portfolios are collections of digital artifacts that students create to document their individual learning. In the e-portfolio, they present individual project results, summarize learning content, and reflect on the learning process and goals they have achieved. E-portfolios are similar to online blogs that contain a variety of multimedia content and can be highly personal. In the context of higher education, e-portfolios are generally used as a competency-based learning tool but also as a means to perform holistic assessments of the learning process and learning outcomes. At the University of Education Weingarten, e-portfolios have been used in introductory courses in computer science and learning technologies for over 10 years.

5.1 Teaching and learning scenario based on e-portfolios

A typical scenario on how to integrate e-portfolios in university courses is as follows. Students take part in the lecture and are encouraged to deepen the learning content independently. They choose their own focus topics and work on these independently. This includes researching relevant information as well as carrying out small projects to apply what they have learned in practice. Students document the entire learning process, rephrase the knowledge they have synthesized, and develop content in their personal e-portfolio. They can share their e-portfolios: It is up to the students to decide who they grant access to the e-portfolio. By doing so, they can receive feedback on the e-portfolio presented in the composition system from their fellow students or the teacher and use the feedback to improve the e-portfolio. At the end of the semester, students submit the completed e-portfolio. The composition system is, in the case of the University of Education Weingarten, the widely used Mahara platform[3].

Latest, at the end of the semester, the teachers assess the e-portfolio based on predefined criteria. The assessment is typically done based on rubrics [28]. In the rubrics, all relevant assessment criteria are listed along with a description of different performance level characteristics. **Figure 1** shows an extract of an example of a rubric for e-portfolio evaluation.

5.2 AISOP: AI-supported observation of e-portfolios

In the AISOP project, we have developed a web application that carries out an AI-based analysis of the e-portfolio contents. Every time the user accesses their e-portfolio in the composition system, they can request an automatic analysis and see the result of this analysis in the AISOP web application. The web application employs thematic classification and concept maps to allow for an interactive concept-based coverage analysis and navigation as depicted in **Figure 2**. It will also provide different perspectives on the e-portfolio contents based on linguistic characteristics such as text complexity, lexical variety, or coherence (see Ref. [29]).

5.3 Design and development process

The AISOP web application has been designed and developed using the scenario-based design approach as proposed by Rosson and Carroll [30]. In the design process,

[3] Mahara is an e-portfolio platform maintained by Catalyst.NET.

Criteria	Beginner	Intermediate	Advanced	Proficient
Complete presentation of relevant concepts	A subset of the relevant concepts are described, and/or relevant concepts are partly described.	Relevant concepts are stated. Descriptions are taken from the available learning materials.	Relevant concepts are described and partially enhanced with additional materials and with explanations in own words.	All relevant concepts are described technically correct and in sufficient detail. Completely independent work.
Indepently created artifacts	Artifacts (graphics, code extracts etc) are taken from the available learning materials.	Some independently created artifacts are presented. Artifacts show/apply basic concepts and their relationships.	Independently created artifacts are presented. Artifacts apply advanced concepts and their relationships.	Independently created artifacts are presented. Artifacts are fully elaborated and described proficiently.
Appropriate use of digital media	The portfolio contents is mainly presented in text format.	Some media artifacts are integrated. The artifacts are selected and included based on the thematic context.	Various media artifacts are integrated that illustrate the presented contents and enhance the understanding of the contents.	Various media artifacts are judiciously selected, well elaborated and provide new perspectives on the underlying contents.

Figure 1.
A part of the rubrics to evaluate e-portfolios.

various scenarios have been developed that illustrate the main usage scenarios for the analysis system from the perspective of the target users (see Ref. [31] for example scenarios). The resulting scenarios are the basis for system design and development and have been used to derive test scenarios for evaluating the application in a real-life context at the university. The evaluations yielded a number of experimental results as presented in Gantikow et al. [32].

The project giving birth to the AISOP system was created so as to offer a reproducible approach that can be summarized by the following steps to obtain a similar system in other teaching opportunities based on e-portfolios (the AISOP "recipe"):

- Formulate *proposed scenarios* of use that reflect the concrete teaching situation at hand. Make sure to consider all aspects that encourage a trusting use of the web application (e.g., inspired by the key questions in the assessment list by the AI HLEG [7]).

- Have an e-portfolio *composing system ready* for the students, including the possibility of sharing with selected users.

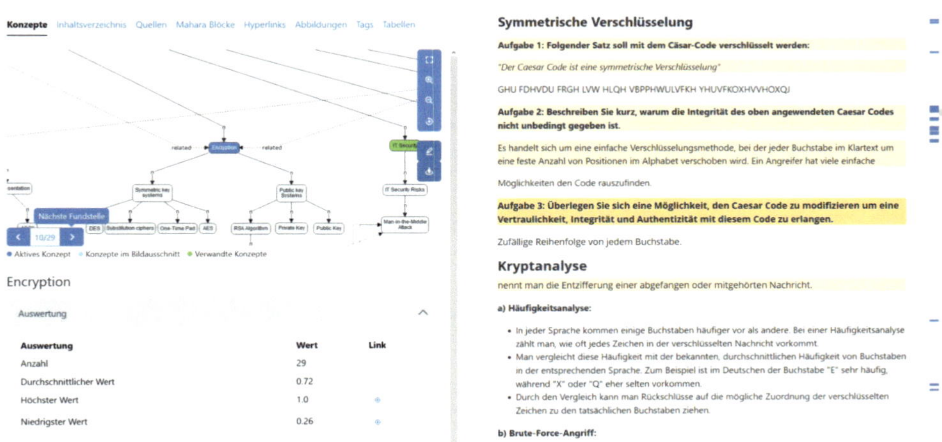

Figure 2.
Concept-based navigation: An interactive concept map generated by the result of the classification with its corresponding e-portfolio navigation.

- Make sure the e-portfolio composing system can be *interfaced* with the AISOP web app (this may need to configure web services, authorize them, or write custom interfaces). This is the step where the users will express their authorizations and thus express their trust. Thus, a clear scenario is useful to envision the trust of the authorization.

- *Identify the courses* where this is to be applied. Create concept maps for representing the knowledge domain of each course (e.g., using CmapTools[4]). Scenarios of usage of the e-portfolios in the course of a term should be available.

- *Collect* textual materials relevant to the course content, such as course slides or earlier e-portfolios, and make sure you are allowed to process them. This processing is necessary to generate training data for the natural language processing (NLP) pipeline incorporated in the e-portfolio analysis system. It is an internal process and can be made with protected content (copyrighted, personal data...).

- *Extract* all the relevant text fragments within text files (e.g., using a clipboard tracker[5]).

- Perform the manual *annotations* of the topic classification of all the fragments (e.g., using Explosion AI's Prodigy[6]).

- *Train the text classifier* and refine the training. This creates a classification model specialized to the course learning content (e.g., using Explosion AI's Prodigy).

- *Install and configure* the classification model as well as the concept map as a new course in the AISOP web application (see web application documentation[7]).

- *Test* the system implementation based on the *proposed scenarios of use* (see step 1). Assess whether the criteria for trustworthiness are met or whether the system needs to be optimized.

All e-portfolios of the newly integrated course can now be analyzed and visualized in the web application by any user who has access to the e-portfolio composition system.

The approach applies fairly generic tools (such as the topic classification) and manages a pool of data so as to train the classifiers, one of the cornerstones of the machine learning approach to developing artificial intelligence tools. As depicted in the recipe, the process starts by defining appropriate usage scenarios considering criteria for trustworthiness and ends with a practical evaluation of the solution based on the scenarios defined beforehand. If the evaluation results do not meet the defined criteria, a new development cycle will be initiated.

---

[4] CmapTools is a freely available concept-maps editing system, https://cmap.ihmc.us.

[5] Such a clipboard tracker is available open-source at https://gitlab.com/aisop/aisop-hacking/-/tree/main/aisop-clipboard-extractor.

[6] Prodigy is a commercial tool to support the annotation of texts for several classical NLP tasks, see https://prodi.gy/.

[7] The AISOP web application is available open-source at https://gitlab.com/aisop/aisop-webapp.

This approach was elaborated and experimented with in the AISOP project. Among the experiments, we ran several rounds of marking supported by the AISOP tool so as to elucidate how the tool could support the teacher's review process. Some of these experiments and their results are described in Gantikow et al. [32] and the papers cited therein. Another round of experiments is in preparation where the interpretation of the students of the colored topic maps and the induced navigation, which are a way to present the output of the text classification, is in focus.

5.4 OECD assessment of the AISOP AI service

Before discussing the ethical and trust-building aspects of the AISOP approach, we first take the time to assess it as an artificial intelligence application according to OECD which "provides a structured way to assess AI systems' potential to promote the development of human-centric, trustworthy AI" [8]. The complete assessment is in Appendix 1.

The assessment covers the five key dimensions: People and planet, economic context, data and input, AI model, task and output. It qualifies the trustworthiness of the AI system embedded as a web application service. Being a system made for supporting the learning, the usage of the AISOP system carries core dimensions that can be reformulated as in **Figure 3**.

The highlights of this assessment include the following observations:

The service must be seen as a complete service, although the AI component (the topic recognition) is a modest part of the process: Indeed, multiple criteria, such as the optionality, the impact on critical processes (such as giving a mark), the agency of persons, or the personal nature of data, are only valid because of the way they are assessed as a service delivering a visualization.

The transparency of the AI results cannot be offered. This lies in the relatively hidden neuronal network nature of the spaCy models but also in the probably homogeneous nature of the texts used for training the classifier. While transparency could become better defined in the scientific literature, there appears to be no pressing need to offer users a more transparent classification, instead, the paper [32] presents a study about the usability of the interactive concept map and highlights that better integrations could be closer to support the students' in their use.

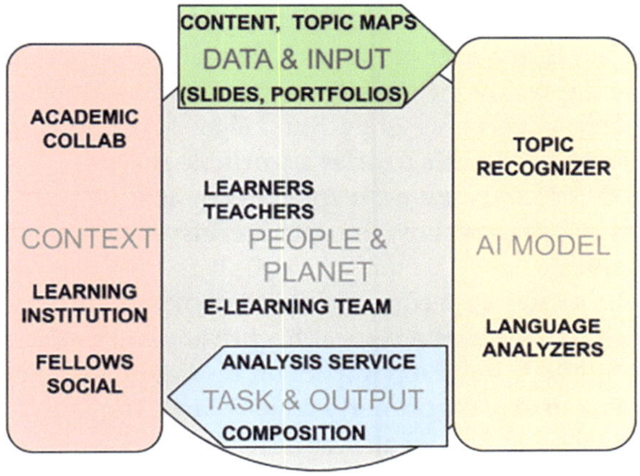

Figure 3.
The cycle of usage of the AISOP web application, adapted from the cycle of usage of a generic AI system of OECD [8].

Rights handling with training corpora for learning relevant material is a multifaceted process. While a university could be handling only its internal data, it is difficult for newcomers to embark, and the reuse of existing corpora is important. For this reason, reusable corpora (e.g., from course contents and from existing e-portfolios) are desirable. Repositories such as Germany's research data repository in education,[8] which allows access to limited researchers' circles, can offer a solution. The highly personal nature of e-portfolios makes it so that, even if anonymized, a student would recognize their e-portfolio immediately. Thus, sharing in a completely open form is rare and needs explicit permission. However, there is no risk in terms of possible divulgation of training content in the AISOP case (contrary to the case of generative AI systems).

Finally, it is important to acknowledge that the AISOP recipe involves course-specific data and thus a course-specific classification system. This implies that each application of the recipe operates for its restricted focus. We claim that, beyond the cold-start problem mentioned above, this allows every institution to carry responsibility for the relevance of the AI service, which is a fundamental value of a course and the services around it.

The assessment of the OECD has given us the opportunity to ask ourselves how the software's artificial intelligence dimensions (such as the flow of data and the personal data protection aspects) are being monitored. Based on this assessment, one can easily answer the European Union's AI Act's classification of the service [10]. This leads us to evaluate the AISOP web application as a limited-risk system for which there may be registration requirements.

6. Making a trustworthy process

The proposed recipe to create an artificial intelligence is rather following common steps: It involves the reuse of software, the reuse of datasets (NLP corpora), the enrichment with context-specific data, and the interfacing so that students submit their own data and obtain, thus, a service powered by artificial intelligence. It can be seen as a typical system without employing large artificial intelligence models of which only a few exist on earth and for which the privacy terms are rarely respectful.

The process can be assessed as trustworthy and respectful of the AI goals of the OECD. That means showing what data is stored, where it is transmitted, and how it is being analyzed. We claim that the AISOP experience has proven that the use of scenarios makes it clear how a user perceives how their data is exchanged and processed. This is a very important lever to attract trust and is somewhat independent of the assessment of the governance of data and algorithms. However, both are of fundamental importance to be able to offer a trustable service.

As shown in the OECD assessment, it appears just as fundamental to give users freedom of choice as it is to show how the data is exchanged in a transparent and comprehensible manner.

While some of the AISOP experiments have shown very little concern about privacy on the part of the students, the respect for privacy can be the subject of a sudden breach of trust that would have a fatal impact on the use of a service. Thus, it appears fundamental to be able to express properly which data is transferred, how much, to whom, for which purpose, and to what extent the user is obliged to use the service.

[8] The research data repository in education is accessible from https://www.forschungsdaten-bildung.de/.

Due to the interplay of multiple systems, it is not uncommon for users to feel overwhelmed by the selection options and simply click on "ok" in an authorization dialog, without actually understanding what they are giving their consent to. But this may stop at any time (e.g., when the news arouses mistrust about a certain aspect, which generally provokes the entire rejection reaction), and only a careful explanation may convince them otherwise. We claim that assessing the trust in workflows through scenarios even before a finalized software is available is an appropriate method to ensure long-term trust and long-term evolution of the software.

7. Conclusion

In this paper, we have attempted to define trustworthiness and trustability for artificial intelligence applications based on the definitions of the literature. The wide spectrum of contributions and recommendations that we could encounter have not yet provided methodologies that have proven themselves as applicable in practice for learning systems.

We have described the design and development process that we followed to build an AI-based web application service of which one can assess the trustability. Through the use of scenarios, we have been able to highlight challenging points of trust and the presentation of what to expect of a system and thus make sure that they are clear to all stakeholders.

In our process, we realized that some uses by students or teachers may have been missed by our scenarios. While it is good for a development to limit its scope, some scenarios are unavoidable as they are fundamental to building trust, and some are even an obligation by law. Examples include the scenarios to operate in case of a request to be forgotten (as is a fundamental right) or the reactions as a teacher against fears of using the service (teachers could explain the web application's privacy guarantees better, but they could also adjust the configuration).

Among the few discoveries that appeared is the establishment of principles of "who should be able to decide whether an AI system is used to analyze an e-portfolio?": While it appears natural to leave this choice to the authors of the e-portfolios, this is not what is done in practice: Any person who is reviewing an e-portfolio is in a position to submit the content to an AI system. Expressing this possibility (or its prohibition) as a scenario is an excellent way to evaluate its desirability.

Acknowledgements

This research was partially funded by the grant 16DHBKI015 (AISOP) of the German Federal Ministry of Research and Education.

We wish to thank the collaborators of the AISOP team, including Thierry Declerck†, Alexander Gantikow, Andreas Isking, Pierre Günthner, and Simon Ostermann, as well as the many students who helped by lending their e-portfolios.

Annex 1: OECD assessment of the artificial intelligence AISOP web application.

Tables A1–A5

People and Planet		
Characteristic	**Question**	**Response**
Users of AI system	*What is the level of competency of users who interact with the system?*	Amateur / Apprentices
Impacted Stakeholders	*Who is impacted by the system?*	Students, Teachers
Optionality and redress	*Can users opt out, e.g. switch systems? Can users challenge or correct the output?*	Usage is optional Correction requires re-running steps.
Human rights and democratic values	*Can the system's outputs impact fundamental human rights?*	No because usage is optional and the information is only indicative for teachers.
Well-being, society and the environment	*Can the system's outputs impact areas of life related to well-being (e.g. job quality, the environment, health, social interactions, civic engagement, education)?*	Enhancement of the review process (support of the education process)
Displacement potential	*Could the system automate tasks that are or were being executed by humans?*	(only enhance the time taken)

Table A1.
Section "People and Planet" of the OECD assessment of the artificial intelligence AISOP web application.

Economic Context		
Characteristic	**Question**	**Response**
Industrial sector	*Which industrial sector is the system deployed in (e.g. finance, agriculture)?*	Education
Business function	*What business function(s) or functional areas is the AI system employed in (e.g. sales, customer service, human resources)?*	Learning, teaching
Business model	*Is the system a for-profit use, non-profit use or public service system?*	Part of the teaching process (public/for-profit)
Impacts critical functions / activities	*Would the disruption of the system's function or activity affect essential services?*	No
Breadth of deployment	*Is the AI system deployment a pilot, narrow, broad or widespread?*	Narrow (becoming broad)

Table A2.
Section "Economic Context" of the OECD assessment of the artificial intelligence AISOP web application.

Data & Input		
Characteristic	**Question**	**Response**
Detection and collection	*Are the data and input collected by humans, automated sensors, both?*	Human
Provenance of data and input	*Are the data and input from experts; provided, observed, synthetic or derived?*	Yes (collected using, e.g. copy-and-paste)
Dynamic nature	*Are the data dynamic, static, dynamic updated from time to time or real-time?*	No, except enhancements by teachers.
Rights associated with data and input	*Are the data proprietary (privately held), public (no intellectual property rights) or personal data (related to identifiable individual)?*	Fragments need allowance but could be shared in corpora. Fragments can be personal. Anonymized fragments can be used and shared for training.

Data & Input		
Characteristic	**Question**	**Response**
Identifiability of personal data	*If personal data, are they anonymised or pseudonymised?*	personal or *pseudonymised*
Data quality and appropriateness	*Is the dataset fit for purpose? Is the sample size adequate? Is it representative and complete enough? How noisy are the data?*	according to cross validation: fit for the purpose (~90%). But course specific.
Structure of the data and input	*Are the data structured, semi-structured, complex structured or unstructured?*	Semi-structured (lines of texts, annotated)
Format of data and metadata	*Is the format of the data and metadata standardized or non-standardized?*	standardized for the annotations.
Scale	*What is the dataset's scale?*	Small

Table A3.
Section "Data & Input" of the OECD assessment of the artificial intelligence AISOP web application.

AI Model		
Characteristic	**Question**	**Response**
Model information availability	*Is any information available about the system's model?*	Limited (spacy's classification model, probably a simple multi-layer-perceptron
AI model type	*Is the model symbolic (human-generated rules), statistical (uses data) or hybrid?*	Statistical
Rights associated with model	*Is the model open-source or proprietary, self or third-party managed?*	Inference tools are open-source (spacy), preparation tools are proprietary (prodigy)
Discriminative or generative	*Is the model generative, discriminative or both?*	Discriminative (and generates visualizations)
Single or multiple model(s)	*Is the system composed of one model or several interlinked models?*	One model
Model-building from machine or human knowledge	*Does the system learn based on human-written rules, from data, through supervised learning or through reinforcement learning?*	Supervised learning based on an annotated corpus
Model evolution in the field (applicable only to machine-learning systems)	*Does the model evolve and / or acquire abilities from interacting with data in the field?*	No But an actualized run of the recipe can be done at the end of the semester.
Central or federated learning (applicable only to machine-learning systems)	*Is the model trained centrally or in a number of local servers or edge devices?*	Centrally (based on existing language models)
Model development and maintenance	*Is the model universal, customisable or tailored to the AI actor's data?*	Customizable
Deterministic and probabilistic	*Is the model used in a deterministic or probabilistic manner?*	Probabilistic
Transparency and explainability	*Is information available to users to allow them to understand model outputs?*	No. (a score is provided)

Table A4.
Section "AI Model" of the OECD assessment of the artificial intelligence AISOP web application.

Task & Output		
Characteristic	**Question**	**Response**
Task(s) of the system	*What tasks does the system perform (e.g. recognition, event detection, forecasting)?*	Topic recognition.
Combining tasks and actions into composite systems	*Does the system combine several tasks and actions (e.g. content generation systems, autonomous systems, control systems)?*	Yes (recognition is followed by presentation on the interactive concept map)
Action autonomy	*How autonomous are the system's actions and what role do humans play?*	Analysis is on request of the user (reviewer) The system only generates visualizations.
Core application area(s)	*Does the system belong to a core application area such as human language technologies, computer vision, automation and / or optimisation or robotics?*	Human language technologies and visualizations

Table A5.
Section "Tasks & Output" of the OECD assessment of the artificial intelligence AISOP web application.

Author details

Sandra Rebholz[1*], Paul Libbrecht[2] and Wolfgang Müller[3]

1 University of Education Weingarten, Ostbayerische Technische Hochschule Amberg-Weiden, Germany

2 University of Education Weingarten, IU International University of Applied Sciences, Germany

3 University of Education Weingarten, Germany

*Address all correspondence to: rebholz@md-phw.de

References

[1] Gantikow A, Isking A, Libbrecht P, Müller W, Rebholz S. On the creation of classifiers to support assessment of E-portfolios. In: International Workshop on Multimedia in Technology Enhanced Learning. Laguna Hills CA: IEEE Inc; 2023. pp. 297-302. DOI: 10.1109/ISM59092.2023.00057

[2] Marsh S, Dibben MR. Trust, untrust, distrust and mistrust - An exploration of the dark(er) side. In: Herrmann P, Issarny V, Shiu S, editors. International Conference on Trust Management. Berlin, Heidelberg: Springer; 2005. pp. 17-33

[3] Slade S, Prinsloo P, Khalil M. "Trust us," they said. Mapping the contours of trustworthiness in learning analytics. Information and Learning Sciences. 2023;**124**(9/10):306-325

[4] ISO/IEC. ISO/IEC 24028:2020. Information Technology - Artificial Intelligence - Overview of Trustworthiness in Artificial Intelligence. Geneva, Switzerland: International Organization for Standardization; 2020

[5] HLEG. High-level expert group on artificial intelligence set up by the European Commission. Ethics Guidelines for Trustworthy AI. 2019;**EN**:41. Available from: https://digital-strategy.ec.europa.eu/en/library/ethics-guidelines-trustworthy-ai [Accessed: October 17, 2024]

[6] UNESCO. Recommendation on the Ethics of Artificial Intelligence. Adopted on 23 November 2021. Paris: United Nations Educational, Scientific and Cultural Organization; 2022. Available from: https://www.unesco.org/en/articles/recommendation-ethics-artificial-intelligence [Accessed: October 17, 2024]

[7] HLEG. High-level expert group on artificial intelligence set up by the European Commission. The Assessment List for Trustworthy Artificial Intelligence (ALTAI) for Self Assessment. 2020:34. Available from: https://digital-strategy.ec.europa.eu/en/library/assessment-list-trustworthy-artificial-intelligence-altai-self-assessment [Accessed: October 17, 2024]

[8] OECD. OECD Framework for the Classification of AI Systems. OECD Digital Economy Papers, No. 323. Paris: OECD Publishing; 2022. DOI: 10.1787/cb6d9eca-en

[9] NIST. Artificial Intelligence Risk Management Framework (AI RMF 1.0). 2023. Available from: https://airc.nist.gov/AI_RMF_Knowledge_Base [Accessed. October 06, 2024]

[10] AI Act. Regulation (EU) 2024/1689 of the European Parliament and of the Council. 2024. Available from: https://eur-lex.europa.eu/legal-content/EN/TXT/?uri=CELEX%3A32024R1689 [Accessed: October 18, 2024]

[11] Knowles B, Richards JT. ACM TechBrief. Trusted AI. ACM Technology Policy Council, Issue 9, Fall 2023. New York, NY, USA: ACM; 2023. DOI: 10.1145/3641524

[12] Doroudi S. The intertwined histories of artificial intelligence and education. International Journal of Artificial Intelligence in Education. 2023;**33**(4):885-928. DOI: 10.1007/s40593-022-00313-2

[13] Schank R, Edelson D. A role for AI in education: Using technology to

reshape education. Journal of Artificial Intelligence in Education. 1989;**1**:3-20

[14] Baker RS. Artificial intelligence in education: Bringing it all together. In: OECD, editors. OECD Digital Education Outlook: Pushing the Frontiers with AI, Blockchain, and Robots. Paris: OECD Publishing; 2021. pp. 43-56. DOI: 10.1787/589b283f-en

[15] Anderson JR, Kline PJ. A learning system and its psychological implications. In: IJCAI'79: Proceedings of the 6th International Joint Conference on Artificial Intelligence. Vol. 1. IJCAI; 1979. pp. 16-21

[16] Holmes W, Tuomi I. State of the art and practice in AI in education. European Journal of Education. 2022;**5**(4):542-570. DOI: 10.1111/ejed.12533

[17] Coeckelbergh M. AI Ethics. Cambridge, MA: The MIT Press; 2020. 248 p. ISBN 9780262538190

[18] UNESCO. Beijing Consensus on Artificial Intelligence and Education [Outcome Document of the International Conference on Artificial Intelligence and Education 'Planning Education in the AI Era: Lead the Leap']. Paris: United Nations Educational, Scientific and Cultural Organization; 2019. Available from: https://unesdoc.unesco.org/ark:/48223/pf0000368303 [Accessed: November 25, 2024]

[19] Michel-Villarreal R, Vilalta-Perdomo E, Salinas-Navarro DE, Thierry-Aguilera R, Gerardou FS. Challengesandopportunitiesofgenerative AI for higher education as explained by ChatGPT. Education Sciences. 2023;**13**(9):856. DOI: 10.3390/educsci13090856

[20] OECD. Initial Policy Considerations for Generative Artificial Intelligence. Paris: OECD Publishing; 2023. DOI: 10.1787/fae2d1e6-en

[21] Vincent-Lancrin S, van der Vlies R. Trustworthy Artificial Intelligence (AI) in Education: Promises and Challenges (No. 218; OECD Education Working Paper). Paris: OECD; 2020. DOI: 10.1787/19939019

[22] Li B, Qi P, Liu B, Di S, Liu J, Pei J, et al. Trustworthy AI: From principles to practices. ACM Computing Surveys. Jan 2023;**55**(9):46, Article 177. DOI: 10.1145/3555803

[23] Lu Q, Whittle J, Xu X, Zhu L, Responsible AI. Best Practices for Creating Trustworthy AI Systems. Addison-Wesley Professional. London, UK: Pearson Education; 2023. 291 p. ISBN: 9780138073947

[24] Friedman B, Hendry D. The envisioning cards: A toolkit for catalyzing humanistic and technical imaginations. In: Proceedings of the SIGCHI Conference on Human Factors in Computing Systems (CHI '12). New York, NY, USA: ACM; 2012. pp. 1145-1148. DOI: 10.1145/2207676.2208562

[25] Google AI. Responsible AI practices. 2024. Available from: https://ai.google/responsibility/responsible-ai-practices/ [Accessed: September 19, 2024]

[26] Amershi S, Weld D, Vorvoreanu M, Fourney A, Nushi B, Collisson P, et al. Guidelines for human-AI interaction. In: Proceedings of the 2019 CHI Conference on Human Factors in Computing Systems (CHI '19). New York, NY, USA: ACM; 2019. Paper 3. pp. 1-13. DOI: 10.1145/3290605.3300233

[27] IBM. Design for AI. 2022. Available from: www.ibm.com/design/ai [Accessed: September 19, 2024]

[28] Brookhart SM, Chen F. The quality and effectiveness of descriptive rubrics. Education Review. 2015;**67**(3):343-368. DOI: 10.1080/00131911.2014.929565

[29] Günthner P, Rebholz S. Implementierung von Textanalyse in der E-Portfolio-Bewertung. EPEPLA Workshop DELFI. 2024;**2024**:9

[30] Rosson MB, Carroll JM. Usability Engineering: Scenario-Based Development of Human Computer Interaction. San Francisco, CA, USA: Morgan Kaufmann; 2002. ISBN 978-0-08-052030-8

[31] Isking A, Libbrecht P. Szenarien für eine automatische Analyse von E-Portfolios. EPEPLA Workshop DELFI. 2024;**2024**:7

[32] Gantikow A, Durski S, Isking A, Libbrecht P, Müller W, Ostermann S, et al. KI-basierte Analyse von E-Portfolios. In: Proceedings of the DELFI 2024. Fulda: GI e.V.; 2024

Chapter 5

Unlocking the Potential of Artificial Intelligence in Academic Libraries

Abid Hussain

Abstract

The objective of this paper is to explore the utilization of Artificial Intelligence (AI) within library services to enhance efficiency, accuracy, and personalization for patrons, as well as to facilitate decision-making processes and improve overall operational performance. Using a qualitative research approach, this study reviews existing literature from sources such as Taylor and Francis Journals, Emerald Insights, Science Direct, Google Scholar, and Springer Link. The findings demonstrate that while AI has been widely applied in sectors like health, agriculture, finance, manufacturing, and education, its integration into academic libraries promises significant improvements in operations such as search and discovery, cataloging, circulation, digital preservation, and Chatbot services. Despite these positive outcomes, the study also highlights limitations, including a reliance on literature without direct input from librarians and patrons, which could provide deeper insights. The research offers practical implications for librarians in both public and private universities, showcasing the potential benefits and challenges of AI implementation. Additionally, it serves as a guideline for academic libraries and encourages stakeholders to consider AI adoption to enhance library services. The study addresses a gap in understanding the role of AI in library services and calls for future research to expand on these findings across diverse library contexts.

Keywords: artificial intelligence, AI-awareness, AI-academic libraries, developing countries, academic libraries, AI and libraries

1. Introduction

Libraries have encountered numerous challenges since their inception, continually adapting to the evolving needs of society. They have undergone remarkable transformations, progressing from the era of clay tablets and stone inscriptions to the modern age of digital information. Throughout history, the mediums through which information is stored and accessed have varied widely, from ancient scrolls and manuscripts to printed books and electronic databases. Originally, libraries served as repositories of knowledge, aiming to provide patrons with access to the latest information available.

However, in the twenty-first century, the pace of technological advancement has accelerated, leading to unprecedented changes in the way information is created, disseminated, and consumed. Today, libraries are recognized as pivotal players in the dissemination of modern technology, serving as dynamic hubs where traditional resources coalesce with cutting-edge digital tools and services [1]. In the nineteenth century, books held sway as the primary conduits of knowledge, but as society progressed, so too did the formats and mediums through which information was transmitted. Just as the book evolved, adapting to new printing technologies and cultural shifts, the nature and shape of information itself continue to undergo rapid evolution in response to technological innovations and changing societal needs.

The present era of technology has brought about many advancements and innovations in education and libraries. Some of the most prominent technologies in these fields include learning management systems (LMS), virtual and augmented reality (VR/AR), cloud computing, big data, and analytics, blockchain technologies, mobile devices and artificial intelligence (AI), etc., among the use of AI is being used in education to personalize learning, automated grading, such technology provide students with personalized feedback [2]. In libraries, AI automates tasks, improves discovery and access to resources, and enhances the user experience [3]. These technologies are transforming how we teach, learn, and access information, and they hold tremendous potential for improving educational outcomes and increasing access to information and resources [4]. The present-era technologies have affected the entire ecosystem of organizations, and with novice applications, a business can grow in the right direction and the standard of living [5]; as technology grows with rapid speed, which affects the ecosystem of entire businesses like health, finance, manufacturing, education and libraries [5]. John McCarthy (An American computer scientist), in 1956, coined the word AI. He organized a Dartmouth conference and invited a group of researchers to create a machine that thinks like a human. This conference marked the birth of AI research, and the term artificial intelligence was used in the conference proposal. John McCarthy is, however, known as the father of AI for his pioneering work in the field [5]. AI has been deployed in various businesses like healthcare, transportation, finance, agriculture, robotics, manufacturing, gaming zones, education, etc. However, the use of AI in library services has proved to be a milestone for the entire operations associated with libraries.

Interestingly, cutting-edge technology has evolved the shape of modern libraries; similarly, the role of AI has been witnessed as the most sophisticated technology of our age. As every technology has its pros and cons, definitely AI is also not free from certain challenges; however, experts in this age are endeavoring to overcome the consequences of this technology. It is said that the deployment of AI will undoubtedly bring positive changes in academic libraries. Another scholar [6] postulated that AI has paramount benefits for library operations and is known as the promising technology of the current century. Applying AI systems in libraries will reduce human costs and labor. It is believed that AI is a technology that provides 24 hours/7 days without getting tired like humans. It can be used to leverage library services effectively. Many scholars have their views that AI in libraries will bring charm to the library services, and it will enhance the experience of both library staff and patrons.

1.1 Academic libraries

Academic libraries are attached to higher education institutions, such as colleges and universities [6]. These institutions serve the information needs of students, faculty, and staff and typically focus on providing access to a wide range of academic resources, such as scholarly journals, books, databases, and multimedia materials. The primary goal of academic libraries is to support teaching, learning, and research by providing access to high-quality, diverse, and relevant information resources [7]. In addition to traditional library services such as reference, circulation, and inter-library loans, academic libraries may also offer specialized services such as data management, digital scholarship, and instruction in research methods and information literacy.

Academic libraries play a crucial role in supporting the academic mission of their parent institutions and contribute to the advancement of knowledge by providing access to the latest research and fostering a culture of lifelong learning. The fundamental goals of libraries are to offer high resources for learning, research, and intellectual growth. Libraries are transforming the conventional way of services to modern information networking. Librarians are utilizing innovative technologies to enhance user experience and remain competitive in the twenty-first century. Digital tools such as open access efforts, mobile apps, beacon technology, and AI have transformed the way libraries serve their users. Librarians must unleash the new possibility by replacing the old traditional services with modern information technology. Libraries with conventional methods will no longer survive until they adopt cutting-edge technologies like cloud computing, the Internet of Things, VR, open access initiatives, and AI. The present paper highlights the function of emerging technologies exclusively AI and its impact on academic libraries.

1.2 Nexus of academic libraries and ICT

Academic libraries play an important role in facilitating the academic pursuits of patrons (students and faculty members). It has always been considered the integral pillar of degree-awarding institutions. Academic libraries are crucial parts of academic institutions to promote cultivating future leaders. These libraries are great hubs of vital information and sources of dissemination and retrieval of scholarly information. The integration of Information and Communication Technology (ICT) within university libraries has been a subject of ongoing discourse since the inception of the internet. ICT, encompassing a spectrum of technologies facilitating information processing, coding, storage, retrieval, dissemination, and transmission [7], is recognized as a multifaceted tool for information production, transmission, and processing [5]. The evolution of technology within library services has seen notable advancements, with automated cataloging, circulation, and acquisition systems enhancing operational efficiency in the twenty-first century. In the contemporary landscape of information technologies, academic libraries stand as pivotal hubs meeting the diverse informational needs of their patrons. The advent of the internet has heralded a paradigm shift, propelling libraries into agents of innovation and technological adaptation. The symbiotic relationship between libraries and technology underscores their joint mission to cater to patrons' information requirements. The emergence of Web 2.0 technology has instigated profound transformations in the realm of information and communication technologies. As technology evolves, so do the practices within academic libraries, necessitating continuous up-skilling among library professionals to navigate new competencies demanded by the market. Librarians in academic settings operate within an ever-evolving technological milieu, providing access to an array of digital resources such as e-books, e-journals, and electronic articles [8]. The exponential growth of technology in library usage has engendered a reevaluation of librarians' perceptions, beliefs, and opinions regarding its implications and applications. To adapt to the dynamic landscape of technological innovation, librarians undergo continual training to acquire the requisite competencies essential for meeting the evolving information needs of their patrons. This proactive stance is vital for addressing the associated challenges and opportunities posed by the integration of technology within library workflows.

1.3 Use of AI in library services

Before going into detail, it is necessary to know about AI. A computer scientist known as John McCarthy, organized a conference in Dartmouth where he introduced the word, coined the word AI. Since that time, AI has been introduced as a field of study. Initially, it was considered as part of the computer system. It was envisioned that AI would perform different tasks like human intelligence. Slowly and gradually, AI has evolved in many shapes like expert systems, neural networks, and machine learning algorithms. It is an astounding fact that the use of AI in education and libraries is increasing exponentially. Numerous applications of AI have been found, ranging from personalized learning systems to online tutoring systems. Many scholars have ascertained that AI-based learning has brought tremendous revolutions in modern library services. A few popular examples of AI applications in advanced countries include the use of automated cataloging, search algorithms, and online reference services via Chatbots. The status of AI varies across advanced and developing countries. Advanced countries like China, the USA, and some European countries have made substantial investments in AI research services, while on the other hand, developing countries are facing numerous challenges due to its high costs, IT infrastructure, and scarcity of skilled manpower; however, still with limited resources many countries in developing nations have adopted different applications of AI like Chatbots, geographic information system (GIS), radio frequency identification (RFID), and other applications of web technologies. Interestingly, some free applications of AI like Turnitin, social media networks, Grammarly, search engines, and location of libraries have already been incorporated; however, developing nations are still working to catch up with cheap applications to satisfy the information needs of their patrons. Countries with robust AI ecosystems, tech companies, and supportive governmental policies are leading the developing nations. It is perceived that the development of AI will likely continue to be shaped by technological advancement. Still, a few issues like the impact of automation on employment, privacy, and ethical concerns are a few considerable issues that need a proper solution. AI technology has great potential to harness library operations for the benefit of humanity; librarians in both developed and developing countries should cope with the surge of technology to meet the information needs of their patrons. Libraries in advanced countries have incorporated advanced applications of AI in their library operations. The librarians in developing countries must follow in the footsteps of advanced countries to deploy various applications that can bring positive changes in the library services of academic libraries.

The present study offers a snapshot of AI in academic libraries and presents the following contents in detail literature review, research methodology and design, applications of AI in academic libraries, digital resilience of the librarians, implications of AI in academic libraries, challenges of AI in academic libraries, conclusion and recommendations of the research.

2. Research objectives

The present research addresses the following three objectives

1. To explore and evaluate how the integration of AI in academic libraries can enhance library operations effectively.

2. To examine the AI-driven tools that can be used to improve users' experience in academic libraries.

3. To analyze the ethical considerations and privacy concerns associated with the use of AI in academic libraries.

3. Significance of the study

1. The present study is useful to explore the integration of AI in academic libraries. The research will explore various features of AI and identify how AI can enhance library operations most effectively. The studies also describe the more streamlined process that reduces operational costs and improves service delivery to meet the academic environment;

2. The present study will examine the AI-driven tools that can be used to enhance users' experience in an academic environment. The study further elaborates that the use of AI in academic setup will create more personalized, accessible, and user-friendly services due to which users will engage with the library resources and will get satisfaction;

3. The present study will explore ethical and privacy concerns associated with AI in academic libraries. As each technology has its pros and cons, similarly, AI also has some concerns for the user's privacy and data privacy. Highlighting them is a vital factor in safeguarding user rights and maintaining trust. These kinds of concerns will formulate a policy guide that can foster responsible and sustainable AI implementation for future use. Hence, the study will contribute positive knowledge for policymakers and stakeholders of organizations to consider these concerns before implementing them into academic libraries.

4. The present study encompasses the deployment of AI in academic libraries; hence, the study will bridge the gap between theory and practices in academic libraries. The findings of this study will contribute a handsome knowledge that will be used for future projects. Although only university libraries have been covered, the result should be generalized to entire geographical locations of the world and is not specific to a single country.

4. Literature review

4.1 RO 1: Integration of AI in an academic library

The library community began to pay attention to the potential use of robotic technology and similar applications of AI in late 1980. In their research, Chen and

Chen [9] revealed that books in libraries are increasing at an alarming rate, so there should be an expert system that can be based on AI to process all library operations, including cataloging, classification, indexing, and abstracting systems to deal with complex problems. In his paper, Ref. [10] articulated that the use of robots in libraries could smoothly alleviate library operations. Language process technology and reduction of hardware costs, such as semantic analysis and computer processors, brought tremendous revolutions in library operations. The successful implementation of AI in other fields, particularly in higher education and libraries, will catalyst library activities more robustly. In their research, Ref. [11] postulated that the use of AI in libraries was not yet widespread; however, it is believed that the next few years will be more crucial for academic librarians to implement AI in academic setup. Another study conducted [12] explored the 25 most influential universities in the United States and Canada have responded positively to AI and its applications in academic libraries. Similarly, Ref. [13] has proposed that some university libraries have already implemented a few applications of AI in their academic environment such as 3D printing, data visualization, Chatbots, and RFID technology. The study also reveals that over the next few years, the penetration of AI in academic libraries will accelerate their library activities. The study by Ref. [14] reveals that library commentators, directors, and publishing began to hold positive attitudes and agree to incorporate AI-related technologies in libraries to foster library activities in more sophisticated ways. Ref. [7] also stated that AI and similar technology can help libraries move forward to smart libraries that can be used for resource discovery, machine-readable collection, resource discovery, and machine-readable collection. Ref. [1], in his study, has stated that libraries are changing agents of innovative technologies, and AI is a promising technology that can impart better services in academic setups. Ref. [15], in their study, discovered that AI provides better opportunities in discovering new knowledge in libraries and can be used as an information literacy tool in academic environments. In their study, Ref. [16] stated that developing countries like Pakistan are lagging behind developed countries in incorporating AI in their academic libraries for many reasons. A few reasons are lack of proper finance for IT tools, lack of professional staff, data privacy, and less attention from stakeholders. Considering this in mind, the present study is an attempt to formulate a policy document that can be used as a guiding rule for implementing AI in academic setups.

4.2 RO2: AI-driven tools for library users

AI is one of the fastest-growing technologies that can be used to leverage library operations more effectively. Their study Ref. [17] discovered that numerous applications are highly useful for users in academic libraries like *Chabot*. The AI-powered Chatbots can provide round-the-clock assistance to patrons, addressing common queries and guiding them to relevant resources [18]. According to Ref. [19], in information retrieval, the concept of *Text Mining is particularly important in the rapid growth of web applications. The scholar further highlighted that* AI-powered text mining tools can extract valuable insights from vast amounts of unstructured data present in library catalogs, databases, and digital collections. *Image Recognition*: AI-powered image recognition tools facilitate the classification and cataloging of images, enhancing accessibility for patrons [18]. In their study, Ref. [18] have defined that *Natural Language Processing (NLP) is a smart tool of AI that can be used to understand text and spoken words*. These AI-powered NLP tools enable the users to analyze and comprehend the text in multiple languages, thereby improving search capabilities and facilitating insights extraction from multilingual data. Ref. [20] have deduced that *Recommender Systems is yet another* AI-powered tool that offers books, journal articles, and video lectures to library users based on their past search and reading history. In their study, Ref. [17] explored that modern libraries used AI *Automated Circulation*; these AI-powered tools automate circulation tasks such as check-ins and check-outs, enabling staff to allocate more time to provide personalized assistance to patrons. In essence, the use of AI tools in academic libraries has brought tremendous revolutions. Utilizing such applications not only provides the fastest services to its end users but also reduces the labor cost of the library staff. **Figure 1** below shows the AI applications and their usage in academic libraries.

4.3 RO 3: AI ethical and privacy concerns for academic libraries

The AI is an advanced technology that revolutionizes the user's experience in academic setup. Libraries are always user-centric, and deploying AI means that how libraries operate and provide services to their users. AI has its prospects and challenges for library users, hence, academic librarians must address the ethical and practical concerns before implementation. The AI deals with data, algorithms, and user privacy. The library staff should interpret and explain the AI-generated results. AI is becoming increasingly integrated into libraries of developed countries to provide maximal services to its end users without wasting their time. Some examples of AI that have already been deployed in developed countries are for the users; these are auto-summarization tools for literature reviews. The study of Ref. [7] discovered that AI is useful for borrowing library material without the involvement of library staff. Ref. [21] have examined that AI is useful for technical services of library operations like classification and cataloging which ultimately provides quick services to its users. Similarly, in a study, Ref. [22] discovered that AI can also be used for library management processes like decision-making, reference services, and information literacy services of its users. Ref. [22] have described that without modern technology, no libraries can impart better services; AI has been deployed in different library services, which attract potential users to the library, still, it is essential to consider user privacy concerns when implementing AI into libraries. In their study, Ref. [23] indicated that tailored AI-based services must be according to the user's needs for maximum usage. Ref. [17] have defined that AI has great potential for academic libraries; however, issues like data privacy and ethical concerns should be kept in mind before deploying them into academic libraries. In their study, Ref. [24] have deduced that AI in

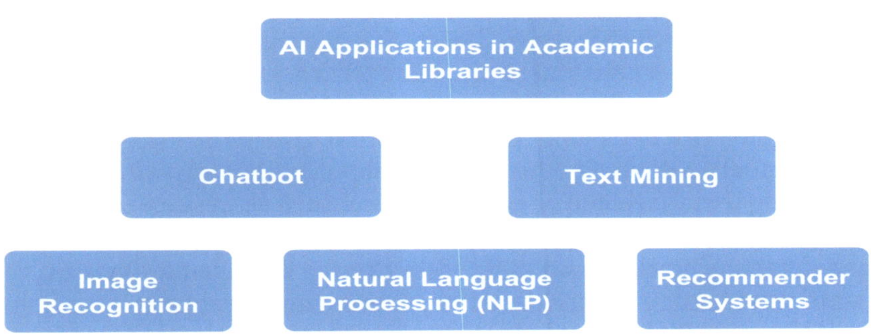

Figure 1.
Use of AI in academic libraries (self-generated).

Keyword development	• The researcher employed a comprehensive keyword strategy to identify relevant literature. Core keywords include AI and libraries, AI applications in libraries, and AI use in academic libraries. • Additional relevant keywords were identified through an initial literature scan.
Database selection	• A systematic search was conducted across the following academic databases: Taylor & Francis, Springer Link, Science Direct, Wiley Inter-science, Emerald Insight, Project Muse, Proquest, and Google Scholar.
Inclusion and exclusion criteria	• Only studies published in English were included. • Studies focusing specifically on AI applications within academic libraries were prioritized. • Literature that directly addresses the research questions was included. • Studies that do not meet the inclusion criteria, such as those focusing solely on general AI applications or those in languages other than English, were excluded.
Data collection	• Relevant articles, books, and conference proceedings identified through the database search were collected. • Full-text versions of selected articles were obtained.
Data organization	• The collected literature was organized systematically based on the research questions. • A coding framework was developed to identify key themes and patterns within the data.
Data analysis	• Content analysis was employed to systematically examine the collected data. • The range of AI applications in academic libraries. • The benefits and challenges associated with these applications. • The impact of AI on library services and users. • Emerging trends and future directions in AI for libraries.
Data interpretation	• The analyzed data was interpreted to answer the research questions. • Findings were presented clearly and concisely, supported by evidence from the literature.
Ethical considerations	• The research adhered to the ethical guidelines for academic research. • Proper citation and referencing were used to acknowledge the work of others.

Table 1.
Research methodology and design.

academic libraries has both negative and positive impacts on the user's privacy as well as on library staff. The scholars further discovered that AI can also cause a loss of job opportunities for the library staff. Similarly, the study [18] shows that, on the one hand, AI has positive potential for academic libraries, while on the other hand, AI raises concerns about data security within an academic environment. The scholars further highlighted that deploying AI and algorithm systems on digital platforms can shape information dissemination in a more sophisticated way while, on the other hand, restricting users' freedom of expression, and such expression raises concerns about privacy, consumer, and data protection [14] in their study discovered that unfair and deceptive practices can harm users' privacy in academic libraries. The library staff must address the privacy issues of users through appropriate regulations in a transparent way [25]. It postulated that AI holds great promise for academic libraries; hence, it is necessary to train library staff and users before implanting the AI applications in academic libraries (**Table 1**; **Figures 2** and **3**).

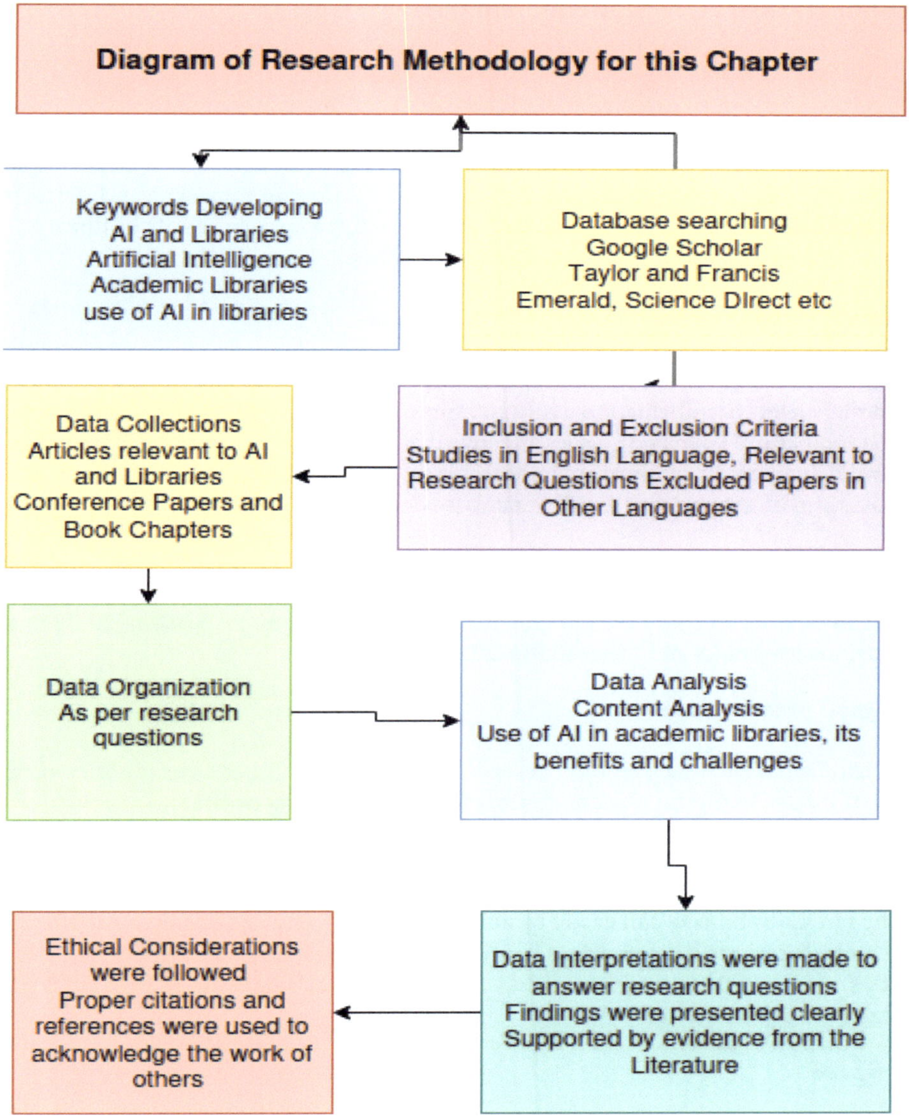

Figure 2.
Diagram of research methodology for this chapter.

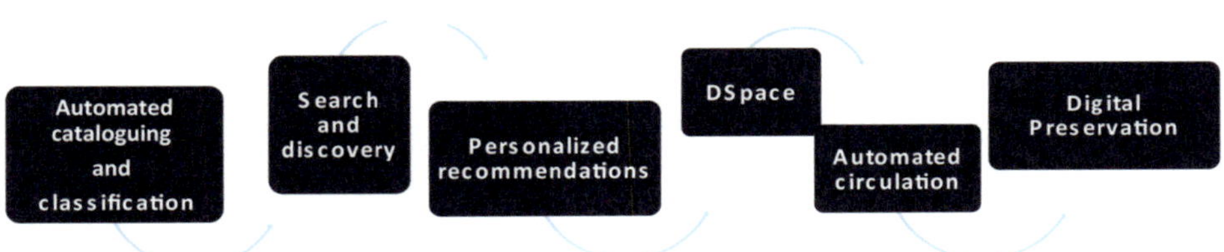

Figure 3.
Applications of AI in academic libraries (self-generated).

5. Application of AI in academic libraries

5.1 Automated cataloging and classification

In their article, Ref. [14] have explained that AI is a useful tool for cataloging and classification of library material. Academic librarians work in stressful and complex environments and create errors and defects while cataloging materials and performing classification tasks in their libraries. AI can perform large amounts of library materials easily and quickly and avoid human errors.

5.2 Search and discovery

Some search engines use AI power tools. These search tools help library users/patrons to find their relevant information easily and more quickly. These search engines use and understand natural language queries and give the most pertinent results; the best example of a search engine is Ebsco-host smart search, which extracts data from numerous databases and directs patrons to other databases for retrieving them.

5.3 Personalized recommendations

AI can be used to analyze a patron's reading habits and make personalized recommendations for books and other materials.

5.4 Digital preservation

AI can be used to analyze and preserve digital collections, such as identifying and mitigating risks to digital objects, detecting, and correcting errors.

5.5 Automated circulation

The circulation tasks can easily be automated using AI Applications. All borrowing materials can easily be checked in and checked out. Using this application will free library staff from other activities, and such applications will provide personalized assistance to the customers.

5.6 DSpace

The modern library uses Dspace library software for open digital repositories. It is an open-source software with open coding. This software uses AI applications that can be used to preserve and manage library repositories. It is the admirable task of AI to provide access to digital collections.

AI applications have transformed library operations effectively; these applications not only provide better services to the patrons but also streamline the library services more effectively and free library services from human errors. AI applications are more useful for both patrons and library staff.

6. Digital resilience of librarians

Librarians of the twenty-first century are resilient to adopt the application of emerging technologies like AI in their respective libraries. These technologies not only effectively support their library operations but also support the academic needs of the patrons. The library staff must understand the potential of AI and other technical skills associated with this technology. Furthermore, librarians also urged that AI is an advanced technology that evolves from time to time, so they should learn the technical and necessary skills. In order to empower and enhance the skills of librarians, some common ways are suggested by scholars to be noted [26].

- Librarians should participate in the professional development program and other training programs to enhance their skills.
- Staying current with the latest developments in AI through reading industry publications and attending conferences and workshops.
- Collaborating with colleagues and peers to share knowledge and best practices for using AI in libraries.
- Experiment with AI tools and technologies to gain hands-on experience and better understand their capabilities.
- Building a network of experts and resources to turn to for support and guidance as needed.

7. Implications of AI in libraries

In the library setup, the adoption of smart technologies, particularly AI is a global phenomenon. However, in developing countries, the deployment of AI in academic libraries lags due to various reasons such as financial constraints, poor IT infrastructure, lack of technical staff, knowledge of IT skills of the librarians, etc. Despite these implications, libraries are still struggling to incorporate AI in the academic realm and exhibit a spectrum of perceptions toward AI. Developed countries have recognized its potential and are endeavoring to enhance its various applications for education and research [27]. On the other side, countries in developing nations still express concerns regarding its impacts on deployment, level of awareness, privacy and security, and access to AI technology varies among stakeholders and academia. Stakeholders and academia must harness the potential benefits of AI in libraries. The authorities and stakeholders must remain informed about the latest developments and best practices offered by AI in academic setup. The authorities must examine its implications, benefits, and risks for the informed decision-making process and its effective implementation in academic libraries. Many scholars have highlighted the potential benefits of AI in academic libraries [15] and ascertained that one of the significant bottlenecks in the deployment of AI in library operations is the digital resilience of librarians. Few have underscored the benefits of AI in academic libraries that should be kept in mind before implementing them. Several open applications of AI hold promise for improving library services at minimal costs. These are:

8. Challenges of AI in the academic libraries

Albeit, before deploying AI in library operations, there might be several challenges associated with artificial intelligence; however, digital resilience of librarians will be overcome while moving forward [28]; some challenges are mentioned below: (1) Limited technical expertise: Librarians may not have the technical skills or knowledge needed to implement and manage AI systems, and may require training and support. (2) Limited funding and resources: Implementing AI systems can be costly, and libraries may have limited funding and resources to support the development and maintenance of AI systems. They may approach the stakeholders and the Higher Education Commission for the funds in this case. (3) Limited access to data: The AI requires high-quality data. It is the job of librarians to invest more time by providing quality data. As AI relies on data, more data would mean more quality services in the library operations. (4) Internet and digital divide: The internet and digital divide is yet another challenge for libraries. In some areas, the internet speed remains quick, while in some places, the speed remains slow. It can also hamper the way the patrons demand. Internet connectivity and digital infrastructure are in high demand for running AI applications smoothly. (5) Limited awareness and understanding: To get benefits from AI applications, libraries may need to be more aware of the potential benefits offered by AI in library services. For awareness of librarians, training

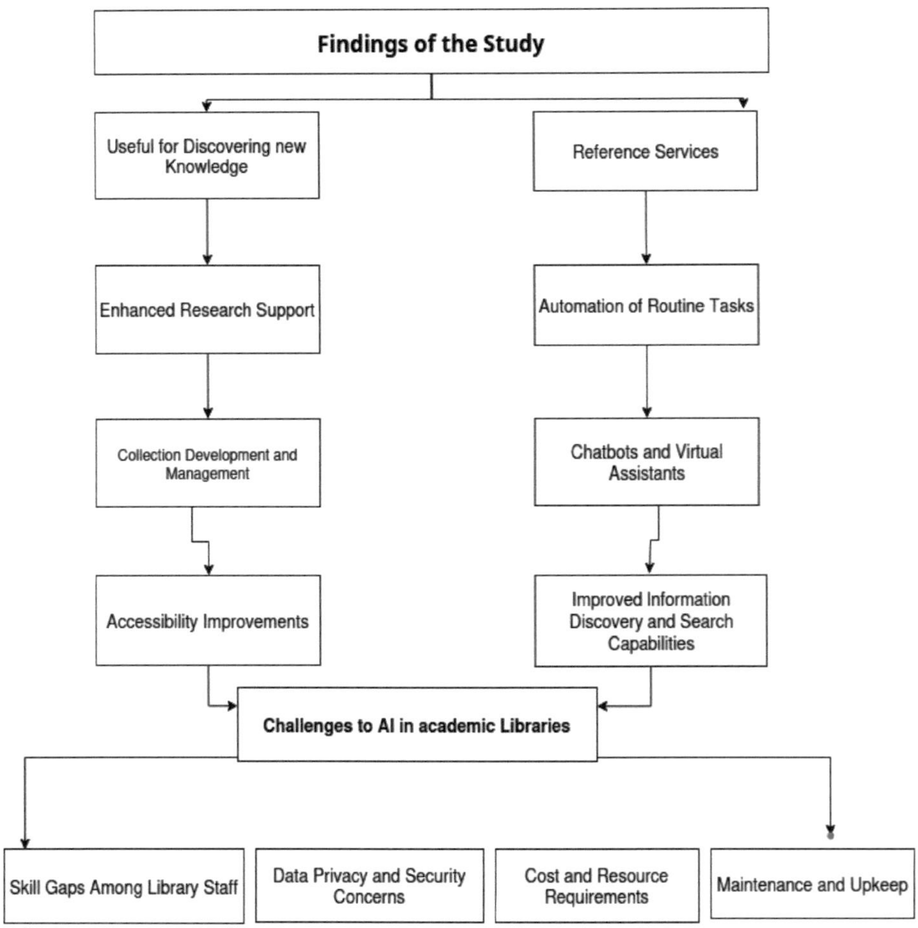

Figure 4.
Findings of the study.

programs should be organized. Because using any new system requires a complete understanding of librarians. (6) Ethical concerns: The AI mostly relies on data. As the libraries deal with huge data, such data may create concerns for the libraries regarding accountability, transparency, and bias. The librarians must know the ethical concerns of AI systems before incorporating them into library operations. Librarians may face different kinds of challenges while adopting AI in their respective libraries; however, keeping in mind the right support, resources, training, and ethical concerns, the librarians may overcome these challenges (**Figure 4**).

9. Findings and discussions

The present research has achieved three objectives of AI and its potential use in academic libraries. The findings of this study show that there is a trajectory of growing interest among librarians to adopt AI in academic libraries. The findings of this study concordance with the study of Ref. [8] who identified that AI has great potential to discover new knowledge within academic libraries context. The scholar further elaborated that AI is the perfect tool for information literacy in any academic environment. The early research identified that AI can effectively address complex library operations. The increasing use of AI-driven technologies in leading academic institutions reflects the growing confidence in AI to enhance library activities. The adoption of AI is not uniform across the globe. The developed nations are leading the way in integrating AI into their academic libraries, while the status of developing countries is a bit slow for many reasons. The study by Ref. [7] highlighted that developing countries are lagging behind developed nations because of limited resources, poor infrastructure, and lack of stakeholders interest while implementing them into academic libraries. The findings of this study also corroborate the study of Ref. [29], who illustrated the lack of librarians' training, data privacy, and finance. The study suggests that there should be tailored strategies and policies that consider the unique challenges in different regions. Over all the literature suggests a positive of the future of AI in academic libraries. The study has also explored that AI will play a critical role in the evolution of library services; however, the adoption will likely vary depending on regional, economic, and institutional factors.

The result of the second objective of the result shows that the integration of AI-driven tools in academic libraries represents significant enhancement and advancement in library operations. The study is in concordance with the study of Ref. [28], which states that numerous applications of AI have been brought into use, such as Chatbots, which provide 24/7 assistance to library users. The study also explores how Chatbots can be used to address different queries asked by patrons. Similarly, the study results also corroborate the study of Ref. [25], who discovered that Chatbot is the most significant tool of AI that streamlines the user's experience with library resources. Their study highlighted the different tools of text mining for information retrieval and discussed that text mining can extract valuable insights from large volumes of unstructured data, which is useful for digital collection and authorized users to access vast amounts of information in more effective ways. The result of this objective is also in concordance with the study of Ref. [20], who deduced that the image recognition tool of AI in academic libraries is useful for cataloging and classifications of images in the libraries. The study also found that the image recognition tool is very helpful for patrons to search and retrieve visual resources more efficiently, thereby improving the overall usability of image collection. The result of this study also corroborates with the study of Ref. [22], who defined the NLP as an AI-driven tool and its usage in the library that enables a user to understand the text and spoken language. It can also be used to analyze and comprehend text in multiple languages; such a function is particularly valuable in academic libraries. The result of this study also meets the study of Ref. [15], who described the recommender systems as an AI-driven tool; the scholar has their views that the recommender system is an essential tool of AI that recommends the user's journal articles, books, and multimedia based on their past search. The study also concordance with the study of Ref. [11], who highlighted the use of automation circulation for library tasks. The study elaborated that automating circulation allows users to check in and check out the library resources without the involvement of library staff. In short, the adoption of AI-driven tools in academic libraries has substantial benefits, including faster service delivery, enhanced user experience, and reduced labor costs. As AI technology continues to evolve, its implementation in academic libraries will undoubtedly meet the changing needs of the libraries in the future. The integration of AI into academic libraries has brought about significant advancements in user services and operational efficiency. However, the adoption of AI technologies also raises critical ethical and privacy concerns that must be carefully considered and addressed by library professionals. The studies reviewed under this objective provide insights into the prospects and challenges of AI in academic libraries, particularly concerning ethical issues, data privacy, and the impact on users and staff.

The result of the third research objective indicates the ethical and privacy concerns of AI in academic libraries. The result of this study is closely related to the study of Ref. [5], who identified that data privacy and ethical concerns are significant issues of AI while implementing them into academic libraries. These concerns revolve around the handling of user data, potential bias in AI-generated results, and the transparency of AI algorithms. The result also corroborates with the study Ref. [28], which described that AI has undoubtedly offered positive potential for academic libraries. Still, it raises concerns about data security and the potential for AI systems to restrict users' freedom of expression; similarly, the study also related to the study of Ref. [30], who further explained that AI in academic libraries has both positive and negative impact on user privacy and the library staff. There is a great chance of data security from the user's side while for library staff it can create a tendency of low job opportunities because it will replace human work with robotic operations. The study of Ref. [12] has also discovered that AI can be used to enhance the browsing processes of libraries and allow users to borrow library material without involving the library; however, it also raises questions about the ethical implications of reducing human interactions in the libraries. In their research, Ref. [28] cautioned that in academic libraries, the unfair practices of AI could harm users' privacy, and it is essential for the library library staff to address this privacy to protect the user's data. The result of this data is also in concordance with the study of Ref. [10], who argued that tailoring AI-based services in academic libraries should ensure privacy concerns to protect user trust. Ref. [31] underlined that privacy concerns might give birth to a negative impact on user trust. Ref. [5] points out that in academic libraries, the use of AI may reduce the need for staff roles. This can pose ethical challenges for the librarians to lose job opportunities in the future. A study, suggested that [32–34] librarians should be imparted training before implementing AI in academic libraries because without proper training, librarians might face several challenges like data privacy of library users, fairness of AI algorithms, and the protection of larger data in order to protect the users from breach and misuse of data. In essence, AI offers significant opportunities for enhancing library services; still, librarians need to safeguard the data privacy of users.

10. Implications of the study

As with other research, the present study also has some implications, such as practical implications, theoretical implications, and educational implications. The practical implication of this study will provide library administration and policymakers with an overview of AI and its usage in academic libraries. The result of this study can be utilized to decide for AI in academic libraries. It can also be used to develop user training programs and a guideline for both library staff and users.

The study adds theoretical implications to the growing body of literature on AI and its implementation in academic libraries. Particularly for university libraries that are beyond any geographical location. Furthermore, the result of this study will help the scholars to refine and extend its theoretical framework to other studies in the future. The study will provide insightful knowledge to policymakers, stakeholders, and practitioner librarians who intend to deploy AI in their respective libraries.

The study provides valuable insights for library professionals and scholars in the field. Thus, the educational implication of this study will provide handsome knowledge for library patrons, curricula devised by higher education, and students of library and information science. The study is useful for researchers, academicians, and policymakers who deal with this subject. In short, this study will help educational organizations, particularly academic libraries to use it as a policy framework.

The study also contributes handsome knowledge on the ethical and social repercussions of AI and its usage in academic libraries. Thus, the findings of this study could prompt discussion regarding the social discussion on AI. Similarly, the study describes concerns, biased issues, and power dynamics of AI in an academic environment. In short, the study provides both challenges and opportunities associated with AI use in academic libraries that could inform decision-makers in both national and international organizations.

11. Conclusion

The paper provides a comprehensive overview of the utilization of AI in academic libraries, aiming to enhance efficiency, accuracy, and personalization for patrons while improving operational performance. Through qualitative analysis of existing literature, it elucidates AI's role in various library functions such as search and discovery, cataloging, circulation, and digital preservation. Despite its potential benefits, challenges like limited technical expertise, funding constraints, and ethical concerns are acknowledged. Recommendations emphasize continuous learning, collaboration, and leveraging free AI applications. The study highlights the importance of AI adoption in academic libraries, underscoring its transformative potential amid evolving technological landscapes. Foresee in mind its function and challenges, the following recommendations are made for the academic librarians, stakeholders, and scholars in the field:

Recommendations for AI in academic libraries

1. To make AI an integral part of their libraries, librarians must keep pace with emerging applications of AI. As AI evolves from time to time, librarians should learn these skills.

2. The librarians should experience AI and associated technologies in the age of digital transformation. Such technologies will not only bring ease to their library operations but also equip patrons with the latest technologies.

3. AI introduces numerous free applications for library operations such as Plagiarism software, Google Maps, Dspace, Chatbots, and other similar applications. Librarians should utilize these applications for smooth functioning.

4. To understand the full spectrum of AI applications in library services, librarians must bring diversity to their services to fulfill the demands of their patrons.

5. Training for new applications is highly necessary; the library staff needs to participate in professional development programs and different types of training that enhance their skills in AI.

6. To gain hands-on experience and understand the capabilities of AI applications in library operations, librarians should experiment with AI tools and technologies.

7. The latest developments in AI technologies occur from time to time. Librarians should abreast themselves with these technologies by joining conferences, workshops, and other professional development programs.

Author details

Abid Hussain
Institute of Strategic Studies Islamabad, Pakistan

*Address all correspondence to: abidmardan@gmail.com

References

[1] Habib U. A Survey on Implication of Artificial Intelligence in Detecting SQL Injections. 2023. Available from: https://www.researchgate.net/profile/Usama-Habib-4/publication/378496266_A_Survey_on_Implication_of_Artificial_Intelligence_in_detecting_SQL_Injections/links/65dd7ebac3b52a1170fbe4d6/A-Survey-on-Implication-of-Artificial-Intelligence-in-detecting-SQL-Injections.pdf [Accessed: September 23, 2024]

[2] Yusuf TI, Adebayo OA, Bello LA, Kayode JO. Adoption of artificial intelligence for effective library service delivery in academic libraries in Nigeria. Library Philosophy and Practice (e-journal) (Nebraska, USA). 2022:6804

[3] Application of artificial intelligence for reference services in academic libraries: A global overview through a systematic review of literature. Journal of Library Resource Sharing. **32**(1-5). Available from: https://www.tandfonline.com/doi/abs/10.1080/26915979.2023.2281668 [Accessed: September 23, 2024]

[4] Nawaz N, Gomes AM, Saldeen MA. Artificial intelligence (AI) applications for library services and resources in COVID-19 pandemic. Journal of Critical Reviews. 2020;**7**(18):16-28

[5] Ali MY, Naeem SB, Bhatti R. Artificial intelligence (AI) in Pakistani university library services. Library Hi Tech News. 2021;**38**(8):12-15

[6] Okunlaya RO, Abdullah NS, Alias RA. Artificial intelligence (AI) library services innovative conceptual framework for the digital transformation of university education. Library Hi Tech. 2022;**40**(6):1869-1892. DOI: 10.1108/LHT-07-2021-0242

[7] Omame IM, Alex-Nmecha JC. Artificial intelligence in libraries. In: Managing and Adapting Library Information Services for Future Users. USA: IGI Global; 2020. pp. 120-144. Available from: https://www.igi-global.com/chapter/artificial-intelligence-inlibraries/245111 [Accessed: September 23, 2024]

[8] Oyetola SO, Oladokun BD, Maxwell CE, Akor SO. Artificial intelligence in the library: Gauging the potential application and implications for contemporary library services in Nigeria. Data and Metadata. 2023;**2**:36-36. DOI: 10.56294/dm202336

[9] Chen CC. Libraries in the New Information Age. North Carolina Libraries; 1987

[10] Lu Y. Artificial intelligence: A survey on evolution, models, applications and future trends. Journal of Management Analytics. 2019;**6**(1):1-29. DOI: 10.1080/23270012.2019.1570365

[11] Adesina AS, Zubairu AN. Contemporary Library and Artificial Intelligence Technology; 2023. Available from: https://journals.sagepub.com/doi/abs/10.1177/09557490241231483 [Accessed: September 23, 2024]

[12] Hussain A. Strategy of libraries and librarians during COVID-19. The International Journal of Law, Humanities & Social Science. 2021;**5**(1):40-49

[13] Hussain A. Cutting edge: technology's impact on library services. In: Innovations in the Designing and Marketing of Information Services. USA: IGI Global; 2020. pp. 16-27. Available from: https://www.igi-global.com/

chapter/cutting-edge/238161 [Accessed: September 23, 2024]

[14] Hussain A. Cutting EDGE: technology's impact on library services. In: Jesubright JJ, Saravanan P, editors. Innovations in the Designing and Marketing of Information Services. IGI Global; 2020. pp. 16-27. DOI: 10.4018/978-1-7998-1482-5.ch002

[15] Gamage I, Nawodya RGI, Ahmed MNT, Aathif MAM, De Silva DI, Dias T. Effectiveness of Cutting-Edge Technology for Library Management System. Rochester, NY: SSRN; 2022. 4279656. Available from: https://papers.ssrn.com/abstract=4279656 [Accessed: September 23, 2024]

[16] Diseiye O, Ukubeyinje SE, Oladokun BD, Kakwagh VV. Emerging technologies: Leveraging digital literacy for self-sufficiency among library professionals. Metaverse Basic and Applied Research. 2024;**3**:59-59. DOI: 10.56294/mr202459

[17] Haq IU, Hussain A, Tanveer M. Evaluating the scholarly literature on information literacy indexed in the web of science database. Library Philosophy and Practice (Nebraska, USA). 2021:5230

[18] Ibrahim H, Okpala AE. Exploring the integration of artificial intelligence in Nigeria library services. International Journal of Knowledge Dissemination. 2024;**5**(1):55-65. DOI: 10.70118/ijkd.0202405010.6

[19] Vasishta P, Dhingra N, Vasishta S. Application of artificial intelligence in libraries: A bibliometric analysis and visualisation of research activities. Library Hi Tech. 2024. DOI: 10.1108/LHT-12-2023-0589 [Vol. ahead-of-print, No. ahead-of-print]

[20] Hussain A. Use of artificial intelligence in the library services: Prospects and challenges. Library Hi Tech News. 2023;**40**(2):15-17. DOI: 10.1108/LHTN-11-2022-0125

[21] Hussain A, Shahid R. Impact of big data on library services: Prospect and challenges. Library Hi Tech News. 2022:000-000

[22] Barsha S, Munshi SA. Implementing artificial intelligence in library services: A review of current prospects and challenges of developing countries. Library Hi Tech News. 2024;**41**(1):7-10. DOI: 10.1108/LHTN-07-2023-0126

[23] De Sarkar T. Implementing robotics in library services. Library Hi Tech News. 2023;**40**(1):8-12

[24] Hussain A. Industrial revolution 4.0: Implication to libraries and librarians. Library Hi Tech News. 2020;**37**(1):1-5

[25] Yoganingrum A, Rachmawati R, Koharudin K. Past, present, and future of artificial intelligence in library services. In: Handbook of Research on Emerging Trends and Technologies in Librarianship. USA: IGI Global; 2022. pp. 91-114. DOI: 10.4018/978-1-7998-9094-2.ch007

[26] Hussain A, Rafiq M. Provision of research support services across the research lifecycle in university libraries. Journal of Librarianship and Information Science. 2023:09610006231207661. DOI: 10.1177/09610006231207661

[27] Hussain A, Ismail M, Usman M. Research contributions of Pakistani LIS scholars: A review of SCOPUS databas. IJoLIS. 2023;**8**:31-47. Available from: https://ojs.aiou.edu.pk/index.php/jlis/article/view/2196 [Accessed: September 23, 2024]

[28] Hussain A. Review of augmented reality in academic and research

libraries. Library Hi Tech News. 2022;**39**(9):23-25

[29] Echedom AU, Okuonghae O. Transforming academic library operations in Africa with artificial intelligence: Opportunities and challenges: A review paper. New Review of Academic Librarianship. 2021;**27**(2):243-255. DOI: 10.1080/13614533.2021.1906715

[30] Gasparini AA, Kautonen H. Understanding artificial intelligence in research libraries: An extensive literature review. LIBER Quarterly: Te Journal of European Research Libraries. 2022;**32**(1):1-36

[31] Hussain A. Use of geographical information system (GIS) application in public libraries. Library Hi Tech News. 2023:32-39. [Ahead-of-print]. Available from: https://www.emerald.com/insight/content/doi/10.1108/LHTN-11-2022-0126/full/(https://ibs.edu.pk/library/ [Accessed: September 23, 2024]

[32] Hussain A. Use of WhatsApp technology in library services: Case study of National Defence University library, Islamabad, Pakistan. Library Philosophy and Practice. 2022:1-11

[33] Hussain A, Jan SU. User perception on electronic resources and services in National Defense University library Islamabad, Pakistan. Pakistan Library and Information Science Journal. 2018;**49**(3):58-68

[34] Abid H. Uses of blockchain technologies in library services. Library Hi Tech News. 2021;**38**(8):9-11. DOI: 10.1108/LHTN-08-2020-0079

Chapter 6

Exploring AI Applications in Essay-Based Assignments: Affordances and Risks

Ahmad Alzahrani and Ying Zheng

Abstract

This study examined the feasibility of employing artificial intelligence (AI) for feedback provision on essay-based assignments in a UK Higher Education setting. Although the critical role of feedback in enhancing students' learning experiences is widely recognised, resource limitations and large student numbers often hinder its quality and timely delivery. Through in-depth interviews with four participants from a university in the UK, this research investigated AI applications in essay evaluation, utilising data from 12 AI-generated essays and their corresponding feedback. The aims of the study are to evaluate tutors' abilities in discerning human and AI-generated essays, as well as evaluating the quality of AI-generated feedback from their perspectives. Findings showed that assessors could detect certain characteristics consistent with AI generation and noted ethical concerns regarding deviations from academic standards. Participants also acknowledged AI's capacity for swift feedback delivery as compared to human. The results of this study help enhance our understanding of AI's affordances and risks in assessment and feedback, particularly in the less explored university essay assignments.

Keywords: artificial intelligence (AI), essay-based assignment, feedback, assessment, ethics

1. Introduction

Quality feedback is recognised as a key factor in improving students' learning experiences and achievements. However, due to resource limitations, providing timely and constructive feedback to many students is a challenging task. Automated feedback systems (AFS) are increasingly seen as a potential solution, but they have been less commonly applied to open-ended writing tasks, such as essay assignments and project proposals [1]. Recent advancements in Generative Pre-trained Transformer (GPT) models, particularly ChatGPT, offer new possibilities for enhancing AFS by providing more natural and context-specific individualised responses.

Additionally, ethical discussions are taking place within educational and scholarly realms. While taking advantages of the methodological advancements in AI, scholars emphasise the need for increased methodological rigour and ethical scrutiny in practice [2]. The emergence of Large Language Model (LLM) powered by AI chatbots, such as OpenAI's, raises scholarly and practical concerns regarding their potential applications, ethical implications, and the distinction between AI- and human-produced texts [3].

Moreover, the widespread use of AI models among students and academics prompts questions about how tutors can adapt course contents and assessment methods to mitigate the impact of students' extensive reliance on them [4]. An alternative perspective suggests empowering educators to incorporate AI for various educational purposes, such as generating lecture topics, demonstrations, exam questions, assignments, content explanations of contents, ideation exercises, and grading essays or programming assignments [5–8].

Similarly, *tutoring*, recognised as a highly individualised and efficient method to improve student learning, faces a shortage of adequately trained tutors [9]. Although tutor training programmes have been developed, a significant gap exists as most programmes lack specific formative feedback, leaving a research void in tutors receiving feedback on their assessment methods. Researchers now advocate emphasising utilising pre-trained Large Language Models to give the tutors precise formative feedback on their tutoring practices, emphasising the assessment of the accuracy of AI-generated feedback in enhancing tutor learning and performance [10].

Integrating AI use as discussed above has been seen as a promising opportunity to improve feedback. This is because creating individualised feedback for assignments is an intricate task [11]. Additionally, recent research recognises the above-mentioned shortcomings of current evaluation approaches and suggests investigating the use of Large Language Models (LLMs) as a potential remedy for automating error identification and facilitating teacher assessments in classroom-based second language (L2) learners' writing assessment [12]. Moreover, research regarding the use of ChatGPT in providing scoring information acknowledges the limitation of directly employing pre-trained models like GPT-3.5 for tasks involving student language and underscores the necessity of fine-tuning on domain-specific data [13].

The study posits that integrating GPT models, like ChatGPT, into automated feedback systems can significantly improve the quality and relevance of feedback for open-ended writing tasks. The research design evaluates this by comparing GPT-based feedback with traditional methods, assessing its impact on accuracy, timeliness, and contextual relevance, while also exploring tutors' views on how AI can enhance their feedback practices. The chapter introduces the challenges of current feedback systems, presents GPT models as a potential solution by reviewing the literature on AI model use in feedback and assessment, and discusses their practical applications and ethical implications, guiding the reader through problem identification, solution evaluation, and future research directions.

2. Literature review

The literature review identified several gaps in understanding how humans detect AI-generated essays and assess the quality of AI-generated feedback from their viewpoints. First, existing studies focused mainly on identifying AI-generated abstracts (e.g. not full essays), which limited understanding due to the greater complexity of full essays. Second, ethical considerations and acceptance of AI tools in education, though gaining more and more attention, have been underexplored empirically so far. Existing opinions vary and lack depth on issues like bias and transparency. Lastly, most studies offered short-term views of AI feedback integration without considering long-term impacts on student learning, teacher practices, and educational quality. Longitudinal studies are needed to evaluate tools' sustainability and evolving effectiveness in education. Addressing these gaps can provide a more comprehensive understanding of AI's role in educational settings, enhancing efficacy of both AI and human contributions to learning and assessment.

In this regard, research revealed a low identification rate among reviewers of research abstracts while assessing scholars' capacity to differentiate between AI- and human-produced abstracts [14]. In a similar vein, these challenges were acknowledged as more significant in identifying AI use in student submissions. In this context, although introducing a novel keyword analysis revealed the potential of detecting ChatGPT's influence on student writings, the output was described as vague, calling for the need for more specific prompting in the detection process [4]. However, the focus on abstracts instead of full essays in these two previous studies limited their scopes, as abstracts did not capture the depth present in full essay assignments.

Similarly, de Winter et al. [4] addressed the challenges of conclusively identifying ChatGPT use in student submissions. The study concluded that although introducing a novel keyword analysis revealed the potential of detecting ChatGPT's influence on student abstracts and academic publications, they acknowledged challenges, such as vague outputs and the need for specific prompting. Moreover, the study by Dai et al. [1] explored the feasibility of using ChatGPT for providing written feedback on a data science project assignment in an Australian university. Their investigation focused on the clarity of the generated feedback, its alignment with instructor-provided feedback, and the inclusion of effective feedback elements. The evaluation included readability, agreement with human instructors using a marking rubric, and application of a theoretical feedback model. Their findings indicated that ChatGPT's feedback readability scores fell within the 3.75–4.0 range, outperforming over 75% of instructor feedback.

Examining assessors' capacity to identify AI is crucial, yet equally significant is evaluating the quality of feedback they provide. In this regard, investigating ChatGPT's feedback clarity, alignment with instructor feedback, and effectiveness revealed its superior scores, especially in providing process-focused feedback, surpassing instructor feedback [1]. Hirunyasiri et al. [10] looked into the ability of GPT-4 to precisely evaluate elements within effective praise given by human tutors to students. Their focus was on comparing the accuracy of GPT-4 assessments using zero-shot and few-shot chain of thought prompting approaches. Results showed that zero-shot and few-shot chain of thought methods produced similar outcomes in which GPT-4 moderately identified specific and immediate praise but struggled to recognise tutors' ability to deliver genuine praise, especially in the zero-shot prompting scenario.

A few studies looked into human voices in this matter. For example, Nguyen [15] investigated the perspectives of English as a Foreign Language (EFL) teacher at Van Lang University in Vietnam on integrating ChatGPT-4 for generating feedback in writing sessions. The study involved 20 EFL teachers who incorporated ChatGPT into language education, collecting quantitative and qualitative data through online surveys and structured interviews. The findings indicated a positive attitude among EFL teachers towards ChatGPT integration, emphasising the importance of professional training, enhancing user understanding of ChatGPT's limitations, and ensuring responsible chatbot usage for effective implementation in language classes. Cao and Zhong [16] investigated the effectiveness of ChatGPT-based feedback compared to traditional teacher feedback and self-feedback in improving Chinese to English translation skills among Master of Translation and Interpretation students. The findings suggested that while traditional feedback methods outperformed ChatGPT in overall translation quality, ChatGPT-based feedback showed strengths in enhancing lexical proficiency and referential cohesion. Therefore, the potential of integrating ChatGPT as an additional resource in translation practice alongside traditional teacher-led methods is worth the effort.

Similarly, Pankiewicz and Baker [11] employed GPT-3.5 model to automate feedback generation for programming assignments, assessing its impact on students. The study compared an experimental group, receiving GPT hints, with a control group. Results indicated that students valued GPT-generated hints, leading to reduced reliance on regular feedback and improved performance in tasks with GPT hints. The experimental group also completed assignments more quickly for tasks with GPT hints.

Another important study, Bewersdorff et al. [12], explored the linguistic analysis of feedback, highlighting challenges in identifying logical errors in complex student experiment protocols. The research investigated the potential of LLMs to automatically identify errors in these protocols. The primary objective was to establish a foundation for generating personalised feedback, evaluating the AI system's accuracy in discerning both fundamental and complex errors, and its practical usability in education. Using a dataset of 65 student protocols, the study built an AI system based on GPT-3.5 and GPT-4, comparing its accuracy to those of human raters. The findings revealed varying levels of accuracy in error detection, with the AI system excelling in identifying fundamental errors but facing challenges with more complex errors. This study provided insights into LLMs' potential applications in education as well as LLMs' capabilities in detecting errors in enquiry-based learning.

3. Method

The four tutors in this study had varying levels of teaching experience, ranging from one year to over 15 years, with two being native English speakers and two non-native. Despite the small sample size, their diverse perspectives and substantial experience in essay evaluation made them suitable for in-depth qualitative analysis. All participants had experience marking essays from the specific postgraduate module under review. The group consisted of one female and three males. They were not informed of the nature of the 12 essays and feedback they were to assess prior to the study. Their task was to evaluate the quality of the essays, assign marks using the marking criteria, and then assess the corresponding AI-generated feedback.

In this study, several ethical considerations were carefully considered, particularly around consent processes and data privacy. First, informed consent was obtained from all tutor participants before conducting the interviews and essay evaluations. The participants were fully briefed about the purpose of the study, the nature of the tasks, and the use of AI-generated essays and feedback without revealing their source until after the assessment to ensure unbiased evaluations. Regarding data privacy, the participants' identities were anonymised to protect their confidentiality, with no personal identifying information disclosed in the reporting of the results. All data collected, including interview transcripts, essay evaluations, and AI feedback assessments, were securely stored, ensuring compliance with data protection regulations. Additionally, participants were given the option to withdraw from the study at any point, guaranteeing their autonomy throughout the research process. These ethical safeguards ensured the protection of participants' rights and privacy during the study.

Phase	Details
Research Design	• Qualitative case-study methodology • Focus on AI (GPT-3.5) application in essay evaluation • Semi-structured interviews with university tutors in the UK
Participants' selection	• 4 university tutors (1 female, 3 males) • Experience in essay marking from 1 to 15+ years • 2 Native English speakers, 2 Non-native speakers
Generating Essays & Feedback	• 12 essays generated using GPT-3.5 based on module guidelines • Essays divided into 3 levels: Excellent, Merit, Pass • AI-generated feedback for each essay
Evaluation Process	• Tutors tasked with evaluating 12 essays across 3 levels and topics • Compare AI feedback with traditional feedback methods • Assess the quality of AI-generated essays and feedback
Data Collection	• Semi-structured interviews • Annotated essays from tutor evaluations collected for comparative analysis

Table 1.
Summary of the research methods.

The study aimed to answer the two research questions, each intertwined with the exploration of AI in academic assessment. First, the study aimed to unveil the perception of human raters, seeking to discern their proficiency in comparing essays organically crafted by students and those generated by AI. Second, the study aimed to contrast traditional assessment modalities with AI-assisted paradigms, particularly focusing on marking and feedback provision within academic modules. A summary of the study methodology is presented in **Table 1**.

4. Results

Nine aspects of the findings are summarised in **Table 2**, which are elaborated in answering the three lines of enquiries in this study, they are, (1) tutors' ability

Aspects	Details	Examples	Contribution to outcome
AI Characteristics	AI-generated essays showed odd language and style.	Flowery language noted by Carl; poetic styles by Helen and Kyle.	Demonstrated the difficulty in distinguishing AI content due to non-academic language and style.
Unreliable Contents	Issues with accuracy and relevance of references.	Questionable references criticised by Omar and Kyle.	Revealed AI's limitations in producing credible, well-supported academic content.
Superficial Analysis	Essays lacked deep insights and meaningful analysis.	Superficial and template-like analysis noted by Helen and Omar.	Showed that AI essays often fail to engage critically with the material.
Not Academic Essays	Essays did not meet academic tone and style standards.	Non-academic language noted by Carl, Helen, and Kyle.	Highlighted the mismatch between AI-generated content and academic writing norms.

Aspects	Details	Examples	Contribution to outcome
Lack of Coherence	Poor logical structure and organisation in some essays.	Disjointed arguments observed by Carl and Omar.	Identified structural deficiencies, impacting readability and argument flow.
Lack of Criticality	Essays lacked critical analysis and had repetitive points.	Repetitive content noted by Kyle and Omar.	Demonstrated AI's failure to provide the critical engagement and original insights needed for high-quality writing.
Efficiency and Identifying Inconsistency	AI feedback was efficient and identified inconsistencies quickly.	Timely feedback for international students; inconsistency highlighted by Helen.	Showed AI's strength in providing rapid feedback and improving workflow efficiency.
Language Support	AI supported language acquisition and provided feedback.	Kyle approved AI tools for enhancing language skills.	Emphasised AI's role in supporting language learning and supplementing traditional methods.
Lack of Constructive Feedback	AI feedback lacked depth and formative guidance.	Inadequate feedback noted by Kyle.	Highlighted the need for human evaluators to provide nuanced, constructive feedback.

Table 2.
Summary of the study results.

to detect AI-generated essays; (2) tutors' evaluation of AI-generated essays against marking rubrics; and (3) tutors' evaluation of AI-generated feedback.

Details, examples, and contributions to the research outcome are provided in the summary, with the first three aspects addressing the first enquiry regarding human raters' ability to detect AI-generated essays, i.e., "AI characteristics", "unreliable contents", and "superficial analysis". "Not academic essays", "lack of coherence", and "lack of criticality" inform the second enquiry, followed by "efficiency and identifying inconsistency", "language support for students and teachers", and "lack of constructive feedback" addresses the third enquiry.

4.1 Tutors' ability to detect AI-generated essays

4.1.1 AI generated

Tutors agreed that some essays displayed characteristics consistent with AI generation, which raised important questions about the role of technology in academic writing. Carl, for example, showed scepticism about the essays' authenticity and authorship as he noted several features that could indicate AI involvement, including "odd language", "flowery expressions", and "inappropriate references".

> *Carl: Well, it's both kind of self-congratulatory saying how wonderful I am, and it's also a ridiculously flowery language*

Carl indicated that the language used in the essay is overly focused on praising the author or the subject matter. It could also imply that the author is more concerned with showcasing their own achievements or opinions rather than providing objective analysis or valuable insights. The term "flowery language" typically refers to writing that is overly exaggerated with excessive use of metaphors, similes, adjectives, and other literary devices. Carl commented that while flowery language can sometimes enhance the beauty of prose, when used excessively, it may obscure the intended message or come across as pretentious, especially in academic writings.

Similarly, Helen expressed her suspicion about the essay's origins, lack of a clear line of argument, and critical evaluation as potential indicators of AI involvement. She suggested that the essay's poetic and idiomatic writing style may be characteristic of AI-generated content, especially when combined with the absence of coherent analysis. She commented that

> *I like this essay, in a good way. However, in terms of the language, it uses a lot of poetic and idiomatic writing. I think that's why it made me feel like it's machine generated, for me as a non-native speaker, I feel I am more sensitive to this type of language.*

Helen highlighted a specific aspect of the essay that she appreciates—its use of poetic and idiomatic language, which suggests if the essay employs creative and expressive language, they might enhance its appeal and make it more engaging to read to some readers. However, this part is interesting because it introduces a contrast. Despite appreciating the poetic and idiomatic writing, the tutor also felt that this style somehow gave the impression of being machine-generated. Furthermore, this tutor added a personal perspective here, indicating that her status as a non-native English speaker might influence her perception of the essay's language. This suggests that she may be more accustomed to certain linguistic features that could be indicative of machine generation, especially if they deviate from typical patterns of second language learners' language use.

Additionally, Kyle argued that the essay's characteristics aligned with those of AI-generated contents and pointed out further that the bland content, inappropriate language, and structural issues as potential indicators of AI involvement.

> *Researcher: So you seriously think it's AI generated? It's likely to be AI generated essay according to you.*
> *Kyle: Yeah, basically because of the sort of blandness of the writing.*

He commented that the "blandness" in writing, to him, means the texts lack depth, creativity, or personal touch. The use of repetitive phrases, generic language, or lack of clear expression could also contribute to this perception of blandness. The use of the word "blandness" implies a lack of distinctive or unique qualities in the writing, which could be interpreted as a deficiency in creativity or originality.

Furthermore, Kyle's use of the phrase "sort of" before "blandness" suggests a degree of hesitation or uncertainty in his assessment, indicating that he may not be entirely confident in his conclusion. This hesitation could stem from the challenge of accurately distinguishing between AI-generated and human-generated content, particularly as AI technologies become more and more sophisticated and capable of mimicking human writing styles.

4.1.2 Unreliable content

The tutors' observations regarding the reliability of the essay's content shed light on the importance of thorough research and accurate referencing in academic writing.

In this regard, Omar, in his comment below, focused on issues related to the accuracy and relevance of the essay's content. He noticed the presence of irrelevant sections, factual inaccuracies, and outdated references, suggesting lack of credibility and academic rigour in the essays that he deems AI generated.

> *Omar: reading through the reference list, some references, for example, "the promise of assessment engineering", didn't sound like a real one to me.*

Omar's doubt about the legitimacy of the reference suggests his concern about the essay's authenticity and reliability. He further commented that in academic writing, references should be precise and credible. The possibility that the reference may have been generated without rigorous academic scrutiny hints at one of the issues with AI-generated text. Omar's critique, therefore, highlights the potential pitfalls of relying on AI-generated content for academic purposes. It serves as a reminder that while AI may be able to assist in generating text, the "hallucinations" it provides often fail to meet the rigorous standards of authenticity and reliability required in scholarly work.

Similarly, Kyle echoed concern about the reliability of the essay's content, emphasising the need for accurate referencing and evidence-based argumentation. Kyle's remarks below indicated his scepticism regarding its reliability and authenticity.

> *Kyle: I'll agree it's well-structured, I think the key points are the sources though. I don't think the arguments presented in the essay are supported by sources.*

His critique centres on three main points: the essay's lack of genuine source support, the coherence of the arguments and their link to the sources. First, Kyle acknowledges the essay's structural soundness, which can be a symbol of strength of AI-generated content. Advanced AI models are adept at creating well-organised texts that mimic human writing to certain extent. However, structural integrity alone does not equate to reliability. The absence of authentic sources is a significant flaw Kyle highlights. AI-generated essays sometimes lack solid citations, which challenge the essay's credibility, suggesting it is not based on genuine research or information.

Second, Kyle's hesitation and repeated phrases, such as "I don't think" and "it's not an argument supported by sources", indicate his uncertainty about the essay's argumentative strength. AI-generated content, while structurally sound, often fails to present compelling, evidence-backed arguments. This deficiency is crucial, as persuasive writing relies heavily on the ability to substantiate claims with credible sources. Without this foundation, the essay's arguments could appear superficial and unconvincing.

4.1.3 Superficial analysis

All four tutors remarked on the superficial nature of the essay's analysis and described the essays as merely scratching the surface of the topic without going into deeper insights or offering meaningful interpretations of the subject matter. Superficial analysis may result from a lack of critical thinking, insufficient research, or a failure to engage with complex ideas or perspectives. For example, Helen's observation below indicated that the essay failed to provide a thorough analysis, suggesting it might be AI-generated.

Helen: However, the problem is, although they mentioned the validity, they didn't go further, or go deeper into the validity, or go to different aspects and with more specific and relevant literature.

Helen noted in one of the essays she evaluated that while the essay briefly mentions the concept of validity, it does not go into deeper aspects of the topic. A comprehensive analysis would typically explore various dimensions of validity, such as construct, content, and criterion validity, and reference-specific relevant literature to support its points. The lack of this depth suggests a superficial treatment of the subject. Similar point was also discussed by Omar who asserted that the essay he referred to was characterised by a superficial analysis.

Omar: I understand you cannot evidence every point in your essay due to word count, but you need to evidence a few critical points, and this one I evaluated reads more like a template.

This template-like nature is indicative of AI-generated text, which often uses a generic structure and adjusts minor details to fit different prompts or topics. The superficiality is further highlighted by the need for only minimal adjustments to make the essay suitable for different tests or bands, suggesting a lack of depth and specificity. Rather than offering deep insights or robust evidence, the AI-generated essay tended to skim the surface, providing just enough to appear coherent without delving into substantial or original thought.

Additionally, Omar's mention of the essay being "more like a template" and the suggestion to "just need to change a few words" reveal a reliance on a pre-structured format that can be easily adapted to various contexts. This template-like nature is indicative of AI-generated text, which often uses a generic structure and adjusts minor details to fit different prompts or topics. The superficiality is further highlighted by the need for only minimal adjustments to make the essay suitable for different tests or bands, suggesting a lack of depth and specificity.

4.2 Tutors' evaluation of AI-generated essays against the rubrics

4.2.1 Not academic essays

In light of the original rubrics of the module under investigation, there is a consensus among the participants regarding the essays' lack of adherence to academic standards, which is indicative of several underlying issues, highlighting various aspects of academic writing that the AI-generated essays failed to meet. For example, Carl's evaluation provided insights into language usage and stylistic elements of the essay. He noted the presence of odd language and expressions, suggesting a departure from the formal tone expected in academic writing.

Carl: some wordings were rather odd. It started with things like "this essay embarks on an ambitious journey. It will surpass conventional boundaries, reflecting excellence and original thought". I mean, this is not typical language of a student essay, or even in any kind of academic.

The above quote provides a critique of the language used in a student essay, noting its atypical phrasing. The critique implies that such ambitious language is unusual and potentially inappropriate for the context, suggesting a mismatch between the essay's language and the expected tone and style of academic work. This analysis underscores the importance of aligning writing style with audience expectations, particularly in academic settings, where clarity and appropriateness are crucial.

Similarly, Helen's assessment below emphasised the absence of a clear argument and critical evaluation in the essay. She pointed out that the essay failed to articulate a coherent thesis or engage critically with the topic. This critique underscored the importance of developing a well-defined argument supported by evidence and analysis in academic writing. Without a clear argument, the essay lacked direction and failed to fulfil the fundamental requirements of scholarly discourse.

> *Researcher: What features help you recognise? ...Can you summarise it please?*
> *Helen: OK, so the first one is from the text itself. It's not written by an L2 student, and there's a really poetic and informatic writing style.*
> *Researcher: When you say poetic, do you mean it is like a poem?*
> *Helen: Yes, a lot of metaphors.... it's not that academic essay to me.*

In her evaluation, Helen provides a clear rationale for why the text in question does not qualify as an academic essay. Her main points revolve around the writing style and the presence of certain literary features that are atypical for academic writing. She notes that the essay is "poetic and informatic", indicating that it employs a style more characteristic of creative writing than of scholarly analysis. Specifically, Helen points out the frequent use of metaphors, which she finds unsuitable for an academic context.

In a similar vein, Kyle echoed concerns about the essay's failure to meet academic standards. He said some of the language would be expected from a storybook, not academic writing.

> *Kyle: The language is articulate and engaging. I mean, I'll certainly describe it as articulate and engaging... But in a story book, you know. It's not an academic style at all.*

His evaluation revealed a critical perspective on its academic validity. Initially, Kyle acknowledges the essay's effective use of language, stating, "The language is articulate and engaging". This suggests that while the essay is well written and likely captivating for readers, its style is more suited to storytelling rather than academic discourse.

He explicitly differentiated between the qualities of effective narrative writing and the requirements of academic writing. Academic essays typically prioritise clarity, objectivity, and evidence-based arguments, adhering to specific structural and stylistic conventions. This evaluation highlights the fundamental difference between engaging narrative and academic rigour. Kyle's critique suggests that while the essay may excel in creativity and readability, it lacks the formal tone, structured argumentation, and scholarly depth, which are the typical characteristics of academic writing.

4.2.2 Lack of coherence

The tutors observed that some essays lacked coherence, which underscored the importance of logical structure and organisation in academic writing. For example, Carl highlighted several structural issues that contributed to the essay's lack of coherence. He noted the presence of random sentences, inappropriate references, and a disjointed structure that hindered reader comprehension.

Carl: In some cases, it's almost like a random collection of sentences, all of which were OK and on topic, but didn't join together properly.
Researcher: That sounds like AI generated it to you?
Carl: Well, if it was generated by AI, it wasn't a very good AI.

Carl's evaluation of the essay highlights a fundamental issue of coherence, indicating that while the sentences were individually acceptable and relevant to the topic, they failed to form a unified, coherent piece. This lack of connection among sentences suggests that the essay lacked a logical flow, making it difficult for readers to follow the argument or narrative. Carl's comment implies that the essay's sentences were disjointed, preventing the text from conveying a clear and cohesive message. It seems the primary issue lies not in the relevance or correctness of the individual sentences but in the essay's inability to weave these sentences into a coherent narrative or argument. Effective writing requires more than just relevant content; it demands a logical progression of ideas, which was evidently lacking in the essay Carl evaluated.

Also, Omar mentioned the essay's lack of coherence and flow, citing issues with the order of presentation and disconnected ideas. In this sense, the essay failed to provide a cohesive narrative or develop ideas in a logical progression, which emphasised the importance of structuring the essay in a way that facilitated smooth transitions between paragraphs and sections. This disjointedness makes it difficult for readers to follow the essay's argument, diminishing its overall effectiveness.

Omar: No coherence, and arguments are not talking about what it promised to talk about in the introduction.

Omar's observation that the arguments do not align with what was promised in the introduction is a critical weakness. The introduction of an essay sets expectations for the reader by outlining the main points or arguments that will be explored. If the body of the essay swings away from these points, it not only breaks the reader's trust but also undermines the purpose of the introduction. This misalignment suggests that the student either did not plan their essay effectively or failed to stay on topic, both of which are detrimental to the essay's overall quality.

4.2.3 Lack of criticality

The tutors' observations about the essay's lack of critical evaluation underscore the importance of analytical thinking and engagement with scholarly literature in academic writing. For example, Kyle's evaluation emphasises the essay's failure to engage critically with the topic or present a coherent argument.

Kyle: I mean, while the argumentation covers the transformative impact on timelines, it may lack in-depth critical analysis, occasionally veering towards a descriptive approach.

Kyle's evaluation highlights that while the essay addresses the transformative impact on timelines, it fails to go into a deep critical analysis. Instead, it tends to adopt a descriptive approach. Criticality in academic writing involves more than just describing or summarising information; it requires engaging deeply with the subject matter, questioning assumptions, evaluating evidence, and considering alternative perspectives. In the absence of criticality, an essay may fall short in several aspects. It may lack originality, merely repeating existing knowledge without adding anything substantial to the academic discourse. Moreover, it may overlook contradictions or biases inherent in the arguments presented, thus failing to provide an understanding of the topic.

Kyle's critique suggests that the student's essay may be superficial in its treatment of the subject matter. While it may acknowledge the transformative impact on timelines, it fails to interrogate the underlying assumptions or implications critically. As a result, the essay may not fulfil the expectations of academic rigour and intellectual depth. To address this deficiency, the student needs to cultivate a more critical mindset, actively questioning assumptions, engaging with conflicting viewpoints, and offering insightful interpretations. By doing so, they can elevate their analysis beyond mere description and contribute meaningfully to the scholarly conversation.

Similarly, Omar noted the presence of superficial analysis and factual inaccuracies, indicating a failure to engage critically with the topic or evaluate the evidence presented. His assessment of the student's essay shows that the essay seems to suffer from a repetitive nature where the same point is repeated without deeper analysis or exploration of alternative perspectives. Criticality in writing involves the ability to evaluate, question, and engage with the material being discussed. It demands a thoughtful examination of ideas, considering various angles, and offering deep insights. Such an absence of criticality in the essay suggests a superficial engagement with the topic, failing to go into its complexities or challenge prevailing assumptions.

Moreover, Omar's observation about the lack of criticality aligning with typical features of AI-generated text underscores the nature of the essay. AI-generated content often lacks the human capacity for critical thinking, relying on algorithms to generate text based on patterns and data inputs rather than genuine analysis. In essence, Omar's evaluation suggests that the AI-generated essay under evaluation falls short of demonstrating critical thinking skills essential for academic discourse. Without criticality, the essay fails to offer meaningful contributions to the conversation, resembling more of a product of automation than genuine intellectual enquiry.

4.3 Tutors' evaluation of AI-generated feedback

4.3.1 Efficiency and identifying inconsistency

The four tutor participants emphasised that AI feedback systems offered unparalleled efficiency and speed in providing feedback on academic writing, taking Omar for example.

> *Omar: Timely feedback is important for international students.*

Timely feedback is crucial for international students, and AI algorithms significantly enhance this process. By rapidly analysing essays, AI can identify grammar errors and provide constructive suggestions much faster than human graders. This speed improves the feedback turnaround time, enabling students to receive prompt guidance on their writing. Timely feedback is particularly important for international students who may face language barriers and cultural differences in academic writing.

Quick and constructive feedback allows them to understand their mistakes and learn how to improve their skills more efficiently. It helps them adapt to academic expectations and standards, reducing the time and stress associated with waiting for tutor grading. Consequently, the ability of AI to deliver immediate, detailed feedback supports international students in making necessary revisions and progressing in their studies more effectively.

Similarly, Helen highlighted the potential benefits of AI in providing feedback, especially in translation work. The conversation begins with the researcher steering the discussion towards exploring how AI might be advantageous in offering feedback. She prompts the participant to consider whether AI could provide any significant affordances or advantages that could be beneficial, specifically asking if AI could offer any "good thing that we can actually benefit from".

Researcher: do you see any advantage that AI could offer in providing feedback? Either in this module or in your translation module, is there any affordances? Is there any advantage? Is there any good thing that we can actually benefit from?
Helen: Yes. They can highlight the inconsistency. I need to read through the translation pieces and find there are some kind of inconsistency, but machine can highlight much more quickly.

Helen responds by pointing out a specific advantage of using AI in translation tasks. She explains that AI can quickly highlight inconsistencies within translation pieces, a task that would typically require a thorough and time-consuming manual review. By automating this process, AI can identify discrepancies and errors rapidly, allowing for a more efficient workflow. This capability is particularly valuable because it helps ensure the accuracy and consistency of translations, which are critical aspects of quality in this field.

The interview emphasises the practical application of AI in enhancing the efficiency and effectiveness of various tasks. In the context of translation, AI's ability to pinpoint issues means human reviewers can focus their efforts on more complex aspects of the translation process. This not only improves the overall quality of the work but also significantly reduces the time and effort required for manual reviews.

Moreover, this discussion illustrates the broader implications of AI in different fields. By automating routine yet essential tasks, AI can optimise workflows and enhance productivity. It allows professionals to allocate their time and skills to more strategic and creative endeavours, thus maximising the value of human input while leveraging the strengths of AI technology. This synergy between human expertise and AI capabilities represents a transformative potential, making processes more efficient and outcomes more reliable.

4.3.2 Language support for students and educators

Tutor interviewees, particularly Kyle, emphasised the valuable language support provided by AI feedback systems.

Kyle: I'd be very happy for students to use AI to help them with their language.

His statement above reflects a positive stance on the use of AI in language learning. He expresses positive attitude towards the idea of students using AI tools to aid their language learning. This perspective aligns with the growing acceptance of technology in education, where AI can offer personalised learning experiences, immediate feedback, and access to a vast array of resources. His approval suggests that he views AI as a beneficial tool to traditional learning methods, enhancing students' ability to practice and improve their language skills. By advocating for AI use, he acknowledges its potential to address individual learning needs and accelerate proficiency. This endorsement highlights a shift towards integrating advanced technologies in educational settings, aiming to make learning more efficient and accessible.

While AI feedback offered many advantages, participants emphasised that it should be used as a supplementary tool for educators rather than a replacement for human feedback. For example, Omar emphasises the potential role of AI in the creative and evaluative processes of brainstorming and writing. He suggests that AI can be employed as a tool to enhance the initial stages of idea generation by providing a critical perspective. The phrase "a pair of eyes" can be interpreted metaphorically as a fresh or unbiased viewpoint that AI brings to the table. This notion highlights AI's capability to assist in refining ideas by offering feedback that is detached from human biases or preconceptions.

> *Omar: you can use AI in the brainstorming stage as a pair of eyes that gives some criticality to your thoughts because you sometimes generate your text, and then you can ask for feedback.*

Omar's mention of using AI for generating text and subsequently seeking feedback underscores a cyclical, iterative process. AI's role in this cycle can be twofold: first, as a collaborator in producing content, and second, as an evaluator that helps to improve and polish the output. This dual functionality allows for continuous refinement and enhancement of ideas and written material. It reflects a growing recognition of AI as a valuable tool, where it can act as a supportive partner rather than a replacement for human creativity.

In summary, Omar advocates for integrating AI into the creative process to provide critical feedback and to foster continuous improvement. This approach not only enhances the quality of the output but also facilitates a more dynamic and interactive creative workflow. By leveraging AI in this manner, users can benefit from an additional layer of critical analysis that complements their own insights and expertise.

4.3.3 Lack of constructive feedback

Although tutor participants argued for the importance of AI in feedback, some tutors, particularly Kyle, noted the absence of constructive feedback provided.

> *Researcher: So, feedback is good, we give human marks, give feedback for formative purposes to help them to learn. But the AI generated feedback won't be able to do that job, at least the current stage of AI generated feedback can't do that.*
> *Kyle: It doesn't. It didn't in the three that you gave me. So that way, yeah.*
> *Researcher: right, right, right.*

This interview brings into focus the current limitations of AI in the realm of educational feedback. The researcher begins by affirming the critical role of human feedback in the learning process, particularly for formative purposes. Formative feedback is essential because it provides students with detailed, personalised insights that help them understand their strengths and areas for improvement. This type of feedback is not just about correcting mistakes but also about guiding students in their learning journey, fostering their development in a supportive manner.

The researcher asserts that AI-generated feedback, at its current stage, cannot perform this function effectively. This claim highlights a significant gap between what

AI can offer and the depth of feedback that humans provide. Human feedback is rich in context, empathy, and understanding, which are crucial elements in education that AI has yet to master.

Kyle's response, noting that the AI feedback he reviewed did not meet necessary standards, corroborates the researcher's point. His statement, "It didn't in the three that you gave me", serves as a concrete example of AI's shortcomings in this area. This practical observation adds weight to the researcher's argument and underscores the importance of maintaining a human touch in educational feedback. The researcher's repeated affirmation, "Right, right. Right. Right", indicates her strong agreement and possibly a sense of urgency about this issue. It suggests that they see this as a significant concern that needs addressing. This repetitive affirmation could also reflect their recognition of the challenges and complexities involved in integrating AI into educational settings.

The conversation between the researcher and Kyle shows a broader debate within educational technology. While AI has shown great promise in various domains, its application in delivering formative feedback remains limited. The dialogue suggests a need for a cautious approach to integrating AI in education. It emphasises that while AI can support certain tasks, the irreplaceable value of human interaction, judgement, and insight into teaching and learning processes must be preserved. This balance is crucial to ensure that the adoption of AI enhances rather than diminishes the quality of education.

5. Discussion

5.1 AI detectability abilities of human raters

The analysis of the four tutor participants' data demonstrated their keen attention to detail and deep understanding of academic writing dynamics. Their evaluations revealed a multifaceted approach, highlighting the complexities involved in differentiating between AI and human content. One key area of focus was the tone of the language used in the essays. Tutors analysed the essays for signs of artificiality, identifying abnormalities such as overly ornate phrasing, disjointed sentence structures, and the presence of unusual idioms or expressions that hinted at non-human origins. These linguistic irregularities served as red flags, prompting further scrutiny to determine the authenticity of the content. This aligns with the findings of Floridi and Chiriatti [17], who discussed common linguistic irregularities in AI-generated text are indicators of non-human authorship.

Beyond linguistic analysis, the assessors examined the essays, searching for signs of AI involvement. They identified important issues, such as a lack of coherent argumentation, superficial analysis, and the absence of original insights, as potential indications of automated generation. Their critiques extended beyond surface-level assessments, exploring the scholarly discourse and the intellectual rigour expected in academic writing. This comprehensive evaluation included examining the depth of analysis, originality of thought, and the overall intellectual engagement demonstrated in the essays. Desaire et al. [18] underscore the importance of these indicators in evaluating academic writing quality, highlighting how the depth of analysis can differentiate human-authored from AI-generated content.

Additionally, the tutor participants paid close attention to the structural coherence and organisation of the essays. They noted deficiencies, such as disjointed arguments, inadequate transitions between ideas, and a lack of logical flow, which detracted from the overall coherence of the work [4]. These observations highlighted the human-like qualities of organisation and coherence that are often lacking in AI-generated content. Crossley and McNamara [19] also emphasise these qualities as hallmarks of skilled academic writing, noting that the absence of well-organised and logically coherent arguments is a significant indicator of AI involvement.

Overall, the human assessors in this study demonstrated an understanding of both linguistic and substantive elements of academic writing, allowing them to identify potential indicators of AI-generated content. This multifaceted approach underscores the importance of a detailed and comprehensive assessment process in distinguishing between human and AI-generated essays and feedback. In this regard, McNamara et al. [20] discussed the role of natural language processing in evaluating writing quality, which can aid in distinguishing human-written content from AI-generated text, reinforcing the need for detailed and thorough evaluation criteria.

The above discussion highlights the need for a detailed approach in detecting AI-generated essays, focusing on linguistic irregularities, such as odd language and disjointed structures, as well as a lack of coherent argumentation and original insights. They also identified structural deficiencies, like poor transitions and logical flow, as indicators of AI involvement. This comprehensive evaluation underscores the importance of analysing both linguistic and intellectual depth to distinguish between human and AI-generated content, aligning with previous research on writing quality assessment.

5.2 AI affordances to feedback and evaluation

In the assessment of academic writing, human evaluators demonstrate a depth of understanding that stems from their ability to recognise distinctions and contextualise their evaluations within the broader landscape of academic standards and expectations. They scrutinise essays, identifying specific shortcomings such as a lack of coherence in argumentation, deficiencies in critical analysis, and the presence of language that falls short of the formal genre expected in scholarly discourse. Drawing upon their individual expertise and experience, human assessors offer personalised feedback tailored to the unique strengths and weaknesses of each piece of writing [21, 22]. This personalised approach enables students to receive targeted guidance for improvement, addressing their specific areas of concern and fostering a deeper understanding of academic writing conventions. For example, human raters can pinpoint nuanced issues in student writing and provide context-specific feedback that AI systems might miss [21]. This level of detailed, contextually rich feedback is crucial in helping students understand and meet the complex demands of academic writing [22].

On the other hand, artificial intelligence (AI) feedback systems offer distinct advantages in terms of efficiency and consistency. Using algorithms to rapidly analyse essays, these systems can provide feedback at a pace unmatched by manual grading processes [23]. This rapid turnaround can significantly enhance the learning process, as students receive timely insights that allow them to quickly address and rectify their mistakes [24]. Moreover, AI feedback ensures a level of consistency and standardisation in evaluation, as it applies predefined criteria uniformly across different student submissions [23]. This standardised approach promotes fairness and transparency in the assessment process, as all students are evaluated according to the same set of guidelines [24].

Furthermore, AI feedback systems can offer personalised support tailored to individual student needs. By analysing writing proficiency levels, learning styles, and specific areas requiring improvement, AI algorithms can adapt feedback to address each student's unique requirements [23]. This personalised feedback enhances the relevance and effectiveness of the guidance provided, ultimately contributing to improved learning outcomes [24]. This capability can be particularly beneficial in large classes where individualised attention from human instructors is limited [20]. Thus, while both human and AI feedback systems have unique strengths, integrating human evaluators' contextual understanding with AI's efficiency and consistency could offer a more comprehensive and effective approach to academic writing assessment [20].

5.3 Risks and ethical issues

Participants evaluating AI-generated feedback compared to human understanding identified several key risks that could impact students' learning and improvement. One major concern raised was the lack of constructive criticism provided by AI systems. Without actionable insights, students may struggle to identify areas for growth and develop their writing skills effectively [25]. Additionally, participants noted issues with the clarity of AI-generated feedback. Clear feedback is essential for students to understand where to improve and how to address those areas. Unclear feedback can lead to confusion and frustration, ultimately hindering students' ability to make meaningful revisions to their work.

Consistency in feedback provision was another area of concern highlighted by the participants. While AI systems offer standardised criteria for evaluation, inconsistencies were still observed in the feedback provided. Inconsistent feedback may confuse students and undermine their confidence in the assessment process, potentially leading to dissatisfaction and mistrust [26]. Moreover, participants expressed worries about the lack of individualisation in AI-generated feedback. Individualised feedback considers the unique strengths and weaknesses of each student's work, providing tailored guidance for improvement. Without this personalised approach, students may feel that their specific needs are not met, which could result in disengagement and frustration [27].

Also, ethical concerns regarding the integrity of academic standards in the face of AI technology were raised, prompting reflections on the potential consequences of relying on AI-generated content without transparent guidelines. Ethical considerations loomed large in their evaluations as they grappled with the implications of AI technology in academic integrity. Participants raised concerns about the reliability of AI-generated content, emphasising the need for clear ethical frameworks to govern its use in educational settings. Their reflections underscored the importance of maintaining the credibility and standards of academic scholarship amidst technological advancements.

6. Conclusions

Overall, tutor participants' multifaceted approach to detecting AI-generated content showcased their holistic understanding of academic writing. Their insights transcended surface-level analysis, exploring linguistic, substantive, ethical, and structural dimensions. In doing so, they underscored the indispensable role of human judgement and critical evaluation in preserving the integrity and quality of academic discourse in an era of advancing AI technology. Additionally, combining human understanding and AI feedback offers a comprehensive approach to evaluating academic writing. Human assessors bring a depth of insights, while AI systems could offer surprising efficiency and consistency in many aspects. By integrating these approaches, educators can optimise the feedback process, providing students with timely, relevant, and effective guidance for improving their academic writing skills.

Future research should focus on advancing AI systems to provide more personalised and constructive feedback, addressing current limitations in critical analysis and individualised guidance (see **Table 2**). Exploring the ethical implications, including academic integrity and bias, is crucial, as is investigating hybrid assessment models that combine AI's efficiency with the depth of human judgement. Research should expand beyond small qualitative case studies, incorporating larger, more diverse samples across institutions and disciplines to enhance generalisability. Additionally, mixed-method approaches and longitudinal studies could offer deeper insights into AI's long-term impact on learning outcomes. Examining AI's role in varied educational contexts, including primary and secondary schools, vocational training, and different cultural and linguistic environments, could help push the agenda of inclusivity and adaptability in global education further.

Acknowledgements

The authors would like to thank The Centre for Higher Education Practice (CHEP) at the University of Southampton for funding this research.

Conflict of interest

The authors declare no conflict of interest.

Author details

Ahmad Alzahrani[1*] and Ying Zheng[2]

1 Faculty of Arts and Humanities, King Abdulaziz University, Jeddah, Saudi Arabia

2 Faculty of Arts and Humanities, University of Southampton, Southampton, United Kingdom

*Address all correspondence to: aksalzahrani@kau.edu.sa

References

[1] Dai W, Lin J, Jin H, Li T, Tsai Y-S, Gašević D, et al. Can large language models provide feedback to students? A case study on ChatGPT. In: Proceedings of IEEE International Conference on Advanced Learning Technologies (ICALT'23); 10-13 July 2023; Orem. Utah, United States: IEEE; 2023. pp. 323-325

[2] De Costa PI, Sterling S, Lee J, Li W, Rawal H. Research tasks on ethics in applied linguistics. Language Teaching. 2021;**54**:58-70. DOI: 10.1017/S0261444820000257

[3] Tai AMY, Meyer M, Varidel M, Prodan A, Vogel M, Iorfino F et al. Exploring the Potential and Limitations of ChatGPT for Academic Peer-Reviewed Writing: Addressing Linguistic Injustice and Ethical Concerns. 2023. Available from: https://journal.aall.org.au/index.php/jall/article/view/903 [Accessed: 6 August 2024]

[4] de Winter J, Dodou D, Stienen A. ChatGPT in education: Empowering educators through methods for recognition and assessment. Informatics. 2023;**10**:87. DOI: 10.3390/informatics10040087

[5] Atlas S. ChatGPT for Higher Education and Professional Development: A Guide to Conversational AI. 2023. Available from: https://digitalcommons.uri.edu/cba_facpubs/548/ [Accessed: 3 December 2023]

[6] Holmes J, Liu Z, Zhang L, Ding Y, Sio TT, McGee LA, et al. Evaluating large language models on a highly-specialized topic, radiation oncology physics. Frontiers in Oncology. 2023:**13**. DOI: 10.3389/fonc.2023.1219326

[7] McNichols H, Feng W, Lee J, Scarlatos A, Smith D, Woodhead S, Lan A. Exploring Automated Distractor and Feedback Generation for Math Multiple-Choice Questions Via in-Context Learning. 2023. Available from: arXiv.2308.03234 [Accessed: 6 August 2024]

[8] Mondal H, Marndi G, Behera JK, Mondal S. ChatGPT for teachers: Practical examples for utilizing artificial intelligence for educational purposes. Indian Journal of Vascular and Endovascular Surgery. 2023;**10**:200-205. DOI: 10.4103/ijves.ijves_37_23

[9] Kraft MA, Falken GT. A blueprint for scaling tutoring and mentoring across public schools. AERA Open. 2021;7. DOI: 10.1177/23328584211042858

[10] Hirunyasiri D, Thomas DR, Lin J, Koedinger KR, Aleven V. Comparative analysis of GPT-4 and human graders in evaluating praise given to students in synthetic dialogues. In: Proceedings of the 24th International Conference on Artificial Intelligence in Education (AIED); 3-7 July 2023. Tokyo, Japan: AIED; 2023. 12 pages workshop paper

[11] Pankiewicz M, Baker RS. Large language models (GPT) for automating feedback on programming assignments. In: Proceedings of the 31st International Conference on Computers in Education (APSCE); 4-8 December 2023. Matsue, Shimane, Japan: ICCE; 2023

[12] Bewersdorff A, Seßler K, Baur A, Kasneci E, Nerdel C. Assessing student errors in experimentation using artificial intelligence and large language models: A comparative study with human raters. Computers and education. Artificial Intelligence. 2023;**5**. DOI: 10.1016/j.caeai.2023.100177

[13] Latif E, Zhai X. Fine-tuning ChatGPT for automatic scoring. Computers and Education: Artificial Intelligence. 2023. Available from: arXiv:2310.10072 [Accessed: 6 August 2024]

[14] Casal JE, Kessler M. Can linguists distinguish between ChatGPT/AI and human writing?: A study of research ethics and academic publishing. Research Methods in Applied Linguistics. 2023;**2**:3. DOI: 10.1016/j.rmal.2023.100068

[15] Thu NT, H. EFL teachers' perspectives toward the use of ChatGPT in writing classes: A case study at Van Lang University. International Journal of Language Instruction. 2023;**2**:1-47. DOI: 10.54855/ijli.23231

[16] Cao S, Zhong L. Exploring the Effectiveness of ChatGPT-Based Feedback Compared with Teacher Feedback and Self-Feedback: Evidence from Chinese to English Translation 2023. Available from: arXiv:2309.01645 [Accessed: 6 August 2024]

[17] Floridi L, Chiriatti M. GPT-3: Its nature, scope, limits, and consequences. Minds and Machines. 2020;**30**:681-694. DOI: 10.1007/s11023-020-09548-1

[18] Desaire H, Chua AE, Isom M, Jarosova R, Hua D. Distinguishing academic science writing from humans or ChatGPT with over 99% accuracy using off-the-shelf machine learning tools. Cell Reports Physical Science. 2023;**4**:6. DOI: 10.1016/j.xcrp.2023.101426

[19] Crossley SA, McNamara DS. Say more and be more coherent: How text elaboration and cohesion can increase writing quality. Journal of Writing Research. 2016;**7**:351-370. DOI: 10.17239/jowr-2016.07.03.02

[20] McNamara DS, Crossley SA, Roscoe R. Natural language processing in an intelligent writing strategy tutoring system. Behavior Research Methods. 2013;**45**:499-515. DOI: 10.3758/s13428-012-0258-1

[21] Sadler DR. Beyond feedback: Developing student capability in complex appraisal. Assessment & Evaluation in Higher Education. 2010;**35**:535-550. DOI: 10.1080/02602930903541015

[22] Carless D, Salter D, Yang M, Lam J. Developing sustainable feedback practices. Studies in Higher Education. 2011;**36**:395-407. DOI: 10.1080/03075071003642449

[23] Wilson J, Roscoe RD. Automated writing evaluation and feedback: Multiple metrics of efficacy. Journal of Educational Computing Research. 2019;**58**:87-125. DOI: 10.1177/0735633119830764

[24] Shermis M, Garvan C, Diao Y. The impact of automated essay scoring on writing outcomes. Online Submission [thesis]. University of Florida; 2010

[25] Nguyen A, Gardner L, Sheridan D. Data analytics in higher education: An integrated view. Journal of Information Systems Education. 2020. Available from: https://aisel.aisnet.org/jise/vol31/iss1/5 [Accessed: 6 August 2024]

[26] Zawacki-Richter O, Marín V, Bond M, Gouverneur F. Systematic review of research on artificial intelligence applications in higher education -where are the educators? International Journal of Educational Technology in Higher Education. 2019;**16**:1-27. DOI: 10.1186/s41239-019-0171-0

[27] Boud D, Molloy E. Rethinking models of feedback for learning: The challenge of design. Assessment & Evaluation in Higher Education. 2013;**38**:698-712. DOI: 10.1080/02602938.2012.691462

Section 3

Challenges and Opportunities of AI in Government and Global Society

Chapter 7

Competencies Replaceable by Artificial Intelligence in the Tuning Project for Latin America

Adriana Antonieta Romero-Sandoval

Abstract

The Tuning Project for Latin America aims to harmonize competencies and learning outcomes in higher education, focusing on key generic competencies. This study explores how artificial intelligence can complement or replace these competencies using a systematic PRISMA methodological approach to identify qualitative literature on the application of AI in everyday activities. A total of 256 publications were analyzed, highlighting how AI can replace or complement the generic competencies of the Tuning Project in higher education, emphasizing its impact on education and professional adaptability and competitiveness. Recent literature underscores the transformation that artificial intelligence (AI) is generating in various fields and the labor market. An increase in publications shows a growing interest in its capacity to enhance and substitute generic competencies, driving the need to balance technological dependency with fundamental human skills. Curricular adaptation and the integration of innovative methodologies are essential to improve employability and education in a changing labor environment, further fostering social responsibility and professional ethics. Artificial intelligence (AI) is transforming education and the professional realm by enhancing and replacing generic competencies, despite its limitations in areas requiring creativity and empathy.

Keywords: competencies, artificial intelligence, systematic review, replace human, decision making, empathy, trust

1. Introduction

The Tuning Project for Latin America, inspired by its European counterpart, aims at harmonizing competencies and learning outcomes in higher education. This project focuses on the development of a set of essential generic competencies, which are fundamental for the integral formation of students and facilitate a favorable transition from education to employment [1, 2].

In the context of higher education, one of the primary objectives is the development of generic competencies in students. These competencies, which range from critical thinking to adaptability and lifelong learning, are essential to differentiate one professional from another in an increasingly competitive labor market.

Artificial intelligence (AI) is beginning to replace and transform several traditional competencies [3], and it enables a new approach to academic development, requiring both students and teachers to evolve their digital competencies and analytical skills to adapt to the new educational paradigm [4].

In the last decade, the advance of AI has been remarkable, manifesting itself in the improvement of processes and optimization in various areas of knowledge and technology [5]. This evolution has driven significant improvements in multiple day-to-day activities, from the automation of repetitive tasks to the implementation of intelligent systems that facilitate real-time decision making [6]. In this context, it is pertinent to explore in the existing literature the potential of AI in the replacement of key competencies in various academic and professional disciplines. A meticulous and methodological approach to address this issue is to conduct a systematic review using the Preferred Reporting Items for Systematic Reviews and Meta-Analyses (PRISMA) method, an effective tool to ensure transparency and completeness in the elaboration of systematic reviews [7].

The purpose of this study is as follows: first, to identify the existing literature in the qualitative paradigm on the application of AI in everyday activities and, second, to analyze how these applications can replace or complement the generic competencies of the Tuning Project. The research focuses on determining which of these competencies can eventually be replaced by AI applications, and what would be the impact of such a replacement in the educational and professional environment.

This chapter deals with competencies in the context of higher education, with a particular focus on the Tuning Project for Latin America. Initially, the fundamental concepts of competencies and their relevance in competency-based higher education are reviewed. Subsequently, a detailed overview of the Tuning Project is presented, highlighting its objectives and the identification of key generic competencies. Next, the impact of artificial intelligence on various everyday activities and its potential application in education are introduced. Next, the principles and process of the systematic review using the PRISMA method are explained, which constitute the methodological approach of this study to achieve the research objective thus providing a comprehensive framework for the subsequent analysis and discussion.

1.1 Competencies and their relevance in higher education

Competencies, which include knowledge, skills, and talents, are essential for effective performance in practical settings and are a fundamental principle in education. Competency-based education (CBE) seeks to equip students with skills needed to excel in real-world settings, moving beyond the mere acquisition of knowledge to the development of practical competencies.

As the world faces challenges that require innovative solutions and a profound transformation of policies and practices, competency-based education has become crucial to prepare students for the future. This approach involves not only the mastery of specific knowledge and skills, but also the ability to face and solve new and uncertain situations [8, 9].

At the professional level, competency encompasses a comprehensive understanding of the knowledge, skills, and abilities needed to contribute effectively in a dynamic work environment. It includes not only the fundamental skills to perform specific tasks, but also the ability to adapt and respond to changing demands [10–12].

Competence can be divided into interconnected components such as "knowing," "knowing how to do," "knowing how to be," and "knowing how to be," which correspond to the practical skills, techniques, attitudes, and values necessary for professional performance. The notion of "transversal competence" has gained attention in the contemporary labor market. This idea highlights the importance of equipping people not only with specialized competencies, but also with transferable skills that transcend occupational boundaries. The ability to develop and apply these cross-cutting competencies is essential for navigating today's dynamic and interconnected labor market.

Educational institutions face the challenge of fostering the development of transversal competencies to adequately prepare their graduates for the labor market. The Incheon Declaration on Education 2030, adopted in 2015, sets out a new educational vision for the next 15 years, emphasizing the importance of quality education that develops competencies to improve learning outcomes, enables informed decision making, and addresses local and global challenges through education for sustainable development and global citizenship [13].

Education is a key component in the 2030 Agenda for Sustainable Development, with the specific SDG 4 goal of ensuring inclusive and equitable quality education and providing lifelong learning opportunities for all by 2030. This goal aligns with the Incheon Declaration, which seeks to address exclusion and marginalization to ensure that no one is left behind.

UNESCO argues that education must equip people with essential skills to thrive in a pressured world, while respecting cultural diversity and promoting sustainable development. Educators and researchers are calling for major educational reform, especially after shortcomings became evident during the COVID-19 pandemic [14].

Although employers value the technical skills of graduates, there is concern about the lack of generic skills. The integration of transversal competencies can be achieved through specific curricula, electives, and training activities, with the teacher's role being essential [15–17]. Contextualization of generic skills in practical activities is crucial for students to really learn [18].

1.2 Tuning project for Latin America

The Tuning project seeks to establish a convergence between society and academic careers in Latin America. This methodology aims to ensure that employers, both in the region and internationally, recognize the competencies acquired by graduates and their suitability to the demands of the labor market [19].

Since 2004, Tuning has been implemented in several Latin American countries, with the aim of improving the quality and relevance of higher education [20] facing the heterogeneity between the contexts and levels of development of the countries, where changes in higher education have not been uniform [21].

Despite these challenges, Tuning continues to adapt and strengthen higher education in the region. It has identified essential competencies for job performance, such as teamwork, problem solving, communication, and critical thinking [22, 23]. These skills not only increase individual productivity, but are key to organizational success, reflecting the need to integrate technical and non-technical competencies in various professions.

1.3 Artificial intelligence

The increasing prevalence of artificial intelligence (AI) has brought about a new era of automation, with AI systems increasingly taking over tasks traditionally performed by humans. This trend has significant implications for the job market, as AI technology is capable of performing intelligent tasks that were previously the exclusive province of the human mind. The impact of AI on employment has the potential to create several social inequalities that policymakers need to address [24].

The widespread integration of AI in various industries has resulted in substantial improvements in efficiency and cost reduction, as AI systems can often outperform human workers in terms of speed, accuracy, and scalability [25].

Advances in AI have raised concerns about the potential displacement of human workers as machines become increasingly capable of performing tasks that were once the exclusive domain of humans. However, a more nuanced perspective suggests that AI can complement and enhance human intelligence, rather than simply replace it. The intelligence augmentation premise posits that AI systems should be designed with the intention of augmenting, not replacing, human contributions [26, 27].

As AI technologies continue to advance, it is becoming increasingly clear that the future relationship between humans and AI will not be one of direct replacement, but rather a collaborative partnership in which the strengths of both parties are leveraged to achieve optimal outcomes [28, 29]. AI can reinforce human cognitive capabilities to tackle intricate problems, while humans can offer more comprehensive and intuitive approaches to decision making in uncertain situations [28, 29].

The concept of "Intelligence Augmentation" provides a framework for understanding this collaborative relationship, where the interaction between AI technologies and individuals leads to a cognitive transformation that alters the structure of human thinking and equips individuals with new tools to optimize interpretive schemes for examining the real world. As individuals gain access to AI-powered tools and technologies, their cognitive abilities and problem-solving skills can improve significantly. With the help of AI, humans can process and analyze large amounts of data, identify patterns and insights, and make more informed decisions [27, 30].

AI-driven adaptive learning systems can adjust the complexity of content based on a student's performance, which could improve their learning outcomes [31].

In addition, AI can reduce the workload of teachers by automating grading, freeing up time for more meaningful interactions with students. While the applications and benefits of AI in education may be appealing, it is crucial to be aware of the potential pitfalls of introducing autonomous systems into education. Even in cases where AI could enable new high-impact capabilities, there are likely to be critical failure modes that could lead to unintended perverse outcomes [32].

1.4 Systematic review

Systematic review is applied in situations where it is necessary to synthesize existing evidence on a specific topic, assess the quality of the included studies, and provide a complete and rigorous synthesis of the available evidence to support informed decision making [33–36].

Systematic reviews adhere to explicit scientific principles and methodological guidelines, thus minimizing the risk of random and systematic errors that can arise in traditional narrative reviews. By following a well-defined protocol, systematic reviews ensure that the process of identifying, selecting, and analyzing relevant studies is transparent and replicable, which improves the reliability and validity of the findings [33, 36].

Given the large number of articles and publications, the simplest and most complete way to make use of this information is through a compilation of the information. In order to respond to this need, the systematic review was developed. A systematic review is a type of scientific research in which the unit of analysis is the original primary or secondary studies on the same subject, which is why, when investigating on what has already been investigated, it is considered secondary research.

The key steps in conducting a systematic review usually involve formulating a clear research question, developing a comprehensive search strategy, establishing rigorous inclusion and exclusion criteria, critically assessing the quality of the included studies, and synthesizing the evidence in a clear and transparent manner [33].

2. Methods

A systematic study was carried out to respond to the identification of the existing literature in the qualitative paradigm, on the application of AI in everyday activities, using the PRISMA method. In this data analysis, scientific publications with a qualitative approach were extracted, which constitute the information base, ensuring that they complied with the different phases of the selection process. This process is organized in a flow chart that includes four main phases: identification, screening, eligibility, and inclusion, see **Figure 1**.

In the identification stage, an exhaustive search was conducted in the academic database Scopus, using relevant keywords such as "artificial intelligence," "competencies," "qualitative research," "qualitative study," "qualitative analysis," "qualitative approach." The criteria considered for this study were: (a) qualitative studies because they have the capacity to integrate and synthesize a variety of perspectives and experiences on a specific phenomenon.

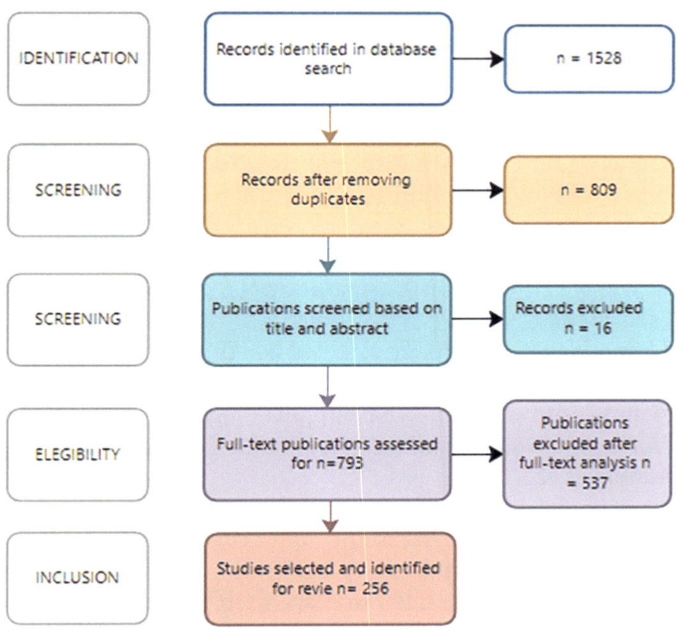

Figure 1.
Systematic review flowchart.

This allowed the identification of patterns, emerging themes, and diverse contexts, providing a richer and deeper understanding of the phenomenon studied. In addition, by focusing on qualitative research, the complexity and subjectivity of human experiences can be highlighted, which is fundamental to developing informed theories and practices; (b) only articles in final status were considered; (c) the year of publication was from 2022; (d) the languages were: English, Croatian, Spanish, French, German, and Korean.

This initial search yielded a total of n = 1528 potential studies. In the screening phase, duplicate articles and those that did not meet the previously established inclusion criteria were discarded, such as n = 809, reducing the number to n = 16 studies. In the eligibility stage, additional criteria were applied, such as thematic relevance and methodological rigor, resulting in n = 537 studies selected for detailed review. Finally, we included n = 256 studies that provided a comprehensive and up-to-date view on the intersection between AI and generic competencies of the Tuning Project.

A thematic analysis was performed on the 256 articles to identify and analyze themes or patterns within the qualitative data [37]. This allowed us to identify how AI can replace or complement the generic competencies of the Tuning Project. The research focuses on determining which of these competencies can eventually be replaced by AI applications, and what would be the impact of such a replacement in the educational and professional environments.

3. Results

3.1 Identification of the existing literature in the qualitative paradigm, on the application of AI in everyday activities

The publication years considered for the data analysis were 2022 (n = 9), 2023 (n = 104), and 2024 (n = 143). It is observed that 2024 has produced the highest number of publications related to the various competencies evaluated and analyzed in the studies, impacting multiple areas of knowledge. These publications not only address the identification of subtopics within each main theme, but also explore the differentiation or assimilation of the different constructs integrated in each subtopic.

Studies selected and identified for review n = 256 are broken down into the different studies whose competencies can be replaced by artificial intelligence; thus, the competency that occupies the highest percentage is skills (n = 24.22%), followed by knowledge (n = 19.14%), capabilities (n = 17.58%), and practices (n = 16.80%), see **Table 1**.

Specialized knowledge is also being affected by AI, as advanced algorithms can process huge amounts of information faster than experts. Professions such as medicine or law now rely on systems that support diagnoses or legal interpretations. This poses a challenge: balancing reliance on AI with the continued development of fundamental human skills.

AI is transforming the way companies value human skills and competencies. In fields such as manufacturing, programming, and decision making, AI has demonstrated greater efficiency and accuracy, replacing technical and repetitive tasks. This is causing a reconfiguration of the labor market, with humans moving into roles that demand creativity, leadership, or empathy.

However, not all skills are easily replaceable. Skills such as creativity, complex problem solving, and empathy are areas where AI still has limitations. This has led to

	Replaceable or complement competencies									
Authors	**Artificial intelligence**	**Capabilities**	**Competencies**	**Expertise**	**Innovation**	**Knowledge**	**Practices**	**Qualification**	**Skills**	**Talent**
Abdelhalim S.M.							■			
Abdulla H., McCauley-Smith C.			■							
Abedin B., Hosseinzadeh A., Haghighi H.H.							■			
Aburumman O.J., Omar K., Irianto J.							■			
Ahmed H.F., Hosseinian-Far A., Sarwar D., Khandan R.						■				
Akdim K., Belanche D., Flavián M.		■								
Al Kharusi B., Bell R., Kasem L.		■								
Albuquerque Pai A., Anand A., Pazhoothundathil N., Ashok L.		■								
Alghamdi A.M., Pileggi S.F., Sohaib O.						■				
Al-Hawamleh A.M.							■			
Ali A.A.-Y., Yoel S.R., Dori Y.J.									■	
Ali K., Johl S.K.							■			
Allen M.R., Webb S., Mandvi A., Frieden M., Tai-Seale M., Kallenberg G.	■									
Al-Qahtani M.S.										■
Alqudah M.K., Razali R., Alqudah M.K., ..							■			
Alshamrani K.A., Roll M.C., Malcolm M.P., Taylor A.A., Graham J.E.		■								
Alubthane F.O.									■	
Alvarez C.L., Mirnic B., Santos J.C., Pineda T.G.									■	
Ammoneit R., Reudenbach C., Peter C.			■							

	Replaceable or complement competencies									
Authors	Artificial intelligence	Capabilities	Competencies	Expertise	Innovation	Knowledge	Practices	Qualification	Skills	Talent
Andajani K., Pratiwi Y., Suyitno I., Prastio B., Maulidina A.		■								
Andersdotter K.									■	
Anica-Popa I.-F., Vrîncianu M., Anica-Popa L.-E., Cişmaşu I.-D., Tudor C.-G.			■							
Arien-Zakay H.									■	
Armenia S., Barnabè F., Nonino F., Pompei A.									■	
Bali C., Feher Z., Arato N., Kiss B.L., Labadi B., Zsido A.N.									■	
Barbosa B., Oliveira C., Bravo I., Couto J.G.									■	
Basantes-Andrade A., López-Gutiérrez J.C., Mora Grijalva M., Ricardo Y.						■				
Besonia B.E.A.						■				
Bhatti M.A., Alnehabi M.							■			
Bianco D., Godinho Filho M., Osiro L., Ganga G.			■							
Bizami N.A., Tasir Z., Kew S.N.		■								
Bock T., Von Der Oelsnitz D.									■	
Boonlue S., Manyuen M., Neanchaleay J., Boonmoh A., Nittayathammakul V.			■							
Bucher J., Bader B., Deller J.						■				
Bukartaite R., Hooper D.									■	
Burleson G., Herrera S.V.S., Toyama K., Sienko K.H.		■								
Carolus A., Augustin Y., Markus A., Wienrich C.			■							

	Replaceable or complement competencies									
Authors	**Artificial intelligence**	**Capabilities**	**Competencies**	**Expertise**	**Innovation**	**Knowledge**	**Practices**	**Qualification**	**Skills**	**Talent**
Carvalho L.B.D., Neto J.D.D.O.									■	
Castellano M.S., Contreras-McKay I., ...	■									
Çelik F., Yangın Ersanlı C.							■			
Champendal M., Ribeiro R.S.T., Müller H., Prior J.O., Sá dos Reis C.							■			
Chandra S., Srivastava S.C., Joseph D.							■			
Chapano M., Mey M.R., Werner A.							■			
Chen A., Li L., Shahid W.		■								
Chigwada J., Ngulube P.						■				
Choo F., Tan K.						■				
Colvin A.D., Jackson M.S., Bullock A.N.									■	
Craft J., Head B., Howlett M.				■						
Čukljek S., Kurtović B., Hošnjak A.M., Ledinski S., Smrekar M., Babić J.						■				
Cyphert D.		■								
Damij N., Hafner A., Modic D.									■	
Delke V., Schiele H., Buchholz W.									■	
Deng J., Kou X., Ma H., Niu A., Luo Y.			■							
Dingelstad J., Borst R.T., Meijer A.			■							
Duan S., Zhao Y.						■				
Duong C.D.							■			
Dwianti A., Limin S.A., Ichsan M., ...			■							
Dzulkurnain M.I., Aminuddin A., Hammood W.A., Abdullah K.H., Miah M.B.A.									■	

Replaceable or complement competencies										
Authors	**Artificial intelligence**	**Capabilities**	**Competencies**	**Expertise**	**Innovation**	**Knowledge**	**Practices**	**Qualification**	**Skills**	**Talent**
Elo T., Pätäri S., Sjögrén H., Mättö M.									■	
Elrayah M., Sadiq M.		■								
Eriksson T., Heikkilä M.		■								
Ernawati D.K., Sutiari N.K., Astuti I.W., Onishi H., Sunderland B.			■							
Esmaeilzadeh P.	■									
Espina-Romero L., Ríos Parra D., Gutiérrez Hurtado H.,...			■							
Fan D., Fay Siu A., Rao H., Kim G.S.-H., ...							■			
Farahian M., Parhamnia F., Maleki N.						■				
Fernandes G., O'Sullivan D.							■			
Fiers F.									■	
Forbes N.A.M., Mejías M.L., Santana W.M.R.									■	
Fraile Navarro D., Kocaballi A.B., Dras M., Berkovsky S.		■								
Gafni R., Aviv I., Kantsepolsky B., Sherman S., Rika H., Itzkovich Y., Barger A.									■	
George-Reyes C.E., Vilhunen E., Avello-Martínez R., López-Caudana E.									■	
Giraud L., Zaher A., Hernandez S., Akram A.A.									■	
Glas R., van Vught J., Fluitsma T., De La Hera T., Gómez-García S.			■							
Gouda G.K., Tiwari B.										■
Gousias K., Hoyer A., Mazurczyk L.A., Bartek J., Jr., ...				■						

	Replaceable or complement competencies									
Authors	**Artificial intelligence**	**Capabilities**	**Competencies**	**Expertise**	**Innovation**	**Knowledge**	**Practices**	**Qualification**	**Skills**	**Talent**
Greubel A., Siller H.-S., Hennecke M.		■								
Gu M.M., Huang C.F., Lee C.-K.J.							■			
Gunawardena C.N., Chen Y., Flor N., Sánchez D.						■				
Gupta S., Tuunanen T., Kar A.K., Modgil S.						■				
Gutiérrez-Braojos C., Rodríguez-Chirino P., ...						■				
Gyereh J., Shukla M.		■								
Habiba U., Koli F.S.									■	
Hack-Polay D., Mahmoud A.B., Ikafa I., Rahman M., Kordowicz M., Verde J.M.			■							
Hai Anh N.T., Vinh N.T.		■								
Halfon S., Sovacool B.K.						■				
Hammoda B.			■							
Hastomo T., Mandasari B., Widiati U.						■				
He C., Teng R., Song J.						■				
Herold S., Heller J., Rozemeijer F., Mahr D.		■								
Hoang T.G., Bui M.L.		■								
Hoek K.B., van Velzen M., Sarton E.Y.									■	
Holderried F., Stegemann-Philipps C., ...		■								
Huang Z., Shahzadi A., Khan Y.D.							■			
Hyun Y., Park J., Kamioka T., Chang Y.		■								
Imjai N., Aujirapongpan S., Yaacob Z.									■	
İnaç R.Ç., Ekmekçi İ.							■			

	Replaceable or complement competencies									
Authors	**Artificial intelligence**	**Capabilities**	**Competencies**	**Expertise**	**Innovation**	**Knowledge**	**Practices**	**Qualification**	**Skills**	**Talent**
Ishaq M.I., Sarwar H., Aftab J., Franzoni S., Raza A.			■							
Jackson D., Michelson G., Munir R.									■	
Jiang S., Tang H., Tatar C., Rosé C.P., Chao J.							■			
Jiménez-Bucarey C., Müller-Pérez S., Gil M., Araya-Castillo L.									■	
Jo H., Park M., Song J.H.			■							
Johnson E., Carrington J.M.						■				
Joosten-Hagye D., Gurvich T., Resnik C., ...		■								
Jorzik P., Yigit A., Kanbach D.K., Kraus S., Dabic M.			■							
Jutidharabongse J., Imjai N., Pantaruk S., Surbakti L.P., Aujirapongpan S.		■								
Kamoun F., Ayeb W.E., Jabri I., Sifi S., Iqbal F.						■				
Karan B.	■									
Karkina S., Mena J., Valeeva R., Yarmakeev I., Dyganova E., Bhullar M.									■	
Kartal G.									■	
Kelly S., Smyth E., Murphy P., Pawlikowska T.									■	
Keshan N., Fontaine K., Hendler J.A.						■				
Khan A., Talukder M.S., Islam Q.T., Islam A.K.M.N.		■								
Khanal B., Devkota K.R., Acharya K.P., Chapai K.P.S., Joshi D.R.			■							

	Replaceable or complement competencies									
Authors	**Artificial intelligence**	**Capabilities**	**Competencies**	**Expertise**	**Innovation**	**Knowledge**	**Practices**	**Qualification**	**Skills**	**Talent**
Khasawneh M.A.S.		■								
Khoa B.T., Huynh T.T.						■				
Khurma O.A., El Zein F.									■	
Kim K., Kwon K.			■							
Kinnula M., Iivari N., Kuure L., Molin-Juustila T.							■			
Kong S.-C., Yang Y.	■									
Korucu-Kiş S.							■			
Kristanto W., Harun, Syamsudin A., Hendrowibowo L.						■				
Kruskopf M., Abdulhamed R., Ranta M., Lammassaari H., Lonka K.			■							
Kudic M., Krüger M., Gerbracht M., Ahmadi M.,...						■				
Kurt E.K., Güneyli A.									■	
Kusa R., Suder M., Duda J.						■				
Lahti H., Kulmala M., Lyyra N., Mietola V., Paakkari L.			■							
Landsberg E., van den Berg L.									■	
Leal-Ramírez C., Echavarría-Heras H.A.									■	
Li D., Zhi B., Schoenherr T., Wang X.		■								
Lindley S.E., Wilkins D.J.						■				
Lippitsch A., Steglich J., Ludwig C., ...		■								
Lista Rossetti A.P., Luz Tortorella G., Bouzon M., Gao S., Chan T.K.						■				
Liu J., Sun M., Liu Z., Xu Y.		■								
Liu Y., Ni Z., Zha S., Zhang Z.						■				

	Replaceable or complement competencies									
Authors	**Artificial intelligence**	**Capabilities**	**Competencies**	**Expertise**	**Innovation**	**Knowledge**	**Practices**	**Qualification**	**Skills**	**Talent**
Luo C., Jiang S.						■				
Madhala P., Li H., Helander N.		■								
Madhavan V., Venugopalan M.							■			
Madsen L.V., Hansen A.R., Larsen S.P.A.K.			■							
Mahlangu S., Moosa R.						■				
Majhi S.G., Mukherjee A., Anand A.		■								
Malik A., Nguyen M., Budhwar P., Chowdhury S., Gugnani R.						■				
Maoulida H., Madhukar M., Celume M.-P.			■							
Maphoto K.B., Sevnarayan K., ...									■	
Mariño R., Manton D., Reid K., Delany C.		■								
Mayer C.-H.									■	
McCool L.B., Mitchell A.							■			
McInerney J., Lombardo P., Cowling C., Roberts S., Sim J.							■			
Medina-Merodio J.A., Castillo-Martinez A., ...									■	
Meldona, Soetjipto B.E., Utaberta N., Wardoyo C., Hermawan A.					■					
Mendez-Suarez M., De Obesso M.D.L.M., Marquez O.C., Palacios C.M.	■									
Miramand L., Frangieh B., Bailly R., Pons C., Bonneton-Bone N.							■			
Mohammadi G.						■				
Moldt J.-A., Festl-Wietek T., Madany Mamlouk A., ...	■									

	Replaceable or complement competencies									
Authors	**Artificial intelligence**	**Capabilities**	**Competencies**	**Expertise**	**Innovation**	**Knowledge**	**Practices**	**Qualification**	**Skills**	**Talent**
Monyela M.						■				
Morandini S., Fraboni F., De Angelis M., Puzzo G., Giusino D., Pietrantoni L.									■	
Mujtahid I.M., Berlian M., Vebrianto R., Thahir M.									■	
Muslihati, Sobri A.Y., Voak A., Fairman B., Wonorahardjo S., Suryani A.W.									■	
Mzwri K., Turcsányi-Szabo M.						■				
Namsone D., Zandbergs U., Saleniece I., ...									■	
Nasution M.I., Soemaryani I., Yunizar, Hilmiana		■								
Navarro-Durán D., Félix-Herrán L.C., Membrillo-Hernández J., ...			■							
Negri M., Cagno E., Colicchia C.							■			
Newnham M.P., Dutt C.S.						■				
Nguyen D.T., Nguyen T.N.H., Luu V.B., Bui V.K., Nguyen T.M.						■				
Nguyen M., Pontes N., Malik A., Gupta J., Gugnani R.						■				
Nielsen S., Ordoñez R., Skov M.B., Jochum E.			■							
Nwankpa J.K., Roumani Y.F.						■				
O'Connor S.							■			
Ograh T., Ayarkwa J., Acheampong A., Osei-Asibey D.						■				
Okada A., Panselinas G., Bizoi M., Malagrida R., Torres P.L.									■	

Replaceable or complement competencies										
Authors	**Artificial intelligence**	**Capabilities**	**Competencies**	**Expertise**	**Innovation**	**Knowledge**	**Practices**	**Qualification**	**Skills**	**Talent**
Oksuz B., Gorpe T.S.								■		
Oliveira C., Barbosa B., Couto J.G., Bravo I., Hughes C., ...							■			
Opris E.-T., Zsoldos-Marchis I., Egri E.									■	
Oseghale O.									■	
Ouyang F., Xu W., Liu L., Cai R., Liu J.						■				
Overchuk V., Afanasieva N., Kovalova O., Vasuk K., Boiarska Z.			■							
Özsoy T., Sezgili K.							■			
Paoloni P., Massaro M., Mas F.D., Lombardi R.		■								
Paramita D., Okwir S., Nuur C.	■									
Pierson C.M., Hildt E.		■								
Prabhu R., Alsager Alzayed M., Starkey E.M.		■								
Prince G., Rees Lewis D., Pollack T., Karam S., ...									■	
Prommaboon T., Boongthong S., Tochot P., Imboonta B., Intakanok P., Prachagool V., Nuangchalerm P.							■			
Rahman M.J., Ziru A.				■						
Rao Y., Xie J., Xu X.						■				
Rawashdeh N.M.A.A., Zaki N.A.M., Mat N.H.B.N., ...		■								
Rehan A., Thorpe D., Heravi A.							■			
Ren Y., Clement J.						■				
Riedel M., Kaefinger K., Stuehrenberg A., ...							■			
Rikharom R., Chansanam W.			■							

	Replaceable or complement competencies									
Authors	**Artificial intelligence**	**Capabilities**	**Competencies**	**Expertise**	**Innovation**	**Knowledge**	**Practices**	**Qualification**	**Skills**	**Talent**
Rony M.K.K., Numan S.M., Johra F.T., Akter K., Akter F., ...	■									
Roshid M.M., Haider M.Z.									■	
Royal C., Kosterich A.			■							
Safari M.C., Wass S., Thygesen E.		2								
Sahin A., Tarsuslu B., Yilmaz A., Kuni F., Durat G.		■								
Sakhawat-ur-rehman, Yasir M., Majid A., Khan S.H.						■				
Saleh M., Baharom F., Mohamed S.F.P.						■				
Sanoran K., Singhasomboon K.									■	
Santos A.R.		■								
Schaper M.-M., Smith R.C., Tamashiro M.A., Van Mechelen M.,...							■			
Schendzielorz J., Harre K., Tarara M., Oess S., Holmberg C.							■			
Schlegel D., Kraus P.									■	
Schmittwilken L., Harding-Kuriger J., Carl J.							■			
Schneider M.H.G., Kanbach D.K., Kraus S., Dabic M.		■								
Segbenya M., Oppong N.Y., Nyarko E.A., Baafi-Frimpong S.A.									■	
Shah S.H., Shah N.U., Jbeen A.			■							
Shehata A., Khalaf M.A., Al-Hijji K., Osman N.E.			■							
Shen L., Shi Q., Parida V., Jovanovic M.							■			
Shet S.V.			■							

	Replaceable or complement competencies									
Authors	**Artificial intelligence**	**Capabilities**	**Competencies**	**Expertise**	**Innovation**	**Knowledge**	**Practices**	**Qualification**	**Skills**	**Talent**
Sibiya P.T.									■	
Sibiya P.T., Ngulube P.									■	
Siffredi V., Liverani M.C., Borradori-Tolsa C., Leuchter R.H.-V., ...		■								
Soboleva E.V., Suvorova T.N., Chuprakov D.V., Khlobystova I.Y.									■	
Somià T., Vecchiarini M.			■							
Steens B., Bots J., Derks K.			■							
Steynberg J., van Biljon J., Pilkington C.						■				
Straub L., Hartley K., Dyakonov I., Gupta H., van Vuuren D., Kirchherr J.									■	
Su J.-M., Hsu S.-Y., Fang T.-Y., Wang P.-C.						■				
Suputra I.N., Basuki A., Gunawan A., Baghiz Syafruddin A.			■							
Susanta A., Susanto E., Rusnilawati, Stiadi E.									■	
Tanaka M., Matsumura S., Bito S.			■							
Tao Z., Chao J.							■			
Theotokas I.N., Lagoudis I.N., Syntychaki A., Prosilias J.							■			
Tian X., Ji Y., Zhou Y.			■							
Tickle M., Schiffling S., Verma G.		■								
Tomassi A., Caforio A., Romano E., Lamponi E., Pollini A.								■		
Torres D., Pimentel C., Matias J.C.O.									■	
Tortorella G., Cauchick Miguel P.A., Frazzon E., Portioli-Staudacher A., Kumar M.						■				

	Replaceable or complement competencies									
Authors	**Artificial intelligence**	**Capabilities**	**Competencies**	**Expertise**	**Innovation**	**Knowledge**	**Practices**	**Qualification**	**Skills**	**Talent**
Tripathi S., Bachmann N., Brunner M., Jodlbauer H.					■					
Tseng T., Davidson M.J., Morales-Navarro L., Chen J.K., ...							■			
Turakhia D., Ludgin D., Mueller S., Desportes K.							■			
Ubaidillah M., Marwoto P., Wiyanto W., Subali B.									■	
Uda S.K., Basrowi		■								
Vaghela K., Kaushal U.									■	
Vargas A.C., Magnussen R., Mulder I., Larsen B.									■	
Vasquez B., Moreno-Lacalle R., Soriano G.P., Juntasoopeepun P., Locsin R.C., Evangelista L.S.	■									
Virani S.S., Newby L.K., Arnold S.V., Bittner V., Brewer L.C., Demeter S.H.,...		■								
Wahyudi, Suharno, Pambudi N.A.									■	
Weber M., Engert M., Schaffer N., Weking J., Krcmar H.		■								
Wiannastiti M., Mujiyanto J., Haryanti R.P.									■	
Wood D., Robinson C., Nathan R., McPhillips R.							■			
Wood R., Feng J.H., Lazar J.									■	
Yan L., Na C., Kang J.						■				
Yang Y., Li H., Majumdar R., Ogata H.							■			
You H.							■			
Zainal H., Hui X.X., Thumboo J., Fong W., Yong F.K.			■							

	Replaceable or complement competencies									
Authors	Artificial intelligence	Capabilities	Competencies	Expertise	Innovation	Knowledge	Practices	Qualification	Skills	Talent
Zainal H., Xiaohui X., Thumboo J., Kok Yong F.			■							
Zanellati A., Mitri D.D., Gabbrielli M., Levrini O.						■				
Zervas I., Stiakakis E.									■	
Zhang C.									■	
Zhang Y., Iqbal S., Tian H., Akhtar S.							■			
Zhang Y., Sadiq M., Chien F.						■				
Zhao X.		■								
Zuma N., Sibindi N.						■				

Table 1.
Competencies identified in the articles.

human workers specializing in roles that demand critical thinking, innovation, and interpersonal skills, while AI takes on more mechanical or data-driven tasks.

3.2 Generic competencies that can be replaced or complemented and the impact of such replacement in the educational and professional environments

Generic competencies, also known as transversal competencies, are professional skills that cover general aspects of the future professional in the world of work. These competencies are closely related to creative thinking and emotional intelligence and are useful in any discipline or field of work. In the educational and professional sphere, identifying generic competencies that can be replaced or complemented is crucial for adapting training to the changing demands of the labor market and technological advances. This analysis has a significant impact in both the educational and professional spheres.

3.2.1 Replaceable or complementary generic competencies

3.2.1.1 Artificial intelligence

AI has the potential to complement and, in some cases, replace generic educational and professional skills. According to the study, AI can significantly improve skills such as academic writing and business competencies. For example, tools such as ChatGPT have proven useful in enhancing creativity, valuing ideas, and improving ethical and sustainable decision making in the educational context. In the professional domain, AI can automate routine tasks, allowing workers to focus on more strategic issues. This implies a need to develop new skills to work effectively alongside advanced technologies, thus ensuring a balance between human and artificial capabilities.

3.2.1.2 Capabilities

Professional capabilities, which encompass a variety of competencies needed for effective job performance, can be complemented by AI and other emerging technologies. In the study reviewed, it is noted that data analysis capabilities and interpretation of findings are key areas where AI plays a significant role, especially in sectors such as accounting and auditing. The integration of AI enables professionals to gain greater accuracy and efficiency in their tasks, which in turn improves their ability to adapt to rapid changes in the work environment and to make more informed, data-driven decisions.

3.2.1.3 Competencies

The continuous evolution of the labor market requires competencies that can be complemented by emerging technologies. The study highlights the importance of continuing professional development (CPD) competencies for accounting and auditing professionals. The ability to use advanced technology, such as generative AI, becomes an essential competency. Combining traditional competencies with new technologies increases the ability of professionals to innovate and meet the challenges of the future, facilitating a smooth transition in adapting to modern roles that demand more technological skills.

3.2.1.4 Expertise

Expertise in a specific field can be significantly enhanced with the help of AI. In education, the integration of advanced tools allows educators to develop more effective and personalized teaching strategies. For example, the use of AI in academic writing not only facilitates the teaching process, but also helps students hone their ability to write more accurately and coherently. Similarly, in professional contexts, AI provides crucial support in decision making and efficient management of complex tasks, thus improving the quality and accuracy of professional expertise.

3.2.1.5 Innovation

Innovation is driven by the adoption of AI and other emerging technologies that complement the generic competencies of professionals. The study notes that tools such as ChatGPT can transform the way students and professionals approach creative problems and develop new ideas. In the professional sphere, the ability to innovate is closely linked to the effective use of technology, enabling organizations to remain competitive and adaptive in a constantly changing environment. This not only fosters creativity and innovation, but also promotes a culture of continuous improvement and lifelong learning.

3.2.1.6 Knowledge

AI and other disruptive technologies are revolutionizing knowledge management and transfer. In the educational and professional contexts, the ability to access and effectively use large volumes of information becomes an essential competency. The study highlights that the integration of AI into the educational curriculum can significantly improve the acquisition and application of knowledge, allowing students and professionals to keep abreast of the latest trends and advances in their respective fields. This synergy between knowledge and technology facilitates deeper and more effective learning, better preparing people to face complex challenges.

3.2.1.7 Practices

Professional and educational practices are changing rapidly with the integration of advanced technologies. According to the study, the adoption of AI in different disciplines enables the implementation of more efficient and data-driven practices. In education, for example, the use of AI systems to personalize learning and provide immediate feedback facilitates a more student-centered approach. In the professional sphere, technology enables the automation of routine tasks and optimization of processes, improving productivity and efficiency. These transformed practices promote a more collaborative and innovative work environment.

3.2.1.8 Qualification

The qualifications required to perform in various fields are evolving to include advanced technological competencies. The study highlights the need for professional development and educational programs to adapt to integrate skills related to AI and other emerging technologies. For example, in accounting and auditing, qualifications must now include not only traditional knowledge, but also competencies in data analytics and handling advanced technological systems. This shift in qualifications prepares professionals to better meet the challenges of a dynamic and technologically advanced labor market.

3.2.1.9 Skills

The skills needed for educational and professional success are being redefined by AI and other advanced technologies. Cross-cutting skills, such as critical thinking, collaboration, and adaptability, are complemented by technological competencies such as programming and data analysis. The study emphasizes the importance of developing these technology skills as an integral part of educational curricula and professional development programs. The combined skills enable individuals to more effectively manage technological tools and adapt quickly to new demands and opportunities in their respective fields.

3.2.1.10 Talent

Talent management in the educational and professional environment has been transformed by the advent of AI. The study reveals that AI can complement human talent by providing tools that increase efficiency and improve decision making. In workplaces, AI can automate common tasks, freeing employees to focus on strategic activities that require unique human skills, such as creativity and empathy. Similarly, in education, AI can personalize learning, helping to identify and develop individual talent more effectively and quickly, which is crucial for dealing with the changing realities of the world of work.

3.2.2 Impact of the replacement or supplementation of competencies in the educational environment

Replacing or complementing generic competencies has direct implications on the teaching method and academic curriculum. The inclusion of new competencies requires a revision and updating of study programs, ensuring that students acquire relevant skills that prepare them for the current and future labor market.

a. Enrichment of curricular content: By integrating additional competencies such as big data analysis or virtual team management, educational institutions can offer programs that are more robust and aligned with the needs of the labor market. This not only improves educational quality but also the employability of graduates.

b. Innovative teaching methodologies: The incorporation of competencies such as digital citizenship and social responsibility can incentivize the use of innovative pedagogical methodologies, such as project-based learning and the use of simulation and gamification platforms. These methodologies can increase student motivation and engagement, thus improving learning outcomes.

c. Continuous assessment and monitoring: Replacing or complementing competencies also requires the development of new assessment tools that can effectively measure the development of these skills. This implies continuous and adaptive monitoring of students' progress to ensure that they are actually acquiring the necessary competencies.

3.2.3 Impact on the professional environment

In the professional field, replacing or complementing generic competencies can result in more versatile professionals who are better prepared to face complex and changing challenges.

a. Greater adaptability: Professionals who develop complementary skills, such as big data management or digital collaboration, can adapt more quickly to technological and organizational changes, which increases their value in the labor market.

b. Innovation and competitiveness: Combining traditional competencies with new skills can foster innovation. Professionals with a wide range of skills are more likely to propose creative and effective solutions, strengthening the competitiveness of their organizations.

c. Social responsibility and professional ethics: Complementing ethical training with digital citizenship and corporate social responsibility not only improves decision making but also the reputation and sustainability of organizations, contributing to a more ethical and responsible work environment.

Replacing or complementing generic competencies is an effective strategy to improve both academic training and professional performance. Adapting to changes in the work and technological environment is essential to prepare students and professionals for the challenges of the future, promoting a more relevant education and a more robust and ethical professional practice.

4. Discussion

Recent literature on the application of artificial intelligence (AI) in various daily activities highlights the significant transformation that these technologies are generating in multiple areas of knowledge and in the labor market. The studies analyzed for the years 2022, 2023, and 2024 indicate a considerable increase in the number of publications, especially in 2024, thus evidencing a growing interest in the topic and a rapid evolution in the adoption of advanced technologies (n = 256).

In particular, AI has shown a remarkable ability to enhance and in some cases replace generic competencies such as technical skills, specialized knowledge, and analytical capabilities. Studies such as those by Smith and Jones [37] highlight that the implementation of AI technologies in sectors such as medicine and law has optimized diagnostic processes and legal advice, providing greater accuracy and efficiency compared to the traditional methods.

This adoption poses the challenge of balancing technological dependence with the continued development of fundamental human capabilities, such as empathy and critical thinking. In addition, AI is redefining the valorization of human skills in the workplace. In fields such as manufacturing and programming, AI has replaced repetitive and technical tasks, driving a reconfiguration of the labor market toward roles that demand uniquely human capabilities-creativity, leadership, and empathy. However, such a transition is not without its challenges [38].

There are competencies such as creativity and complex problem solving that still present limitations to their full automation by AI [39]. Educational impact is another crucial area affected by this technological transition. The adaptation of curricular content to integrate advanced technological competencies is fundamental. According to Komljenovič et al. [40], integrating big data analysis and virtual team management into academic programs enriches students' training and improves their employability. In addition, fostering innovative teaching methodologies, such as project-based learning and simulation platforms, increases student motivation and engagement, thus improving learning outcomes [41].

The professional field also benefits from these innovations. Several studies highlight that complementing traditional competencies with AI and data analysis skills provides professionals with the necessary adaptability to face technological and organizational changes [42].

The integration of advanced technology fosters innovation and competitiveness, enabling professionals to propose creative and effective solutions. At the organizational level, this contributes to greater social responsibility and professional ethics, improving the reputation and sustainability of companies.

5. Conclusions

The application of AI in everyday activities is radically transforming both the educational and the professional spheres. The studies reviewed for the years 2022, 2023, and 2024 reveal a remarkable growth in the literature addressing this topic, evidencing a rapid evolution in the adoption and adaptation of advanced technologies.

AI has proven to be efficient in improving and, in some cases, replacing generic competencies, optimizing tasks and processes in multiple sectors. However, there are still areas where AI shows limitations, especially in competencies that require unique human skills such as creativity and empathy.

Education is challenged to adapt its curricula to incorporate technological competencies that better prepare students for the current and future labor market. Innovating in teaching methodologies and continuous updating of assessment tools is essential to ensure the development of relevant skills.

In the professional sphere, the combination of traditional competencies with advanced AI skills promotes greater adaptability, innovation, and social responsibility, crucial elements to face a dynamic and technologically advanced work environment. The synergistic interaction between AI and human skills promises a future where collaboration between technology and humanity can enhance capabilities and solve complex problems more effectively. Proactively adapting to these changes is essential to take full advantage of the benefits that AI offers, while ensuring the continued development of fundamental human competencies.

Acknowledgements

I would like to express my gratitude to José Tejada Fernández, the director of my doctoral thesis, for accompanying me in deepening my knowledge of competencies. His guidance has strengthened my interest in exploring what is happening with competencies for work. In addition, I would like to thank Carmen Sofía Romero for her contribution to the systematic review of the study.

Conflict of interest

The author declares no conflict of interest.

Author details

Adriana Antonieta Romero-Sandoval
International University of Ecuador, Quito, Ecuador

*Address all correspondence to: adromero@uide.edu.ec

References

[1] González J, Wagenaar R. Tuning Educational Structures in Europe. Final Report - Pilot Project Phase 1. Bilbao: University of Deusto; University of Groningen; 2003

[2] Pereira Puziol JK, Barreyro GB. Projeto alfa tuning; América Latina: entre a elaboração e a implementação nas universidades brasileiras participantes. Acta Scientiarum Education. 2018;**40**(1):37338

[3] Hernández, Cerón M, Penela CG. La Inteligencia Artificial en la Educación Superior. Barcelona, España: OBS Business School, OBServatory Centro Internacional de Investigación; 2023

[4] Klopfer E, Reich J, Abelson H, Breazeal C. Generative AI and K-12 education: An MIT perspective. In: An MIT Exploration of Generative AI. United States: MIT; 2024. DOI: 10.21428/e4baedd9.81164b06

[5] Abegglen S, Nerantzi C, Martínez-Arboleda A, Karatsiori M, Atenas J, Rowell C, editors. Towards AI Literacy: 101+ Creative and Critical Practices, Perspectives and Purposes. Londres: #creativeHE; 2024. DOI: 10.5281/zenodo.11613520

[6] Kaplan A, Haenlein M. Siri, Siri, in my hand: Who's the fairest in the land? On the interpretations, illustrations, and implications of artificial intelligence. Business Horizons. 2019;**62**(1):15-25

[7] Moher D, Liberati A, Tetzlaff J, Altman DG. Preferred reporting items for systematic reviews and meta-analyses: The PRISMA statement. Journal of Clinical Epidemiology. 2009;**62**(10):1006-1012

[8] Mulder M. In: Mulder M, editor. Competence-Based Vocational and Professional Education. 1st ed. Cham: Springer International Publishing; 2016

[9] Shakirova MA, Zamaletdinov RR, Fahrutdinova AR, Fahrutdinov RR. Competence approach as a basis of professional training for higher education students in conditions of implementing new educational standards. The Journal of Social Sciences Research. 2018;**SPI 1**:61-64

[10] Ananda F. Implementation of the pedagogic competence of Islamic religious education teachers. Jurnal Pendidikan Agama Islam Indonesia (JPAII). 2023;**4**(1):1-4

[11] Muharromah M, Syarif H. Reporting verbs in academic articles written by English teachers in Sumatera Barat: A study of professional competence of English teachers. In: Proceedings of the Eighth International Conference on Languages and Arts (ICLA-2019). Paris, France: Atlantis Press; 2020

[12] Harding AD, Walker-Cillo GE, Duke A, Campos GJ, Stapleton SJ. A framework for creating and evaluating competencies for emergency nurses. Journal of Emergency Nursing. 2013;**39**(3):252-264

[13] Mokshein SE. Education for sustainable development (ESD) in Malaysia: Policy, program and evaluation. In: Proceedings of the 3rd International Conference on Current Issues in Education (ICCIE 2018). Paris, France: Atlantis Press; 2019

[14] Zhao Y, Watterston J. The changes we need: Education post COVID-19. Journal of Educational Change. 2021;**22**(1):3-12

[15] Alrifai AA, Raju V. The employability skills of higher education graduates: A review of literature. International Advanced Research Journal in Science, Engineering and Technology. 2019;**6**(3):83-88

[16] Bridgstock R. The graduate attributes we've overlooked: Enhancing graduate employability through career management skills. Higher Education Research & Development. 2009;**28**(1):31-44

[17] Sedlan-König L, Hocenski M, Turjak S. Graduates are from venus, employers are from mars: A croatian study on employability. Poslovna izvrsnost - Business Excellence. 2018;**12**(2):9-23

[18] Bath D, Smith C, Stein S, Swann R. Beyond mapping and embedding graduate attributes: Bringing together quality assurance and action learning to create a validated and living curriculum. Higher Education Research & Development. 2004;**23**(3):313-328

[19] Isaza JP, Rush H. Emerging industry-university trends, challenges, and interventions for Latin America. In: 2011 Atlanta Conference on Science and Innovation Policy. Atlanta, Georgia: IEEE; 2011. pp. 1-15

[20] Pérez-Sánchez L, Lavandera-Ponce S, Mora-Jaureguialde B, Martín-Cuadrado AM. Training plan for the continuity of non-presential education in six Peruvian universities during COVID-19. International Journal of Environmental Research and Public Health. 2022;**19**(3):1562

[21] Iturrieta OS. Crossroads of higher education in troubled times facing the future of work and the subjective well-being of professionals in Latin America. In: Higher Education - New Approaches to Accreditation, Digitalization, and Globalization in the Age of Covid. IntechOpen; 2022

[22] Pillutla RS, Narayana MGPL. Framework integrating multiple dimensions of competency and related pedagogies: A case for IT industry. In: 2013 12th International Conference on Information Technology Based Higher Education and Training (ITHET). United States: IEEE; 2013. pp. 1-8

[23] de Bruno-Faria MF, Brandão HP. Competências relevantes a profissionais da área de T & D de uma organização pública do Distrito Federal. Revista de Administração Contemporânea. 2003;**7**(3):35-56

[24] Kaur A, Wadhawan K. AI: Job creator or jobless future. International Journal for Multidisciplinary Research. 2023;**5**(4):1-9

[25] Frank MR, Autor D, Bessen JE, Brynjolfsson E, Cebrian M, Deming DJ, et al. Toward understanding the impact of artificial intelligence on labor. National Academy of Sciences of the United States of America. 2019;**116**(14):6531-6539

[26] Hassani H, Silva ES, Unger S, TajMazinani M, Mac FS. Artificial intelligence (AI) or intelligence augmentation (IA): What is the future? AI. 2020;**1**(2):143-155

[27] Barile S, Piciocchi P, Bassano C, Spohrer J, Pietronudo MC. Re-defining the role of artificial intelligence (AI) in wiser service systems. In: Advances in Artificial Intelligence, Software and Systems Engineering. Cham: Springer; 2019. pp. 159-170

[28] Chakraborti T, Kambhampati S. Algorithms for the greater good! On mental modeling and acceptable

symbiosis in human-AI collaboration. 2018:1-9. arXiv:1801.09854v1

[29] Jarrahi MH. Artificial intelligence and the future of work: Human-AI symbiosis in organizational decision making. Business Horizons. 2018;**61**(4):577-586

[30] Hao R, Liu D, Hu L. Enhancing human capabilities through symbiotic artificial intelligence with shared sensory experiences. 2023:1-21. arXiv:2305.19278v1

[31] Chinonso OE, Theresa AME, Aduke TC. ChatGPT for teaching, learning and research: Prospects and challenges. Global Academic Journal of Humanities and Social Sciences. 2023;**5**(02):33-40

[32] Kamalov F, Santandreu Calonge D, Gurrib I. New era of artificial intelligence in education: Towards a sustainable multifaceted revolution. Sustainability. 2023;**15**(16):12451

[33] Paré G, Kitsiou S. Chapter 9 Methods for Literature Reviews [Internet]. 2017. Available from: https://www.ncbi.nlm.nih.gov/books/NBK481583/ [Accessed: July 1, 2024]

[34] Sampaio R, Mancini M. Estudos de revisão sistemática: um guia para síntese criteriosa da evidência científica. Revista Brasileira de Fisioterapia. 2007;**11**(1):83-89

[35] Haines T, McKnight L, Duku E, Perry L, Thoma A. The role of systematic reviews in clinical research and practice. Clinics in Plastic Surgery. 2008;**35**(2):207-214

[36] Cohen Hubal EA, Frank JJ, Nachman R, Angrish M, Deziel NC, Fry M, et al. Advancing systematic-review methodology in exposure science for environmental health decision making. Journal of Exposure Science & Environmental Epidemiology. 2020;**30**(6):906-916

[37] Smith J, Jones L. Social media manipulation in the defense sector: An analysis of AI powered tactics. Uttar Pradesh, India. Cybersecurity Quarterly. 2023;**18**(3):112-128

[38] Hussein BR, Halimu C, Siddique MT. El futuro de la inteligencia artificial y sus consecuencias sociales, económicas y éticas. Universidad de Cornell; 2021. DOI: 10.48550/arxiv.2101.03366

[39] Bengio Y et al. Managing AI Risks in an Era of Rapid Progress. Cornell University; 2023. DOI: 10.48550/arxiv.2310.17688

[40] Komljenovič J, Sellar S, Birch K. Turning Universities into Data-Driven Organisations: Seven Dimensions of Change. Springer Science+Business Media; 2024. DOI: 10.1007/s10734-024-01277-z

[41] Song Y. Analysis on Existing Project-Based Learning Application in Various Education Levels and Technology-Integrated Project-Based Learning; 2023. DOI: 10.54254/2753-7048/2/2022325

[42] Butler T, Espinoza A, Angelina A, Seppälä S. Towards a Capability Assessment Model for the Comprehension and Adoption of AI in Organisations. Cornell University; 2023. DOI: 10.48550/arxiv.2305.15922

Chapter 8

From Bias to Balance: Navigating Gender Inclusion in AI

Gloriana J. Monko and Mohamedi M. Mjahidi

Abstract

This chapter explores the intersection of Artificial Intelligence (AI) and gender, highlighting the potential of AI to revolutionize various sectors while also risking the perpetuation of existing gender biases. The focus is on the challenges and strategies for achieving gender inclusivity within AI systems. By examining the progress made by organizations in addressing gender bias, the chapter identifies key technical, ethical, legal, and social barriers and outlines approaches for integrating gender inclusivity throughout the AI lifecycle. Utilizing a narrative literature review supplemented by industry case studies, the chapter critically analyzes selected literature to address these issues. The findings underscore persistent challenges in identifying and mitigating gender bias in AI systems alongside complex ethical and legal implications. Nevertheless, notable advancements in gender-specific algorithm design and inclusive data practices are highlighted. The chapter concludes that achieving gender inclusivity in AI requires a coordinated effort across developers, researchers, and policymakers, offering actionable recommendations to ensure AI systems are fair, transparent, and equitable, thus contributing to a more just and inclusive society.

Keywords: navigating gender, inclusive AI, fairness in AI, addressing biases in AI, gender gap

1. Introduction

Artificial Intelligence (AI) holds great potential to address significant challenges and transform our lives and work. However, alongside this promise, AI also risks exacerbating existing inequities and digital divides. Reflecting the biases inherent in society, AI has already contributed to gender-based discrimination, introducing a new dimension to the digital divide [1]. This chapter seeks to answer critical questions about the challenges and progress made by organizations in addressing gender bias in AI systems and how the technical, ethical, legal, and social barriers hinder achieving gender balance in AI development.

Gender bias in AI refers to the systematic discrimination against individuals based on gender, which can manifest through algorithms, datasets, and the interaction of these technologies with social norms. These biases often perpetuate existing gender stereotypes and inequalities, reducing the fairness, accuracy, and effectiveness of

AI systems, particularly for women and other marginalized groups [2]. Addressing this bias involves understanding which methodologies can be employed to integrate gender inclusion throughout the AI development process.

Gender bias can emerge at multiple stages of the AI lifecycle, from data collection and algorithm design to deployment and interpretation of outputs. The historical roots of this issue date back to the early days of computing, where predominantly male perspectives shaped the foundation of the field. In the mid-nineteenth century, tasks like programming and software development were considered clerical and often assigned to women [3]. As the field gained prestige, the shift toward male-dominated spaces resulted in long-term effects on women's representation in technology. The most significant question to ask ourselves is, what is the potential of AI to address these disparities and promote societal equity?

According to the Global Gender Gap Report of 2023, women make up only 30% of professionals in the global technology industry, and this figure drops to 22% in the field of artificial intelligence [4]. These statistics reflect the persistent gender imbalance in tech, which raises the need for actionable steps for developers, researchers, and policymakers to promote gender inclusivity in AI.

The societal impact of biased AI profoundly affects employment, access to services, legal systems, and public trust in technology. AI systems in hiring, healthcare, and education risk perpetuating discriminatory practices when gender biases are embedded. Understanding these barriers and exploring strategies to mitigate them will be vital to ensuring equitable outcomes.

Figure 1 illustrates the importance of intentionally considering gender in the development of AI systems and highlights the negative impact of neglecting this consideration, which may lead to the unintentional exclusion of certain groups. Gender-inclusive AI addresses immediate biases and fosters a transformative shift in societal structures and interactions. This vision for the future emphasizes an AI-enhanced society that values and upholds the principles of fairness and equity, ensuring that every individual has the opportunity to succeed and contribute meaningfully to society, regardless of gender.

To explore this topic further, the chapter addresses the following research questions:

- What challenges are encountered and progress made by organizations in addressing gender bias in AI systems?
- What technical, ethical, legal, and social barriers hinder achieving gender balance in AI?
- What approaches can be applied to integrate gender inclusion in the AI development process?
- What is the potential of artificial intelligence to address gender disparities and promote societal equity, considering both immediate applications and long-term impacts?
- What actionable steps can developers (industry), researchers (academia), and policymakers (government) take to promote gender inclusivity in AI development, research, and regulation?

The remainder of this chapter is structured as follows: First, we explore the theoretical framework behind the intersectionality of gender and AI, covering key concepts and

Figure 1.
Gender inclusivity and exclusivity in AI design.

historical context. Next, we present the methodology that discusses case studies highlighting both the successes and challenges organizations face in fostering gender-inclusive AI, the challenges in achieving gender balance in the field, approaches for gender inclusion in the AI lifecycle, and the societal impact of gender-inclusive AI. Finally, we conclude with a discussion of a comprehensive blueprint for action aimed at industry, academia, and policymakers to create more equitable AI systems and processes.

2. Intersectionality in gender and AI

The complex interplay of intersecting social identities such as race, gender, socio-economic status, disability, and sexual orientation profoundly impacts the design and development of AI systems. This intersectional lens reveals how compounded disadvantages faced by marginalized groups can lead to disproportionate outcomes when these systems are not designed with their unique needs and challenges in mind. Without integrating intersectionality into AI design, we risk creating systems that reflect and amplify existing social inequalities and biases, further entrenching systemic barriers [5].

Intersectionality, a concept first introduced by Kimberlé Crenshaw in 1989, provides a crucial framework for understanding how various dimensions of identity interact to produce unique experiences of discrimination and disadvantage [6, 7]. When applied to AI, intersectionality offers a critical lens for examining the compounded effects of bias that emerge in AI systems and helps ensure these technologies serve all individuals fairly, particularly those at the intersection of multiple marginalized identities. For instance, AI algorithms trained on biased data can disproportionately misclassify or disadvantage women of color, who face both racial and gender biases, more so than white women or men of color [8].

AI systems that fail to account for these intersecting identities may reinforce existing stereotypes and social hierarchies. For example, facial recognition technologies have been shown to perform poorly for individuals with darker skin tones, particularly women, due to a lack of diversity in training datasets [9]. Moreover, decision-making algorithms used in sectors like healthcare or criminal justice can result in biased outcomes that disproportionately affect marginalized groups. For instance, predictive policing tools may over-police communities of color, or healthcare algorithms might underdiagnose conditions in minority populations due to historical underrepresentation in medical research datasets [5, 8].

Incorporating intersectionality into AI design entails addressing biases at every stage of the AI lifecycle, from data collection to algorithm development to deployment. This means developing diverse and representative datasets that capture the full range of human experiences, including those of marginalized communities. Failure to do so risks perpetuating historical biases and widening existing social disparities [5]. For example, an AI model used for hiring decisions that is trained predominantly on resumes from men will likely perpetuate gender biases, thereby disadvantaging women applicants, particularly women of color or women with disabilities [8].

An intersectional approach also necessitates the development of fairness frameworks that go beyond traditional metrics. Many fairness measures in AI focus on single-attribute classifications, such as gender or race, but fail to consider the compounding nature of multiple, intersecting identities. Newer frameworks, such as differential fairness, attempt to address this by ensuring fairness across multiple protected attributes simultaneously, providing better protection for minority groups who are often neglected in conventional fairness approaches [5].

The consequences of neglecting intersectionality in AI design are significant. Without careful attention to how gender, race, and other identities intersect, AI systems can exacerbate inequalities, leading to unfair outcomes in employment, healthcare, education, and beyond. For example, biased AI systems may misidentify or unfairly assess individuals based on their gender or racial identity, leading to discriminatory practices in hiring, law enforcement, or medical treatment [8]. These flaws undermine the effectiveness of AI systems and contribute to the further marginalization of vulnerable groups, deepening societal inequities. By adopting an intersectional approach, AI designers can mitigate these risks and ensure that these systems are inclusive, fair, and capable of advancing social equity.

3. Methodology

This chapter employed a narrative literature review to investigate gender inclusion in AI. The narrative review methodology was chosen for its ability to synthesize diverse perspectives, identify emerging themes, and facilitate an in-depth exploration of both historical and contemporary trends. These features make it particularly well-suited for examining the multifaceted issues surrounding gender inclusion in AI. The review explored case studies of persistent challenges and progress made, obstacles to achieving gender balance, approaches for fostering inclusion throughout the AI lifecycle, and the societal impacts of gender-inclusive AI.

A systematic approach was employed to ensure the quality and relevance of the selected literature, as illustrated in **Figure 2**. The process began with a targeted literature search using carefully chosen keywords related to the core concepts of the study. These included terms such as "Artificial Intelligence," "Gender," "Navigating Gender Balance in AI," "Gender Inclusion in AI," "Gender Equity and Inclusion in AI," "Addressing Biases in AI," "Gender Gap in AI," and "Fairness in AI." The search terms were used independently and in various combinations across four scholarly databases (i.e., Google Scholar, IEEE Xplore, ACM DL, Springer, Science Direct, and Tylor & Francis) and from reports of leading platforms such as the World Economic Forum, Google Research, and Spotify Newsroom. These sources were selected due to their intersection coverage of AI and gender-related literature.

The literature search covered the last eight years, from 2016 to 2024, ensuring the inclusion of recent advancements and discussions. The articles retrieved were refined to exclude those not directly addressing the intersection of AI and gender. Initial screening involved reviewing the titles and abstracts of potential articles for relevance, followed by full-text examinations. Further screening was conducted to eliminate duplicates, non-peer-reviewed publications, non-English articles, and unrelated literature.

Following this careful selection process, 36 pieces of literature were chosen for thorough review. Each literature was analyzed to extract the main findings that address the research questions. The findings were narratively synthesized and presented in sections addressing the key themes identified. This systematic approach to the narrative literature review ensured a comprehensive and critical examination of the current state of knowledge regarding gender inclusion in AI, providing a solid foundation for addressing the research questions and informing future directions in this field. The findings are presented in the subsequent sections, organized into case

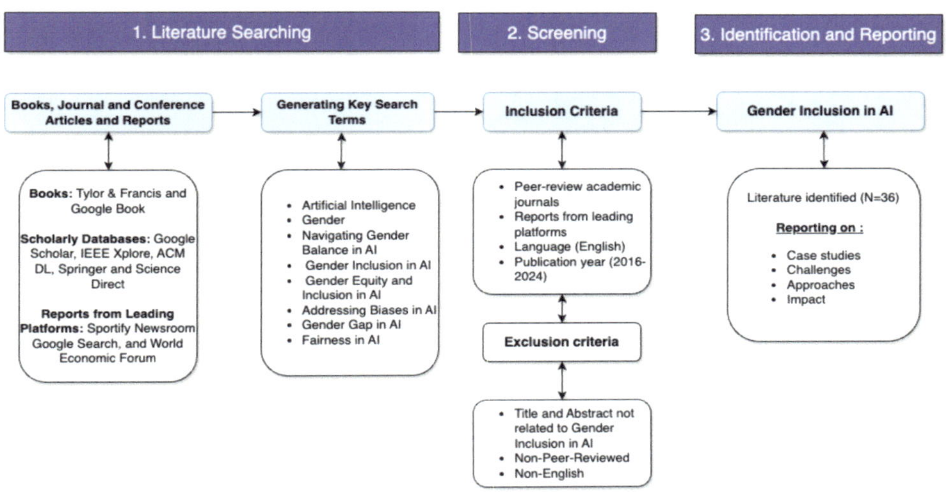

Figure 2.
Literature review structure.

studies on the challenges and progress, barriers to gender balance, approaches for fostering inclusion in the AI lifecycle, and the societal impact of gender-inclusive AI.

3.1 Case studies

In recent years, the tech industry has made significant strides toward developing more inclusive AI systems, particularly in addressing gender bias. This effort spans various areas, including language processing, healthcare, entertainment, and search algorithms. While progress has been made, challenges persist, highlighting the complex nature of bias in AI and the ongoing need for vigilance and improvement. Highlighting the successful case studies, Google Translate exemplifies both progress and lingering issues in language processing. The platform now offers gender-specific translations for some gender-neutral languages, providing both "he" and "she" options for sentences like the Turkish "o bir doktor," meaning he/she is a doctor in English (**Figure 3a**) [10]. However, this approach has yet to be uniformly applied, with translations from low-resource languages like Swahili, "Yeye ni daktari" still defaulting to male pronouns (**Figure 3b**), underscoring the need for more comprehensive solutions.

In healthcare, IBM's Watson for Oncology incorporated diverse clinical data and insights across gender demographics to provide equitable treatment recommendations [11, 12]. This approach recognizes the critical importance of gender considerations in medical care and sets a positive precedent for AI applications in healthcare.

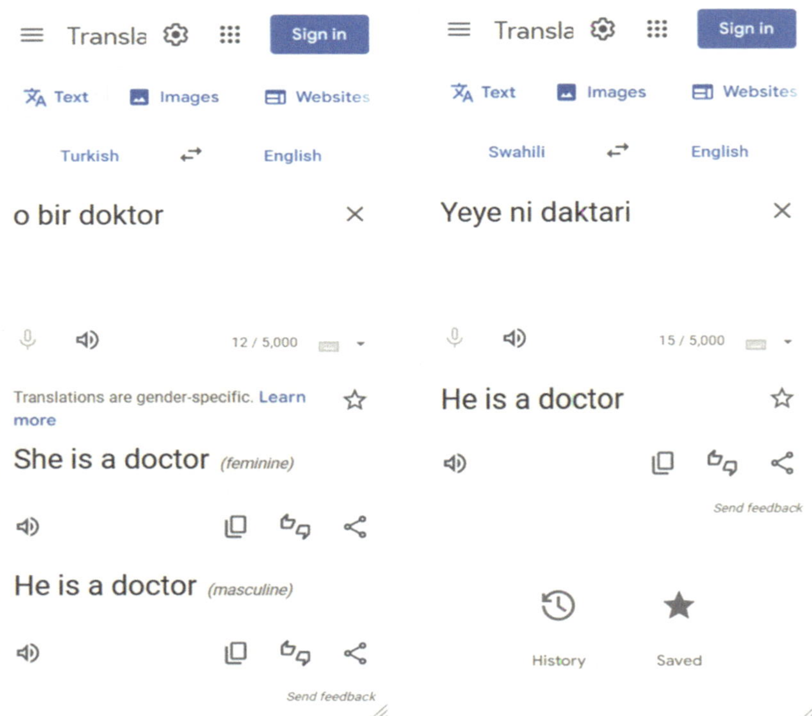

a. Feminine and masculine translation **b.** Masculine translation

Figure 3.
Google translations. a. Feminine and masculine translation. b. Masculine translation.

The entertainment industry has also seen initiatives to address gender imbalances. Spotify's Equalizer Project, for instance, aims to promote gender parity in curated playlists by highlighting underrepresented female artists [13]. This increases visibility for diverse talents and challenges systemic gender disparities in the music industry. In the fashion industry and search algorithms, a good example is Pinterest, which has updated its search algorithms to promote more inclusive results [14], particularly in beauty-related searches, thereby challenging traditional beauty standards and promoting diversity across races, ethnicities, and gender expressions.

Despite these positive developments, significant challenges remain, as evident in Amazon's AI recruitment tool [15, 16]. The tool discovered to be biased against women for technical positions serves as a stark reminder of how AI can perpetuate and even amplify existing societal biases. This case underscores the importance of rigorous testing and diverse input in AI development processes. Additionally, the rapid degradation of Microsoft's Tay chatbot into producing offensive and sexist content within 24 hours of its launch on Twitter in 2016 [17, 18] highlights the vulnerability of AI systems to malicious input and the need for robust safeguards. Similarly, early versions of Apple's Siri voice assistant were criticized for responses that reinforced gender stereotypes, particularly in handling queries related to women's safety and harassment. Facial recognition technologies have also been found wanting in terms of gender and racial equity. A landmark study [19] revealed significant error rates in systems from major tech companies, particularly for women of color. These inaccuracies not only raise concerns about privacy and misidentification but also point to deeper issues of representation in AI training data and development teams.

The financial sector has yet to be immune to these challenges. For instance, Apple's credit card algorithm, developed with Goldman Sachs, faced accusations of gender bias, with reports of women receiving lower credit limits than men with similar financial profiles [20]. This case highlighted potential biases in financial algorithms and the need for transparency and fairness in AI-driven financial decisions. Social media platforms have also grappled with algorithmic bias. Notably, [21–23] highlighted that Facebook's advertisement algorithm reinforced gender stereotypes in job advertisements, potentially limiting opportunities based on gender. These case studies illustrate how AI systems can inadvertently perpetuate societal biases, emphasizing the need for ongoing scrutiny and adjustment of these algorithms.

These case studies collectively paint a picture of an industry in transition. While there have been notable successes in addressing gender bias in AI, persistent challenges remain, as summarized in **Table 1**. As AI continues to play an increasingly prominent role in our lives, ensuring these systems are fair and inclusive for all genders is not just a technical challenge but a fundamental ethical imperative.

3.2 Challenges in achieving gender balance

Achieving gender balance in artificial intelligence presents numerous technical, ethical, and legal challenges. Addressing these challenges is crucial for developing AI systems that are not only effective but also fair and equitable. Ensuring gender balance involves creating algorithms and systems that do not favor one gender over another, which requires a multifaceted approach encompassing various domains. Here is a deeper look into each of these critical areas:

References	Challenge persisted	Progress made	Industry area	Organization
[9]	Defaulting to male pronouns for low-resource language	Gender-specific translations	Language Translation	Google
[10, 11]	Not trained with real patient data	Equitable treatment recommendations	Healthcare	IBM's Watson
[12]	Unfair presentation of female artists	Gender-curated playlists	Entertainment/ Music	Spotify
[13]	Unfair search results for women of color	Improved search to promote diversity across races, ethnicities, and gender expression	Fashion	Pinterest
[14, 15]	Biased against women for technical positions	Abandoned	Job Recruitment	Amazon
[16, 17]	Creating offensive and sexist content	It was shut down	Conversational AI Chatbot	Microsoft
	Responses that reinforced gender stereotypes	Provision of various Assistant voice options	Voice Assistant (e.g., Siri)	Google, Apple and Twitter
[19]	Lower credit limits for women with similar financial profiles to men	Refined algorithm and transparency to ensure equal treatment	Financial (Credit cards)	Apple
[20–22]	Reinforced gender stereotypes in job advertisements, favoring men	Implemented stricter guidelines, such as limiting microtargeting based on gender	Advertisement	Facebook

Table 1.
Challenges persisted and progress made in addressing gender bias in AI solutions.

3.2.1 Technical challenges

De-biasing AI algorithms is a complex and nuanced task that involves several intricate steps, each presenting unique technical challenges. These challenges arise from the inherent complexity of AI systems and the subtle nature of biases that can be embedded within them.

3.2.1.1 Identification of bias

The first step is to recognize and measure the bias present in AI systems. This often requires comprehensive analysis and auditing of the training data and algorithms. Recognizing bias involves identifying obvious disparities and more subtle forms of bias, such as indirect discrimination or latent stereotypes. Indirect discrimination occurs when seemingly neutral policies or practices disproportionately affect a particular group, while latent stereotypes refer to ingrained societal assumptions that can inadvertently influence AI outcomes. This complexity makes the identification process particularly challenging, as it demands a deep understanding of both technical and social dimensions. As noted by O'Connor and Liu [24], hidden biases in data can often go undetected, leading to significant challenges in identifying bias [24].

3.2.1.2 Modification of algorithms

Once biases are identified, the next step is to modify algorithms to mitigate them. This can involve techniques such as re-weighting training data to ensure under-represented groups are appropriately emphasized, using fairness-aware algorithms designed to correct biases during the learning process, or applying adversarial training methods where the model is trained to perform well even when challenged with inputs that expose biases. Each method has trade-offs between maintaining the algorithm's performance and reducing bias. Shrestha and Das [9] highlight the difficulty in achieving both fairness and accuracy in AI, particularly when balancing performance and the need for bias reduction [9].

3.2.1.3 Continuous monitoring

De-biasing is not a one-time fix. AI systems must be continuously monitored for biases as they learn and evolve over time. This ongoing process requires robust frameworks and tools to ensure that biases do not re-emerge or new types of biases are not introduced. Ovalle et al. [25] stress the need for continuous monitoring and the integration of ethical oversight to ensure long-term fairness [25].

3.2.2 Ethical challenges

Striking a balance between accuracy and fairness in AI systems is one of the most pressing ethical challenges. There are multiple definitions of fairness, and choosing the appropriate one for a specific context is difficult. Whether it is demographic parity, equality of opportunity, or individual fairness, each definition has implications for AI decision-making processes. Kong [26] underscores the complexity of defining fairness in a way that accommodates intersectional identities, especially for marginalized groups like women of color. Increasing fairness can sometimes reduce accuracy, posing a critical challenge in areas such as healthcare or criminal justice [26].

Additionally, there is an ethical need for transparency in how AI systems make decisions. Users and stakeholders should be able to understand the decision-making process, which requires explanations from AI systems that are both accurate and understandable. Figueroa et al. [8] explore how transparency is crucial for ensuring that AI systems are not only technically sound but also ethically aligned with societal values [8].

3.2.3 Legal and social implications

AI systems must operate within the bounds of existing legal frameworks, which include laws designed to prevent discrimination. Understanding legal requirements varies from country to country; different nations have distinct laws and regulations regarding discrimination, and AI systems used globally must comply with these diverse legal landscapes. Carter et al. [27] and Fosch-Villaronga and Poulsen [28] address the legal responsibilities that AI developers must adhere to prevent discrimination through biased systems [27, 29].

Beyond legal compliance, there is a broader social responsibility to ensure that AI systems do not perpetuate or exacerbate social inequalities. Shams et al. [30] highlight the importance of engaging with diverse communities to understand their needs and ensuring that AI technologies are developed in an inclusive manner to benefit all societal segments [30]. Additionally, Piskopani et al. [31] emphasize the significance of socially responsible AI in other domains, pointing out that all sectors should address ethical and legal challenges related to fairness and inclusivity [31].

Addressing these challenges is essential for advancing AI technology that respects gender equality and promotes a more inclusive society. Each area requires dedicated focus from stakeholders across disciplines to ensure that AI serves the good of all without reinforcing existing disparities.

3.3 Approaches for gender inclusion in the AI lifecycle

Realizing gender balance throughout the AI lifecycle requires a multifaceted and proactive approach. The complex nature of gender bias, deeply rooted in societal structures and often manifesting unconsciously, presents a significant challenge in AI development. These biases, along with existing socioeconomic disparities, can inadvertently be encoded into algorithms and training datasets, perpetuating and potentially amplifying gender inequalities. To counter this challenge, several approaches for gender inclusion in AI can be adopted. These approaches are illustrated in **Figure 4**, encompassing a range of interconnected practices designed to create AI systems that are fair, equitable, and representative of diverse populations. Key approaches include gendered user-centric design, data diversification, building an inclusive AI team of experts, implementing gender-focused AI algorithm design, conducting thorough gender impact assessments, and formulating AI policy and governance frameworks. Each approach plays a crucial role in addressing the unique challenges of gender inclusion, from the initial concept phase to real-world application. By systematically integrating these approaches, AI technology can advance in a way that avoids perpetuating existing

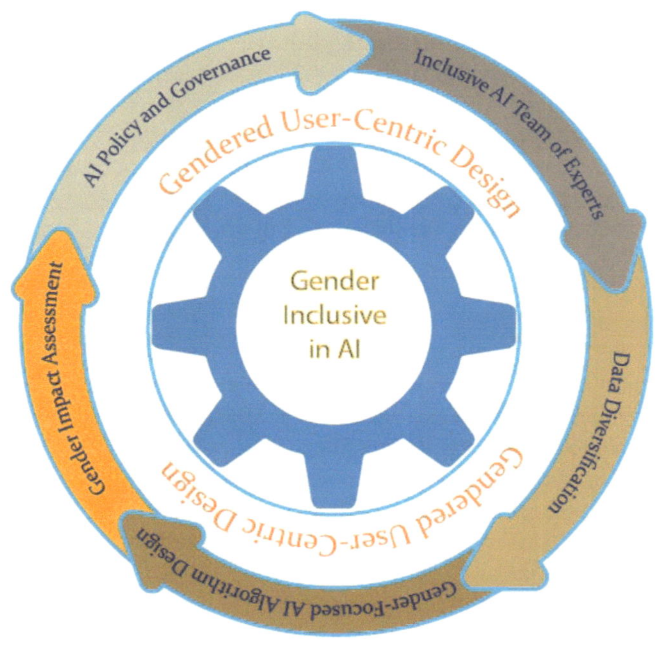

Figure 4.
Gender-inclusive approaches in the AI lifecycle.

biases and actively promotes gender equality, ultimately benefiting all users regardless of their gender identity. This holistic strategy represents a shift from merely mitigating bias to proactively fostering inclusivity and equity in AI systems.

3.3.1 Gendered user-centric design

Gendered user-centric design is fundamental to ensuring gender inclusivity in AI development. This approach involves actively engaging diverse users throughout the design process, from conception to deployment. By capturing perspectives, needs, and preferences across various gender identities, developers can uncover and address subtle gender-related issues that might otherwise be overlooked. This process goes beyond simple feedback collection; it involves immersive techniques such as participatory design workshops, where users become co-creators of the AI solutions [28, 32, 33]. Through iterative testing and refinement based on user input, developers can create AI systems that are technically proficient, socially aware, and responsive to the specific needs of different genders. This approach helps bridge the gap between technological innovation and real-world applicability, ensuring that AI solutions are inclusive and user-friendly across the gender spectrum.

3.3.2 Building an inclusive AI team of experts

Diversity within AI development teams is crucial for promoting gender inclusion. Building an inclusive team of experts goes beyond mere representation; it involves creating an environment where diverse perspectives are valued and integrated into every aspect of the development process [28, 32, 34, 35]. This means assembling multidisciplinary teams with expertise in AI and machine learning and gender studies, ethics, sociology, and other relevant fields will ensure representation from various genders, backgrounds, and cultures within the team fosters a rich environment for innovation and problem-solving. Moreover, implementing ongoing diversity and inclusion training for team members helps create a culture of awareness and sensitivity. This inclusive approach challenges assumptions, identifies potential biases early in the development process, and leads to AI solutions that resonate with a broader user base. The synergy of diverse viewpoints within the team often results in more creative and comprehensive approaches to gender inclusion in AI.

3.3.3 Data diversification

The quality and diversity of training data significantly impact the fairness and inclusivity of AI systems. Effective data diversification strategies are crucial for mitigating biases and ensuring comprehensive representation. This involves not just curating datasets with balanced representation across gender identities but also regularly auditing these datasets for hidden biases or underrepresentation. Developers must go beyond existing data sources, actively seeking out or generating data that fill gaps in representation. This might involve collaborating with diverse communities to source more representative data or creating synthetic data to balance datasets [28, 32, 36, 37]. The process of data diversification is ongoing, requiring constant vigilance and updates to keep pace with evolving societal understandings of gender. By actively managing and diversifying data, developers can create AI models that more accurately reflect the complexities of gender in society, reducing the risk of perpetuating stereotypes or exclusionary practices.

3.3.4 Gender-focused AI algorithm design

Developing algorithms with gender inclusivity at their core is critical in creating fair AI systems. This approach involves implementing fairness-aware machine learning techniques such as equalized odds and demographic parity to ensure that the algorithm's predictions are equitable across different gender groups. However, gender-focused algorithm design goes beyond these technical solutions. It requires a holistic approach that considers the entire lifecycle of the algorithm, from initial concept to deployment and beyond. This includes continuously monitoring and adjusting models to address emerging biases, incorporating explainable AI methods to enhance transparency and build trust with users, and designing flexible algorithms that can adapt to evolving understandings of gender [28, 34, 36, 37]. By prioritizing gender considerations at every algorithm development stage, AI systems can be created to avoid perpetuating existing biases and promote gender equality.

3.3.5 Gender impact assessment

Conducting thorough gender impact assessments is critical for understanding and mitigating the potential effects of AI systems on different genders. This process involves a comprehensive analysis of how an AI system might affect various gender groups directly and indirectly [28, 32]. It requires identifying potential unintended consequences and developing strategies to mitigate negative impacts before they occur. In addition, engaging with gender experts and affected communities is crucial for gaining deeper insights into the subtle ways AI might influence gender dynamics. Moreover, establishing ongoing monitoring and evaluation processes post-deployment ensures that the system's impact is continually assessed and adjusted as needed. Transparent communication of assessment findings to stakeholders is essential, as it fosters accountability and builds trust in the AI system [35, 37–39]. This approach provides a framework for continuous improvement, allowing AI systems to adapt as societal norms and understandings of gender evolve.

3.3.6 AI policy and governance

AI developers often focus primarily on solving specific problems, sometimes overlooking the potential risks and harm their products may impose on society. Meanwhile, society tends to prioritize the benefits gained from using AI products without necessarily considering whether those benefits are advantageous in the long term [28, 32]. By considering both the developer's and society's perspectives, AI policies, guidelines, and regulations can play a crucial role in promoting gender diversity and inclusion in AI. These frameworks provide clear guidance for AI's ethical design and deployment, ensuring fairness, transparency, and accountability. Additionally, they help mitigate risks associated with AI, such as unintended consequences, biases, and vulnerabilities, thereby protecting individuals and organizations from harm [28, 32, 34, 36, 38, 40].

3.4 Impact of gender-inclusive AI on society

The influence of AI on society is profound and wide-reaching. As we strive to integrate gender inclusivity into AI, the impacts can be observed in the short and long term, ultimately steering us toward a more equitable future.

3.4.1 Short-term impacts

Gender-inclusive AI leads to immediate changes in how products and services are designed and delivered. By actively addressing gender bias in AI algorithms, companies can create more effective and inclusive products that cater to a broader audience. For example, voice recognition software has traditionally had higher error rates for female voices than male voices due to the underrepresentation of female voices in training datasets. Dennis Fucci et al. explored the issue of gender imbalance in automatic speech recognition by manipulating pitch [41]. They examined the sensitivity of these systems to the sociolinguistic variability of speech data, emphasizing the significant role gender plays. The study highlighted how this variability can lead to disparities in recognition accuracy between male and female speakers, mainly due to the underrepresentation of female voices in training data. By addressing these biases, technology companies can improve the user experience for all genders, increasing satisfaction and expanding their market reach.

Another area impacted is healthcare diagnostics. AI models trained on gender-diverse data can diagnose conditions more accurately across genders, leading to better health outcomes. Gender inclusivity in AI also prompts changes in marketing strategies. With AI models that do not perpetuate stereotypes, advertising becomes more diverse and inclusive, appealing to a wider demographic and promoting a positive brand image that values diversity [42].

3.4.2 Long-term impacts

Integrating gender-inclusive practices in AI could lead to significant shifts in societal norms and behaviors over time. One key area is the workplace, where AI tools that facilitate unbiased hiring practices can help achieve gender parity across various industries, particularly in STEM fields where gender disparity is prominent [1]. Such tools can screen candidates based on skills and potential rather than unconscious biases, reshaping workforce demographics and promoting a culture of fairness.

Education is another sector where gender-inclusive AI can make a long-lasting impact. Educational software that adapts to the needs of students without bias can help close gender gaps in performance, particularly in areas where one gender historically underperforms. This can encourage a more diverse range of young people to pursue careers they might not have considered previously, altering career trajectories and expanding professional opportunities for all genders.

3.4.3 Vision for how AI can contribute to a more equitable world

Looking forward, the goal of gender-inclusive AI is not just to prevent bias but to actively contribute to a world where gender equity is the norm. AI has the potential to be a great equalizer in society, offering tools that help bridge gaps rather than widen them. For instance, AI-driven analyses can identify gender disparities in pay and job roles across sectors, providing data that can spur changes in corporate and governmental policies.

Furthermore, AI can be instrumental in educational reform by providing personalized learning experiences that adapt to different learning styles across genders, thus fostering an environment where all students can thrive equally [30]. In public policy, AI can help simulate policy outcomes to predict their impact on different genders, guiding more informed decisions that promote gender equity.

4. Discussion

4.1 Overcoming challenges, building progress, and shaping the future for gender inclusion in AI

The results unveiled a complex landscape in addressing gender bias within artificial intelligence (AI) solutions across diverse industries. These analyses highlight both persistent challenges and notable progress in mitigating gender imbalances, developing inclusive methodologies throughout the AI lifecycle, and assessing the societal impact of gender-inclusive AI systems. While some organizations, notably Google and Apple, have implemented commendable measures to mitigate bias through enhanced algorithms, equitable treatment protocols, and increased transparency, others such as Amazon and Microsoft have faced setbacks, necessitating the discontinuation of problematic systems due to intractable bias issues. Key technical hurdles include the identification of bias within intricate models, modifying algorithms to ensure fairness, and establishing robust, continuous monitoring systems to prevent bias. Ethical considerations arise from the need to balance unbiased decision-making processes with privacy concerns and responsible data utilization. At the same time, legal and social implications primarily focus on ensuring AI systems' compliance with anti-discrimination legislation and preventing the reinforcement of detrimental stereotypes.

The achievement of gender balance in AI necessitates the implementation of deliberate methodologies, encompassing gendered user-centric design principles and assembling diverse, inclusive teams of AI experts. Critical to ensuring equitable AI technologies are data diversification strategies and the design of algorithms specifically focused on mitigating gender bias. Comprehensive gender impact assessments and the implementation of robust AI governance frameworks further bolster these efforts. Regarding the impact of gender-inclusive AI on society, in the short term, gender-inclusive AI has the potential to enhance workplace diversity and reduce bias in digital services. Long-term impacts may contribute to developing more equitable societies, with AI playing a pivotal role in dismantling systemic gender discrimination. A progressive vision for AI should aspire to empower all individuals equitably, thereby contributing to the cultivation of a more just and inclusive global society.

4.2 Blueprint for action

Successfully mitigating gender bias in AI requires a triple helix approach, where each stakeholder contributes their unique expertise and perspective. This section outlines actionable steps that developers (i.e., industry), researchers (i.e., academia), and policymakers (i.e., government) can take to promote gender inclusivity in AI.

4.2.1 For developers

Developers are instrumental in shaping the ethical framework of AI technologies. To ensure their AI systems promote gender fairness, developers should incorporate gender analysis throughout the AI lifecycle from conceptualization to deployment, integrating gender impact assessments to identify potential biases and their implications. Diversifying training datasets is crucial, ensuring that datasets are representative of all genders by balancing the number of male and female samples while considering the diversity within gender groups to capture a broad spectrum of gender identities.

In addition, developers should develop and utilize metrics that can quantify gender bias, such as demographic parity and equalized odds, to monitor and minimize bias during the training process. Transparent reporting practices are essential; developers should document data, algorithmic decisions, and methodologies used for bias mitigation in a manner accessible and understandable to all stakeholders.

Engagement in continuous learning is also vital. Developers should stay updated on the latest research and best practices in ethical AI development, participating in forums and workshops focusing on AI fairness to refine and update practices continually. Before deployment, rigorous testing of AI systems under diverse conditions must ensure they operate fairly across different gender groups. This testing should include both quantitative methods and qualitative assessments from human reviewers.

4.2.2 For researchers

Understanding and combating gender bias in AI relies heavily on innovative research; therefore, researchers play a crucial role in deepening our understanding of gender biases in AI and developing more effective methods to counteract these biases. Investigating the underlying mechanisms that lead to gender bias in machine learning algorithms, including the impact of algorithmic choices such as model architecture and hyperparameter settings, is essential. This exploration provides valuable insights into how biases are embedded and perpetuated within AI systems.

An interdisciplinary approach is vital for creating fairer AI systems. Insights from social sciences, cognitive sciences, and ethics can significantly inform AI development. For instance, integrating sociological theories of gender can help researchers understand and model complex gender dynamics within data, leading to more nuanced and equitable AI outcomes.

Innovative de-biasing techniques are also a key focus area where researchers develop and refine methods to detect and mitigate bias, including novel machine learning approaches such as adversarial training or transfer learning. These techniques aim to enhance the fairness and accuracy of AI systems by addressing biases at their root.

Conducting long-term studies to assess the impact of AI systems on gender bias in real-world settings is essential for understanding the evolving nature of these systems and their long-term effects on societal gender norms. Longitudinal research helps track the progress and efficacy of de-biasing efforts over time, ensuring that AI technologies contribute positively to gender inclusivity.

Moreover, considering global perspectives on gender is important to understand how AI impacts gender inclusivity across different cultural and geographic contexts. Gender perceptions vary widely, and AI systems must be adaptable to these nuances to be truly inclusive. Studying these variations helps design AI that respects and accommodates diverse gender identities worldwide.

4.2.3 For policymakers

Policymakers have the authority to create an environment that fosters gender fairness in AI through thoughtful regulation and policies. Establishing legal frameworks is a critical step in this direction. Policymakers can ensure equitable AI by enforcing legal standards requiring fairness in AI applications. The legislation could mandate regular audits and reporting on gender bias in commercially used AI solutions, holding companies accountable for their practices.

It is also essential for these bodies to allocate resources and grants specifically for research into gender bias in AI. Funding for gender inclusivity research would encourage more scholars to focus on this critical area, leading to a deeper understanding and more effective solutions to combat bias in AI systems. More importantly, promoting public awareness and education about gender bias in AI is essential for creating a more inclusive technological landscape. This can be achieved by implementing educational campaigns to raise awareness and encouraging more diverse participation in AI and technology fields to help build a workforce mindful of gender issues and equipped to address them.

Additionally, policymakers can decide to incentivize companies to adopt best practices in gender fairness by offering tax breaks, awards, and recognition for companies demonstrating effective strategies in reducing AI biases. This will not only encourage ethical behavior but also publicly acknowledge and reward companies that are committed to gender inclusivity.

Furthermore, encouraging collaborations and partnerships between government bodies, academic institutions, and the private sector is vital for sharing knowledge and co-creating solutions for gender-inclusive AI. These collaborations can facilitate the exchange of ideas and resources, leading to more comprehensive, sustainable, and effective strategies to address gender bias in AI.

By following these recommendations, developers, researchers, and policymakers can contribute significantly to advancing gender fairness in AI, leading to more equitable technological developments.

5. Conclusion

The journey toward achieving gender inclusivity in AI is fraught with challenges, yet it is an essential endeavor for creating equitable technologies that serve all members of society. This chapter has demonstrated that while significant strides have been made, persistent biases still pose substantial risks, particularly for marginalized groups. Addressing these issues requires a multifaceted approach involving developers, researchers, and policymakers, each playing a critical role in ensuring AI systems are fair, transparent, and inclusive. The chapter advocates for continuous monitoring and refinement of AI systems to prevent the re-emergence of biases and for the implementation of gender-aware policies and frameworks. Ultimately, the successful integration of gender inclusivity in AI will not only enhance the technology's fairness but also contribute to a broader societal shift toward equity and justice.

Acknowledgements

This work was carried out with the aid of a grant from the Artificial Intelligence for Development in Africa Program, a program funded by Canada's International Development Research Centre, Ottawa, Canada, and the Swedish International Development Cooperation Agency (Grant no. 109704-001/002). The Registration was funded by the Anglophone Africa Multidisciplinary Research Lab (AI4D Lab). The author acknowledges the use of Grammarly for grammatical check and correction.

Author details

Gloriana J. Monko* and Mohamedi M. Mjahidi
Department of Computer Science and Engineering, College of Informatics and Virtual Education, The University of Dodoma, Dodoma, Tanzania

*Address all correspondence to: gloriana.monko@udom.ac.tz

References

[1] Nadeem A, Abedin B, Marjanovic O. Gender bias in AI: A review of contributing factors and mitigating strategies. In: ACIS 2020 Proc - 31st Australasian Conference on Information Systems. USA: Association for Information Systems (AIS) eLibrary; 2020

[2] Nadeem A, Marjanovic O, Abedin B. Gender bias in AI-based decision-making systems: A systematic literature review. Australasian Journal of Information Systems. 2022;**26**:1-34

[3] Richardson L. (De) constructing gender with office technology. From typewriter to productivity apps. Techniques & Culture. Revue semestrielle d'anthropologie des techniques. 2022;**10**:4915-4931

[4] World Economic Forum. Insight report [Internet]. World Economic Forum. 2023. Available from: https://www3.weforum.org/docs/WEF_GGGR_2023.pdf [Accessed: June 20, 2024]

[5] Foulds JR, Islam R, Keya KN, Pan S. An intersectional definition of fairness. In: 2020 IEEE 36th International Conference on Data Engineering (ICDE). Dallas, TX, USA: IEEE; 2020. pp. 1918-1921

[6] Crenshaw K. Demarginalizing the intersection of race and sex: A black feminist critique of antidiscrimination doctrine, feminist theory and antiracist politics. Droit et société. 2021;**108**:465

[7] Crenshaw K. Demarginalizing the intersection of race and sex: A black feminist critique of antidiscrimination doctrine, feminist theory and antiracist politics. In: Feminist Legal Theories. USA: Routledge; 2013. pp. 23-51

[8] Figueroa CA, Luo T, Aguilera A, Lyles CR. The need for feminist intersectionality in digital health. The Lancet Digital Health. 2021;**3**(8):e526-e533

[9] Shrestha S, Das S. Exploring gender biases in ML and AI academic research through systematic literature review. Frontiers in Artificial Intelligence. 2022;**5**:976838

[10] Johnson M. Providing gender-specific translations in google translate. Google AI Blog. 2018. Available from: https://research.google/blog/providing-gender-specific-translations-in-google-translate/ [Accessed: June 22, 2024]

[11] Somashekhar SP, Sepúlveda MJ, Puglielli S, Norden AD, Shortliffe EH, Kumar CR, et al. Watson for oncology and breast cancer treatment recommendations: Agreement with an expert multidisciplinary tumor board. Annals of Oncology. 2018;**29**(2):418-423

[12] Liu C, Liu X, Wu F, Xie M, Feng Y, Hu C. Using artificial intelligence (Watson for oncology) for treatment recommendations amongst Chinese patients with lung cancer: Feasibility study. Journal of Medical Internet Research. 2018;**20**(9):e11087

[13] Equalizer Project. Now in its fourth year, makes strides in increasing female representation in music. Spotify, 27 October. 2020. Available from: https://newsroom.spotify.com/2020-10-27/equalizer-project-now-in-its-fourth-year-makes-strides-in-increasing-female-representation-in-music/ [Accessed: July 2, 2024]

[14] Dave P. Pinterest's new algorithms want you to see every body type. In: WIRED. 2023. Available from: https://

www.wired.com/story/pinterests-new-algorithms-want-you-to-see-every-body-type/ [Accessed: July 3, 2024]

[15] Dastin J. Amazon scraps secret AI recruiting tool that showed bias against women. In: Ethics of Data and Analytics. USA: Auerbach Publications; 2022. pp. 296-299

[16] Horodyski P. Recruiter's perception of artificial intelligence (AI)-based tools in recruitment. Computers in Human Behavior Reports. 2023;**10**:100298

[17] Neff G. Talking to bots: Symbiotic agency and the case of Tay. International Journal of Communication. 2016

[18] Vorsino Z. Chatbots, gender, and race on web 2.0 platforms: Tay. AI as monstrous femininity and abject whiteness. Signs: Journal of Women in Culture and Society. 2021;**47**(1):105-127

[19] Buolamwini J, Gebru T. Gender shades: Intersectional accuracy disparities in commercial gender classification. In: Conference on Fairness, Accountability and Transparency. New York, NY, USA: PMLR; 2018. pp. 77-91

[20] Rizzi A, Kessler A, Menajovsky J. The Stories Algorithms Tell: Bias and Financial Inclusion at the Data Margins. Washington, DC, USA: Center for Financial Inclusion, Accion; 2021

[21] Eren Ezgi, Lukas Hondrich, Linus Huang, Basileal Imana, Matthias C. Kettemann, Joanne Kuai, Marcela Mattiuzzo et al. Increasing Fairness in Targeted Advertising. The Risk of Gender Stereotyping by Job Ad Algorithms. Germany: The Alexander von Humboldt Institute for Internet and Society (HIIG); 2021

[22] Blass J. Algorithmic advertising discrimination. Northwestern University Law Review. 2019;**114**:415

[23] Fosch-Villaronga E, Poulsen A, Søraa RA, Custers BH. A little bird told me your gender: Gender inferences in social media. Information Processing & Management. 2021;**58**(3):102541

[24] O'Connor S, Liu H. Gender bias perpetuation and mitigation in AI technologies: Challenges and opportunities. AI & SOCIETY. 2024;**39**(4):2045-2057

[25] Ovalle A, Subramonian A, Gautam V, Gee G, Chang K-W. Factoring the matrix of domination: A critical review and reimagination of intersectionality in AI fairness. In: Proceedings of the 2023 AAAI/ACM Conference on AI, Ethics, and Society. USA: Association for Computing Machinery (ACM); 2023. pp. 496-511

[26] Kong Y. Are "intersectionally fair" AI algorithms really fair to women of color? A philosophical analysis. In: Proceedings of the 2022 ACM Conference on Fairness, Accountability, and Transparency. USA: Association for Computing Machinery (ACM); 2022. pp. 485-494

[27] Carter SM, Rogers W, Win KT, Frazer H, Richards B, Houssami N. The ethical, legal and social implications of using artificial intelligence systems in breast cancer care. The Breast. 2020;**49**:25-32

[28] Fosch-Villaronga E, Poulsen A. Diversity and inclusion in artificial intelligence. In: Law and Artificial Intelligence: Regulating AI and Applying AI in Legal Practice. Vol. 35. The Hague: T.M.C. Asser Press; 2022. pp. 109-134

[29] Zowghi Didar, Francesca da Rimini. Diversity and inclusion in artificial intelligence. arXiv preprint arXiv:2305.12728. 2023

[30] Shams RA, Zowghi D, Bano M. AI and the quest for diversity and inclusion: A systematic literature review. AI and Ethics. 2023:1-28

[31] Piskopani AM, Chamberlain A, Ten Holter C. Responsible AI and the arts: The ethical and legal implications of AI in the arts and creative industries. In: Proceedings of the First International Symposium on Trustworthy Autonomous Systems. USA: Association for Computing Machinery (ACM); 2023. pp. 1-5

[32] Hernández Ernesto Giralt. Towards an ethical and inclusive implementation of artificial intelligence in organizations: A multidimensional framework. arXiv preprint arXiv:2405.01697. 2024

[33] Adler RF, Paley A, Li Zhao AL, Pack H, Servantez S, Pah AR, et al. A user-centered approach to developing an AI system analyzing US federal court data. Artificial Intelligence and Law. 2023;**31**(3):547-570

[34] Gengler E, Hagerer I, Gales A. Diversity bias in artificial intelligence. In: The Digital and AI Coaches' Handbook: The Complete Guide to the Use of Online, AI, and Technology in Coaching. USA: Routledge, Tylor & Francis Group; 2024

[35] Mandhala VN, Bhattacharyya D, Midhunchakkaravarthy D. Need of mitigating bias in the datasets using machine learning algorithms. In: 2022 International Conference on Advances in Computing, Communication and Applied Informatics (ACCAI). Chennai, India: IEEE; 2022. pp. 1-7

[36] Bainomugisha E, Nakatumba-Nabende J. Developing and deploying end-to-end machine learning Systems for Social Impact: A rubric and practical artificial intelligence case studies from African contexts. Applied AI Letters. 27 Aug 2024:e100

[37] Agarwal R, Bjarnadottir M, Rhue L, Dugas M, Crowley K, Clark J, et al. Addressing algorithmic bias and the perpetuation of health inequities: An AI bias aware framework. Health Policy and Technology. 2023;**12**(1):100702

[38] Whittlestone Jess, Jack Clark. Why and how governments should monitor AI development. arXiv preprint arXiv:2108.12427. 2021

[39] Havrda M, Klocek A. Well-being impact assessment of artificial intelligence–A search for causality and proposal for an open platform for well-being impact assessment of AI systems. Evaluation and Program Planning. 2023;**99**:102294

[40] Aldoseri A, Al-Khalifa KN, Hamouda AM. Re-thinking data strategy and integration for artificial intelligence: Concepts, opportunities, and challenges. Applied Sciences. 2023;**13**(12):7082

[41] Fucci D, Gaido M, Negri M, Cettolo M, Bentivogli L. No pitch left behind: Addressing gender unbalance in automatic speech recognition through pitch manipulation. In: 2023 IEEE Automatic Speech Recognition and Understanding Workshop (ASRU). Taipei, Taiwan: IEEE; 2023. pp. 1-8

[42] Golder S, O'Connor K, Wang Y, Stevens R, Gonzalez-Hernandez G. Best practices on big data analytics to address sex-specific biases in our understanding of the etiology, diagnosis, and prognosis of diseases. Annual Review of Biomedical Data Science. 2022;**5**(1):251-267

Chapter 9

Machine Learning in Procurement with a View to Equity

Ishrat Fatima, Roberto Nai and Rosa Meo

Abstract

The application of machine learning to big data from tenders published in Italy provides significant benefits to public administrations and economic operators, including improved procurement processes. Quantitative results from our study show a 96.5% accuracy using XGBoost models for predicting the presence of tender variations during contract execution. These models estimate the likelihood of variations in upcoming tenders: their correct prediction is a valuable tool because variations avoidance reduces completion time and costs of public contracts. Additionally, explainable AI tools help the description graphically and intuitively of the analyzed data. They also allow the analyst to highlight potential biases in tender participation and their awards, contributing to fairer public procurement. The results of their application to public tenders show that strong differences in the Italian country exist with a consequent lack of equity. Finally, the application of recommendation systems on the tender notices shows they are an effective cognitive tool to search for similar tenders and retrieve the actors involved, such as public administrations or economic operators. The precision score of the answers is above the value of 90% for the 74.15% of the queries. The chapter describes the tasks that permit the achievement of the above objectives.

Keywords: tenders, big data, machine learning, explainable artificial intelligence, descriptive models, ethical fairness, predictive models, deep neural network embedding, recommendation systems, prescriptive models

1. Introduction

Thanks to the use of digital information systems, organizations have stored data about their business processes. The large amounts of data collected can be used for many purposes, from monitoring progress and assessing risks to setting targets and making comparisons with other contexts (especially when these data are cross-checked with open data from other realities).

This chapter discusses the Italian case of tender notices published by public administrations.

Public procurement in Italy concerns contracts stipulated by the Public Administration with economic operators for the supply of goods, services, or works.

The award process takes place according to precise rules, mainly regulated by the Procurement Code.[1]

The process of awarding a public contract follows these main phases:

Tender notice: The Public Administration publishes a tender notice that defines the project and the requirements for participation.

Presentation of offers (or bids): Interested economic operators present their offer, which includes technical and economic proposals.

Evaluation of offers: A special commission evaluates the offers according to specific criteria (lowest price or most economically advantageous offer).

Awarding: The contract is awarded to the economic operator who submitted the best offer, compliant with the established criteria.

Execution of the contract: The winning operator executes the contract, respecting the agreed conditions.

The entire process is subject to principles of transparency, competition, and non-discrimination to guarantee fairness and correctness.

Tender notices are published in the Official Gazette and a few data on them is sent by the public administrations to the regional public expenditure observatories or directly to the National Anti-Corruption Agency (ANAC). ANAC was set up by the Italian government in 2010 with the aim of monitoring and reducing public expenditure. The ANAC database on tenders is public and can be queried online [1].

The accumulated big data, consisting of more than seven million notices, on the expenditure of tenders of all the Italian public administrations, whether they are works, supplies, or services, is an extremely valuable resource. It provides data and evidence to help the data analysis expert formulate and test the validity of the hypothesis, from the awarding process to the litigation in front of the Regional Administrative Courts, to the execution of the contract, testing, and so on.

The tenders in the ANAC database are highly diverse, covering works, supplies, and services, and each tender has its specific type and sector. A tender may fall under public works, services like consultancy, or supply contracts. These tenders are significant as they determine the allocation of public funds and play a key role in economic development. Understanding the tendering process is critical to ensuring transparency, competitiveness, and fairness. For instance, consultancy tenders, which are the focus of this chapter, can be prone to variability and require close monitoring to prevent cost overruns. The data collected on these tenders, such as the *CIG* identifier, tender type, and award amounts, serve as a foundation for our study. There are two types of motivations for the focus of the chapter on the analysis of counseling tenders. The first one is Simpson's paradox.[2] According to this principle, a trend or correlation among variables appears in heterogeneous groups of data but it could disappear when the groups are merged. Therefore, we would like to reduce the risk of obtaining erroneous results by restricting the data analysis to a single group composed of more homogeneous types of tenders. The second is the awareness of the fact that the phenomenon of money laundering could be facilitated by the existence of a consultancy cost that is not easy to quantify or limit directly. Finally, we leverage a recent trend in research on Artificial Intelligence (AI) known as "Trustworthy AI" [2] in which ethical values and human rights are taken into account when AI tools are developed and

[1] The text of Procurement Code in Italy, which was updated several times, is available at https://www.codiceappalti.it/

[2] A description of the phenomenon is at: https://en.wikipedia.org/wiki/Simpson's_paradox.

used in society. Among the guaranteed rights, there is the right to obtain explanations for the outcome of a (technological) process, accountability such as the right to find responsibilities for every mistake of the AI tools, equity interpreted as the guarantee that everyone receives equal treatment regardless of ethnic group, the provenance, or other sensible features. In other terms, fairness and non-discrimination have a central role and should be used to evaluate the good performance of a human or technological process in which AI is involved [3].

The situation is particularly delicate in the case of tenders by public administrations (PA) involving the transfer of public funds. On the one hand, there is the right of every citizen of the territory to receive public money as a reward for the commitment and professionalism involved in a project for public administration. On the other hand, there are different contexts in which public administrations and economic operators operate in their territories. Not all situations are comparable, especially if we take into account the different economic backgrounds that exist in the Italian territory. The south, the so-called "Mezzogiorno", is more disadvantaged, but also suffers more from the presence of criminal organizations originating from these regions. Criminals try to exploit and extort money from the legal and public administrations. As a result, southern Italy may suffer more from coexistence with criminal organizations and be suspected of involvement with them. This chapter studies in an objective way the available data on the tendering process on the Italian territory to measure with the lens of data analysts and tools for measuring AI fairness [3] if inequalities and asymmetries exist. Knowledge about the existence of the phenomenon is the first step to correct it.

The secondary objective of this chapter is to demonstrate that the ANAC database is a valuable resource. When analyzed, the available data can be used to improve the tendering process. Two directions are followed. The first uses predictive AI models trained on the ANAC data, to predict whether a contract awarded by a tender will be involved in a variation. This prediction could help public administrations avoid the variation, which often leads to delays and increased costs. In the second direction, a tender recommendation system is being developed on the ANAC database. This is a valuable resource for both the PA and economic operators, who can use it to search for similar cases in the past, similar competitors who could be possible partners for similar projects, and obtain useful information on costs, time, constraints, award procedures, etc. Moreover, recommendation systems help to increase the competitiveness and diversity of the bidding pool by analyzing the companies that typically bid on specific tenders by helping to suggest new companies that have not participated before but might be interested in bidding.

The remainder of this chapter is organized as follows: Section 2 introduces the related works; Section 3 describes the case study; Section 4 describes the study on equity of awarding tenders on the territory; Section 5 provides insights about predicting the presence of a variation in the procurement; Section 6 outlines the recommendation system and the obtained results. Finally, Section 7 concludes the chapter.

2. Related work

In the context of Machine Learning (ML) in procurement, there is a growing focus on leveraging AI technologies both at the National [4] and European level [5]. One study emphasizes the importance of integrating ethical and sustainable sourcing practices into supply chain management, highlighting how ML and big data analytics can improve decision-making processes [6]. These technologies enable more socially responsible procurement by ensuring transparency, reducing biases, and fostering fair supplier selection and contract management [7].

Another perspective is offered through research on supply chain resilience, which examines how AI and ML can enhance information exchange among supply chain partners. This approach reduces risks and supports socially equitable outcomes by promoting transparency and fairness in procurement processes. AI technologies are seen as key to driving social equity by improving supplier diversity and advocating for fair labor practices across supply chains [8, 9].

A systematic literature review of social procurement in the construction and infrastructure sectors explores the evolution of procurement practices to include social value creation. This shift focuses on using government initiatives to mandate social outcomes in procurement contracts. The review identifies barriers and enablers to social procurement and provides strategies for overcoming challenges, highlighting the potential of procurement practices to deliver social benefits and promote equity [10, 11].

Additionally, the role of AI in procurement is explored in terms of its potential to strengthen diversity and inclusion. Data analytics and ML are highlighted as tools to identify opportunities to engage diverse suppliers and ensure equitable procurement processes [12]. This approach aligns with global trends in utilizing technology to support socially equitable procurement practices and underscores the importance of integrating equity considerations into ML models used in public procurement [13, 14].

Recommendation systems are increasingly utilized in the legal domain to swiftly retrieve relevant documents for specific cases. In the study of Dhanani et al. [15], a graph clustering method is proposed to group referentially similar judgments and identify semantically relevant ones within these clusters. In the study of Nai et al. [16], numerical vectors known as *sentence embeddings* [17] were trained using BERT (Bidirectional Encoder Representations from Transformer) [18] to build an abstract and general representation of the semantic content of contract descriptions. Input sentences were taken from the brief descriptions in natural texts of procurement in the ANAC database, resulting in 768-dimensional vectors. Subsequently, for an individual procurement case, the most similar and relevant ones in the rest of the database were searched using SBERT [19] and LaBSE [20]; similarly, in the study of Nai et al. [21], the performance of a recommendation system based on the embeddings provided by two different commercial models was compared.

Bert LaBSE model is a language-agnostic Bidirectional Transformer Sentence Embedding [20]. A transformer has one or more encoders, used to represent in a latent model the context of the sentence, while the decoder parts are usually applied to generate sentences from the abstract representation and to change the language in automatic translation. BERT connects the encoder and decoder through a token-based attention mechanism. In BERT, consecutive sentences from the input are separated into tokens, transformed into numerical vectors from which the system performs different tasks such as learning the words' context through random masked words and learning if sentences are consecutive (or related in a question-answering task).

As regards equity in public procurement, van Dijk and Wilke [22] examined the effect of different interests on public-good provision by adopting the equity theory. The latter aims at determining whether the distribution of resources is fair taking into account the contributions (or costs) and the benefits (or rewards) for each individual in an organization. Decarolis and Giorgiantonio [23] employ ML in studying the effectiveness of indicators used in police investigations on corruption (called red flags) in public tenders for roadworks. The survey [24] provides an overview of the many control measures for fairness that researchers in AI proposed to monitor the fairness of a process. The monitored process might be assisted by AI and ML tools and its fairness needs to be verified with respect to the membership to a group (that expresses a sensitive feature) for some of the involved actors. The measures for fairness are guided by different concepts: (a) parity-based metrics that compare the predictive positive rates across groups. An instance is statistical *independence* between the predicted score and the group; (b) Confusion matrix-based metrics that compare groups by taking into account the potential differences across groups. An instance is *separation* that evaluates the equal opportunity of comparable individuals from the different groups; (c) Calibration-based metrics that compare groups by the probability that the predicted scores are emitted. An instance of this metric is *sufficiency* with tests for fairness. In Section 4.1, we apply the above three concepts to assess the fairness of the participation of economic operators in public tenders and the subsequent award of contracts, taking into account their different origins: north of Italy, center of Italy, or "Mezzogiorno" (south or islands).

3. Case study: Tenders of Italian anti-corruption authority: ANAC

The primary dataset pertains to ANAC, the Italian government authority collecting public tenders. A dedicated section on the ANAC website [1] allows users to access data in a standard format, enabling category selection and downloading in compressed files. In the ANAC Open Data catalog, the central dataset concerns the creation of a *Tender Notice*, organized by year and month. Besides the tender dataset, four additional significant datasets are available: the list of *Contracting Authorities* (CA) that have issued a tender, the list of tenders that have received an *Award*, the *Economic Operators* (EO) who have won a tender, and the *activities* associated with a tender post-award (e.g., *contract-start*, *contract-end*, *subcontract*, etc.). Each of these four datasets is briefly described below. CAs[3] are public bodies or entities acting on behalf of public institutions, responsible for procuring goods, services, or works through tenders. They oversee and manage the entire public tender process. CAs are categorized into three types: Central (e.g., ministries), Regional and Local (e.g., municipalities), and other entities (e.g., hospitals). Awards include a list of awarded tenders, with details such as the final awarded amount, the award date, and the EOs receiving the tender. EOs can be individual enterprises, artisans, partnerships or corporations, cooperatives, etc. A 10-character alphanumeric variable called *CIG* identifies each tender and its related activities. CAs and EOs are recognized by their *tax code* (an alphanumeric string), and CAs also have a unique *ISTAT code*. Finally, the *Variants* dataset contains information on any variation authorized during execution from the original contract, as a result of unforeseen circumstances. **Figure 1** presents a portion of the *Tender Notice* and *Award* where some tenders have not been awarded to an EO (with *DATE_AWARD* and *TENDER_AWARD* fields left empty).

3.1 Main data overview

This section presents a short description of the most relevant features from three tables of ITH, whereas their features are listed in **Table 1**. In the TENDER_NOTICE

[3] Contracting authorities are often referred to more generally as public administrations.

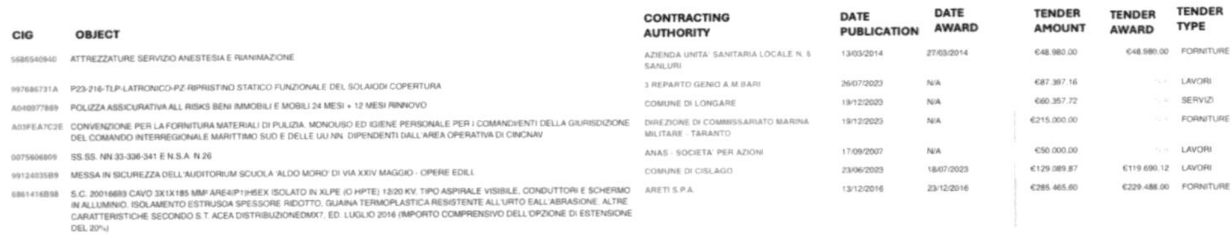

CIG	OBJECT	CONTRACTING AUTHORITY	DATE PUBLICATION	DATE AWARD	TENDER AMOUNT	TENDER AWARD	TENDER TYPE
5686540940	ATTREZZATURE SERVIZIO ANESTESIA E RIANIMAZIONE	AZIENDA UNITA' SANITARIA LOCALE N. 6 SANLURI	13/03/2014	27/03/2014	€48.980,00	€48.980,00	FORNITURE
997686731A	P23-216-TLP-LATRONICO-PZ-RIPRISTINO STATICO FUNZIONALE DEL SOLAIODI COPERTURA	3 REPARTO GENIO A.M.BARI	26/07/2023	N/A	€87.397,16	N/A	LAVORI
A040977889	POLIZZA ASSICURATIVA ALL RISKS BENI IMMOBILI E MOBILI 24 MESI + 12 MESI RINNOVO	COMUNE DI LONGARE	19/12/2023	N/A	€60.357,72	N/A	SERVIZI
A03FEA7C2E	CONVENZIONE PER LA FORNITURA MATERIALI DI PULIZIA, MONOUSO ED IGIENE PERSONALE PER I COMANDI/ENTI DELLA GIURISDIZIONE DEL COMANDO INTERREGIONALE MARITTIMO SUD E DELLE UU.NN. DIPENDENTI DALL'AREA OPERATIVA DI CINCNAV	DIREZIONE DI COMMISSARIATO MARINA MILITARE - TARANTO	19/12/2023	N/A	€215.000,00	N/A	FORNITURE
0075606809	SS.SS. NN 33-336-341 E N.S.A. N.26	ANAS - SOCIETA' PER AZIONI	17/09/2007	N/A	€50.000,00	N/A	LAVORI
99124035B9	MESSA IN SICUREZZA DELL'AUDITORIUM SCUOLA 'ALDO MORO' DI VIA XXIV MAGGIO - OPERE EDILI	COMUNE DI CISLAGO	23/06/2023	18/07/2023	€129.089,87	€119.690,12	LAVORI
6861416B98	S.C. 20016693 CAVO 3X1X185 MM² ARE4(P1)H6EX ISOLATO IN XLPE (O HPTE) 12/20 KV. TIPO ASPIRALE VISIBILE, CONDUTTORI E SCHERMO IN ALLUMINIO, ISOLAMENTO ESTRUSOA SPESSORE RIDOTTO, GUAINA TERMOPLASTICA RESISTENTE ALL'URTO EALL'ABRASIONE. ALTRE CARATTERISTICHE SECONDO S.T. ACEA DISTRIBUZIONEDMX7, ED. LUGLIO 2016 (IMPORTO COMPRENSIVO DELL'OPZIONE DI ESTENSIONE DEL 20%)	ARETI S.P.A.	13/12/2016	23/12/2016	€285.465,60	€229.488,00	FORNITURE

Figure 1.
ANAC Open Data-CSV file data preview, where it is possible to see the main features of a tender. Full-size image available here: https://bit.ly/3M75Pch.

Table	Feature	Description
T_N	CIG	Alphanumeric value (key value)
	Tender object	Textual summary of the tender
	Framework agreement between PA and EO	1 if yes, else 0
	Number of lots	Integer value {1..n}
	Tender type	Supplies (U) Works (W) Services (S)
	Tender area	Ordinary (O) Special (S)
	Tender amount	Float value
	Date of publication	Date in format yyyy-mm-dd
	EO selection mode	Integer value {1..122}
	Execution mode	Integer value {1.19}
	Region	Italian region names + Central Government
	CPV	String ID (XX000000-Y)
	CPV division code (first two digits of CPV)	String ID (XX)
	PNNR flag	1 if yes, else 0
AW	CIG + AWARD_ID	Alphanumeric value (key value)
	EO consortium (group of EOs)	1 if it is a group of EOs, else 0 (individual)
	Award date	Date in format yyyy-mm-dd
	Awarded amount (bid amount)	Float value
	Awarded amount drop (bid drop)	Float value
	Number of bids admitted	Integer value {1..n}
	Subcontracting admitted	1 if yes, else 0
C_A	Tax Code	Alphanumeric value (key value)
	ISTAT Code	Alphanumeric value
	CA denomination	Textual string

Table 1.
Main features of the tables TENDER_NOTICE (T_N), AWARD (AW), and CONTRACTING_AUTHORITIES (C_A).

table, each tender is identified by an alphanumerical value called the *CIG* (the key ID value), which is used to link most of the remaining tables. The main distinction between tenders is their *type* and *sector*: types can be "Services" (S), "Supplies" (U), or "Works" (W), while sectors can be "Ordinary" (O) or "Extraordinary" (E) based on whether they are planned or due to extraordinary events (e.g., floods, earthquakes, etc.). All types of tenders are described by the CPV code, i.e., the *Common Procurement Vocabulary.*[4] These categories are organized into an ontology (a hierarchical organization) whose elements are identified by codes; using the first two digits of the codes (which correspond to the upper part of the ontology and to the coarsest-grain categories), they provide the CPV *divisions* useful for distinguishing the product categories purchased by CAs (e.g., "90" represents cleaning services, while "9040" represents sewer cleaning). A tender can be defined within a *framework agreement*, meaning that the CA and EO have a prior agreement to provide services for further tenders for a defined time (e.g., 1–5 years). Often, a tender is split into *lots*, with a lower amount that can be awarded separately to different companies because they could be pertinent to different economic activities. Finally, each tender has a well-defined *selection criterion* that will be applied by the CA to choose the EO who will be awarded; an *implementation criterion* will also be considered and the winning EO must comply with it.

The table AWARDS contains the list of relevant features related to the tender award, including the awarding entity, date, amount, etc. As expected, non-awarded tenders are not reported in this table (so they are only available in the TENDER_NOTICE table).

The table CONTRACTING_AUTHORITIES contains information about the name of the authority and the main keys that allow to link the information of the tender with other tables. In this respect, the *tax code* determines the type of CA by joining this table with the ISTAT table necessary to study the relationship between the tender process and the regional population and geographical dimensions.

3.2 Italian National Institute of Statistics—ISTAT

An important aspect involves determining the scope of each tender administrative aggregation. The National Institute of Statistics (ISTAT)[5] offers a comprehensive range of statistical information about Italy. Among these are the *Nomenclature of Territorial Units for Statistics* (NUTS)[6] and the distribution of the *population per municipality*. The NUTS system is structured into three hierarchical levels: NUTS 1 comprises socio-economic regions, such as large economic areas (that in this chapter we call macro-areas); NUTS 2 pertains to smaller regions for implementing regional policies, such as provinces or large metropolitan areas; NUTS 3 covers the smallest areas, including regions, provinces, and municipalities.[7] The distribution of inhabitants can be interesting for understanding, for example, the quote of investment per population in a certain area.[8] Including NUTS and population in ANAC Open Data

---

[4] https://ted.europa.eu/en/simap/cpv.

[5] https://www.istat.it/en.

[6] https://www.istat.it/classificazione/codici-dei-comuni-delle-province-e-delle-regioni.

[7] https://www.istat.it/it/archivio/6789.

[8] https://www.istat.it/it/archivio/156224.

facilitates, for instance, the comparison and analysis of territorial investments at the different geographic granularity levels, possibly normalizing costs by the population.

4. Descriptive tasks and fairness study

When analyzing a phenomenon from data, it is suggested to create descriptive models (such as geographical heat maps, histograms, etc.) that allow a first look at the phenomenon with a summary of an immediate interpretation. **Figure 2** summarizes the total amount spent on counseling tenders in the studied period (2016–2019). The outlier over the other regions, whose expenses are instead more similar, is the region Lazio, in the central macro-area. The capital of Italy, Rome, is located in this region and this could be a justification for the higher number of counseling contracts for the government of the country.

In **Figure 3**, we show the result of a predictive model (linear regression) that we trained to predict, as a target, the fraction of tenders for counseling in the same period on the whole Italian territory. The regression model was trained from the predictive features that are macroeconomic variables of the economic richness of the regions. These variables are shown in **Table 2** with the coefficients in the regression model.

These economic variables were chosen by the financial and economic institutions in Italy, like Banca d'Italia and Sistema Conti Pubblici Territoriali [25]. Data on these variables were downloaded from ISTAT.[9] To train the regression, we expressed the

Figure 2.
The heat map of the Italian regions on the total amount of expenditure on contracts awarded to economic operators in the regions. Darker colors indicate higher values and lighter colors have lower values. Full-size image available here: https://bit.ly/3M75Pch.

[9] https://esploradati.istat.it/databrowser/#/it/dw/categories.

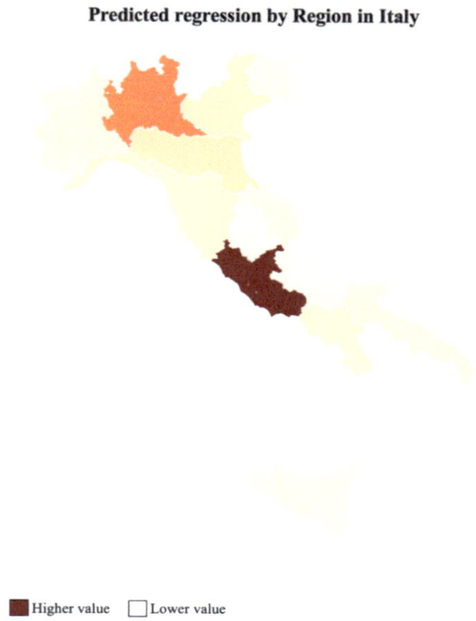

Figure 3.
Predicted fraction of the procurement awarded by economic operators of each region. Darker colors indicate higher values and lighter colors have lower values. Full-size image available here: https://bit.ly/3M75Pch.

Regression variables	Coefficient
Gross Domestic Product of the region (in Italian - PIL)	1.592985
internal consumption	356.007253
expenses for consumption on the territory by families	−273.787177
expenses of private non-profit social institutions serving families	0.275970
expenses for consumption of the public administrations	−44.654956
gross fixed capital formation	−0.661344
number of economic operators resident in the region	0.127807
land area	−0.874896
resident population	0.926562
constant term	0.0145896

Table 2.
Input variables for the regression of the fraction of counseling tenders in the regions with their coefficient.

value of each variable for each region as a fraction of the global value for the Italian territory, so that the ranges of the variables are comparable and none of them can dominate the others in the regression model.

The results of the regression in terms of root mean squared errors (RMSE) are good because RMSE accounts for 0.3%. The intuitive meaning of using linear regression to predict the presence of contracts awarded by economic operators in the regions, based on socio-economic data of the regions, is that the presence of awarded contracts is proportional to the economic wealth of the people living

Region	Macro-area	Amount (Euro)	Predicted fraction
Abruzzo	Mezzogiorno	734,973,355.25	−0.006508
Aosta Valley	North	1,273,734,015.66	0.010198
Apulia	Mezzogiorno	5,881,228,868.15	0.026437
Basilicata	Mezzogiorno	930,324,140.31	−0.006734
Calabria	Mezzogiorno	751,751,372.06	−0.009588
Campania	Mezzogiorno	3,380,554,743.60	0.034156
Emilia-Romagna	North	16,192,602,344.01	0.061392
Friuli Venezia Giulia	North	2,538,965,895.64	0.008922
Lazio	Center	83,322,638,530.51	0.436136
Liguria	North	5,416,448,787.22	0.035922
Lombardy	North	18,370,982,885.57	0.244621
Marche	Center	2,986,739,413.73	0.019560
Molise	Mezzogiorno	147,358,035.15	0.003210
Piedmont	North	3,987,636,944.23	0.014454
Sardinia	Mezzogiorno	10,822,040,833.39	−0.015567
Sicily	Mezzogiorno	3,483,991,756.14	0.014344
Trentino-South Tyrol	North	13,090,022,541.79	0.118560
Tuscany	Center	13,255,987,874.61	0.039263
Umbria	Center	1,819,818,815.68	−0.000578
Veneto	North	7,081,496,000.08	0.049062

Table 3.
[left & center columns] Region, macro-area, and amounts awarded to economic operators in the region shown in ***Figure 2****; [right column] the fraction of tenders in Italy for each region predicted by regression shown in* ***Figure 3****.*

in the region and to the number of economic operators. The coefficients of the regression agree with this interpretation (see right column of **Table 2**). Among the variables, the most important ones are those with a higher and positive coefficient, that are *internal consumption*, *GDP*, and *number of economic operators* while those that are negatively correlated with the target have a large negative coefficient: *expenses for consumption on the territory by families* and *expenses for consumption of the public administrations*.

The total amounts for counseling tenders for each region are shown in **Table 3** together with the proportion of tenders predicted by the regression model. If the predicted value of the fraction of tenders awarded is negative, it means that for those regions, the estimated value is higher than the actual value. This means that in these regions, we would expect proportionally more tenders to be awarded: this is the case for many regions in the Mezzogiorno. In Section 4.1, we go deeper into the analysis by considering the fairness of the distribution of tenders in the three macro-areas mentioned.

4.1 Analysis of the fairness of participation in tenders and the award of contracts to economic operators of different origins

In this analysis, we consider three variables:

1. S represents the sensitive variable, also called group, which, in the case study of this chapter, denotes the macro-region of origin (North, Center, or Mezzogiorno) of the economic operators that won the tenders.

2. Y represents the ground truth of the analyzed process, which, in the case study, denotes the actual proportion of tenders awarded to economic operators in the macro-areas.

3. R denotes the score, i.e., the result of the AI/ML model that predicts the target given the observed characteristics or given an assumption (often called the null hypothesis in statistics). In the case of this chapter, R is the score obtained by the linear regression that predicts the proportion of tenders awarded to economic operators in the macro-area according to the socio-economic characteristics of the area in **Tables 2** and **3**.

The three concepts introduced in the study of Caton and Haas [24] are applied. The formulae that must be satisfied for all groups to prove the fairness of the process are reported.

1. *Independence*: the score of the predictive model must be independent of the sensitive variable: $R \perp S$

2. *Separation*: the score of the predictive model must be independent of the sensitive variable, given the ground truth variable: $R \perp S|Y$

3. *Sufficiency*: the ground truth variable must be independent of the sensitive variable given the predicted score: $Y \perp S|R$

There is some difficulty in testing the statistical independence of the variables because of the limited number of observations (20, the number of administrative regions in Italy). Some statistical tests such as χ^2 [26] give reliable results if data obeys some assumptions that are not always valid in our data (for instance, no value in the contingency table should be less or equal to five but this occurs since data are spread into the different groups according to the macro-area). As a solution [26], we grouped the continuous values of variables R and Y in two bins (low, high) separated by the median value of their frequency distribution. After this transformation, the problem of testing independence according to the above formulae for testing fairness transforms into a new test described as follows.

The test aims to calculate the probability that a Bernoulli process resulted in the given observations shown in **Table 4**. The Bernoulli random events represent the frequency of tender awards to economic operators in a region occurring above or below the median, assuming they are independent and are not different in the country regions.

Since the independence test for separation (sufficiency) is conditional on the Y (R) variable, whose values are divided into two bins, the independence test in the two bins is repeated separately. Each observation on a region is treated as a Bernoulli trial in which we made the null hypothesis that counseling tender awards have the same probability of occurring in the regions of the three macro-areas. The probability that the Bernoulli process results as observed in **Table 4** is given by the well-known formula:

		Y low bin	Y high bin
R low bin	Center	2	0
	Mezzogiorno	6	0
	North	2	1
R high bin	Center	1	1
	Mezzogiorno	0	2
	North	0	7
		R low bin	**R high bin**
Y low bin	Center	2	0
	Mezzogiorno	7	0
	North	1	1
Y high bin	Center	1	1
	Mezzogiorno	0	1
	North	0	8

Table 4.
Distribution of the regions of the three macro-areas to the lower or higher bin for the independence tests according to sufficiency (upper contingency table) and separation (lower contingency table).

$$\Pr = \frac{p^k (1-p)^{(n-k)} n!}{k!(n-k)!} \quad (1)$$

where n is the number of trials (regions, 20) and k is the observed number of occurrences in the lower bin (or the higher) for the regions of the three groups (macro-areas). $p = 0.5$ is the probability that an observation falls in the lower bin according to the null hypothesis. Bins were created on the values of the variables Y (and R) according to the threshold of the median value that, by definition, is the value that leaves half of the observations below it and the other half above. In our case, it is the probability that tender awards occur in a region with values of Y (and R) lower than the median.

Since our sample has a limited size, for the independence tests, Fisher's exact test [10] must be applied using the formula 1 for the three cases in which we observe one or fewer regions in one of the two bins and all the remaining regions in the other. In both the cases of separation and sufficiency, the probability of obtaining the observed results from the Bernoulli process under the null hypothesis is extremely low and equal to $3.433 \cdot 10^{-5}$. For the simpler, independence test $S \perp R$, we grouped the two macro-areas of Center and Mezzogiorno in which the regions tend to have a lower proportion of awarded tenders and kept the regions of the North in a separate category. The above reasoning was repeated and concluded that the probability of observing a situation so unbalanced or more extreme is again very low $\left(6 \cdot 10^{-5}\right)$.

Conclusions are that the estimation of the counseling tender awards by the linear regression model is not fair according to the definitions of fairness in the field of

[10] For the formulation of Fisher's exact test, see for instance: https://en.wikipedia.org/wiki/Fisher's_exact_test.

Explainable AI. The unfairness does not denote limits of the model itself: it can foresee precisely the ground truth of the actual tender awarding process in the three macro-areas. On the contrary, the unfairness of an accurate model in predicting the ground truth denotes the unfairness of the distribution of ground truth variable across groups.

Several other analyses were repeated (which cannot be described here for reasons of space), also taking into account the amount of each tender (with the amount divided into four levels) and the size of the economic operators (divided into four levels) according to the share capital of the company: similar results are always confirmed. Whatever the macro-area of the public administration, and especially when the size of the company is large and the amount of the tender is high, the public administrations tend to award the tenders with a higher probability to the regions of the North (or Center), but not to the Mezzogiorno. This result is particularly unbalanced and unfavorable for Mezzogiorno, given that the total number of enterprises in the Mezzogiorno and in the Center is not proportionally lower than that in the North, but approximately equal (even if the enterprises in the North tend to be larger).

The socio-ethical consequences of the inequalities observed are a lack of equal opportunities for economic operators in the Mezzogiorno. The observations confirm the historical gap that exists in Italy between the Mezzogiorno and the rest of Italy (the so-called southern question). On the one hand, it highlights the increasing difficulty and persistent disadvantage of Mezzogiorno operators in competing at the national level. On the other hand, it could highlight the existence of a possible reduced confidence on the part of contracting authorities in the ability of economic operators in the Mezzogiorno to carry out a public contract successfully, at a reduced cost and in a shorter period of time, given their persistent difficulties of operation and the difficult socio-economic context. The recommendations for the stakeholders are to carefully monitor the fairness indicators of the tender awarding process. For policymakers, it is a matter of proposing regulatory correctives, but also of carefully monitoring the efficiency of the use of resources by economic operators once they have been awarded public contracts. Here too, the large amount of data available in the ANAC database is useful, as it provides many examples of contract performance that can be used for comparison and as examples of best practice.

5. Predictive tasks

In the predictive tasks, several ML models were employed to evaluate their performance and accuracy in handling complex datasets. The models included Logistic Regression (LR), Decision Tree (DT), Random Forest (RF), XGBoost (XGB), and Naive Bayes (NB), each offering distinct advantages and trade-offs explored in this research.

LR, a linear model, is often used for binary classification tasks. It is straightforward and interpretable, making it a suitable baseline model. However, its simplicity limits its effectiveness in capturing complex relationships in high-dimensional or non-linear data [27].

DT, a non-linear model, splits data based on feature importance, making it more flexible than LR. DT is easy to interpret and can handle both numerical and categorical data. However, it tends to overfit the training data if not properly tuned, leading to reduced generalization on unseen data [28].

RF builds on the decision tree model by creating an ensemble of trees, improving robustness, and reducing overfitting. It performs well on complex datasets due to its ability to capture non-linear patterns and interactions between features. RF also provides feature importance scores, making it useful for interpretability in large datasets [29].

XGB, an advanced gradient boosting algorithm, often outperforms other models in terms of accuracy, especially with complex datasets. It builds trees sequentially, optimizing for errors made by previous trees, which allows for a more refined learning process. XGBoost is highly efficient in handling large-scale data but requires careful tuning of hyperparameters to achieve optimal performance [30].

NB is a probabilistic model based on Bayes' theorem, and while it performs well in certain text classification tasks or cases where feature independence can be assumed, it is generally less effective with complex, non-linear datasets. Its main advantage is its computational efficiency, which makes it useful for large datasets with simple relationships [31].

In particular, the described experiment aims to identify procurement that has undergone variations. Variations could be used by economic operators as a "kind of strategy" to gain back part of the lot amount that they originally lowered to have more chances of being awarded the contract. Thus, variations impact the final contract price and time and alter the budget allocations. Specifically, funds allocated to a variant are no longer available for other activities, thus unbalancing the overall expenditure. Therefore, procurement for services (S), namely *consultancy services*, was selected for this experiment. To keep the dataset balanced in the consultancy-related variants, procurement with the same CPV divisions (73 and 85) was chosen 4 years before COVID-19 (2016–2019); the resulting dataset thus consists of 25,732 tenders.

The dataset contains procurement marked by whether they include a variant (*label* = 1) or not (*label* = 0). The two classes are inherently imbalanced, with one possibly more prevalent than the other. The dataset was balanced by sampling equal numbers from each class to address this. This ensures that the ML models do not favor the more frequent class, thus providing a fair evaluation. The balanced data was randomly divided into training, validation, and test sets, with an 80–10–10 split, where the test set was reserved for unseen data to evaluate model performance on new, unobserved examples. Features were standardized and encoded to improve the performance of certain models, ensuring they operate effectively across varying scales of input data. In detail, based on the dataset described in **Table 1**, several preprocessing steps were applied to prepare the data for ML models. *Numerical fields*, such as the Tender amount and Awarded amount, were normalized to bring all values within a standard range, ensuring that no single variable dominated the learning process due to differences in scale. *Categorical fields* like Tender type were encoded using one-hot encoding, which converts the categories into binary vectors for compatibility with ML algorithms. For *boolean fields*, such as the Framework Agreement and Subcontracting admitted, a boolean encoding was used, where 1 indicates true and 0 indicates false. These preprocessing steps are standard in ML to ensure that the data is in a format suitable for training, reducing bias, and improving the accuracy of the models [32]. As described at the beginning of this section, various models were trained: LR, DT, RF, XGB, and NB. These models were chosen for their diverse capabilities, from simple interpretations to handling complex, non-linear relationships. Hyperparameter tuning was conducted on the models using the Hyperopt library to optimize their performance and identify the best combination of parameters for accurately predicting procurement affected by variants. The models were evaluated using *cross-validation* [33] to test their generalization capabilities. This method ensures that models perform well across different subsets of data, reducing the risk of overfitting the training set. Model performance was assessed using Accuracy [34], Precision [34], Recall [34], and F1-Score.[11] These metrics provide insights into how well each model can identify procurement with variations, which is crucial for understanding their budgetary impacts. The data and scripts for this part of the experiments are publicly available.[12]

5.1 Predictive tasks: Results

The cross-validation metrics provide a robust evaluation of model performance by accounting for variability in the data, as highlighted in **Figure 4** and **Table 5**. Among the models analyzed, XGB demonstrates superior performance, with the highest cross-validated accuracy of 0.965 and $F1$-Score of 0.965. This indicates high precision in its predictions and a strong balance between precision and recall, with precision and recall values of 0.983 and 0.947, respectively, making it an ideal choice for datasets where both false positives and false negatives are costly. The RF model also performs well, with an accuracy of 0.947 and an $F1$-Score of 0.948. Although slightly lower than XGB, it still offers a commendable trade-off between recall and precision, reflected in its precision of 0.957. This suggests that RF is reliable in applications where precision is prioritized, albeit with slightly less balance than XGB. The DT model showcases a moderate performance, with an accuracy of 0.953 and an $F1$-Score of 0.954. Despite having lower overall precision than the RF and XGB models, it achieves a high precision of 0.965, indicating its effectiveness in scenarios

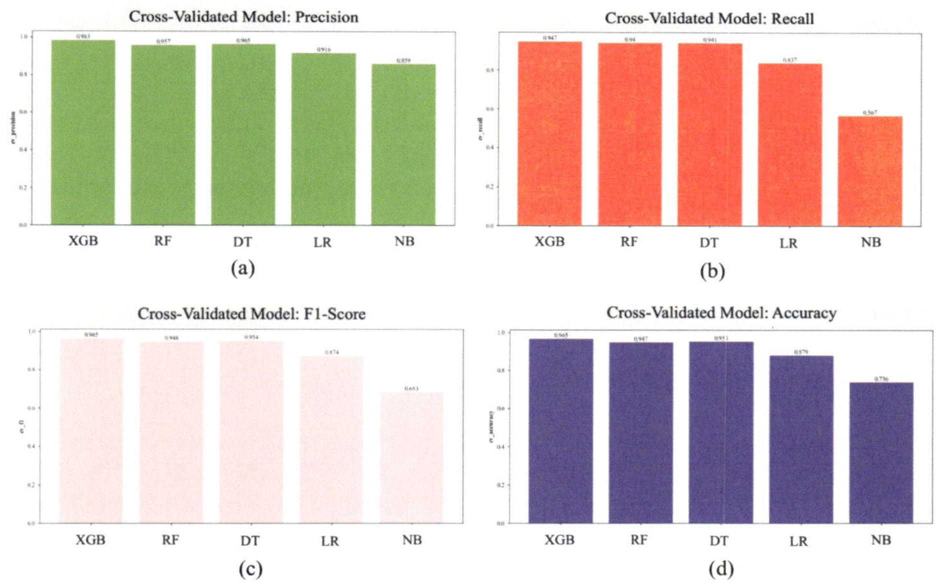

Figure 4.
Predictive model results by metric: (a) Precision, (b) Recall, (c) F1-Score, (d) Accuracy. The x-axis contains the model name while the y-axis contains the obtained value of the metric. Full-size image available here: https://bit.ly/3M75Pch.

[11] F1-Score is the harmonic mean between recall and precision, and it is often used for combining precision and recall in a unique measure of the prediction performance.

[12] https://github.com/roberto-nai/ANAC-OD-ETHICAL.

Model	Accuracy	F1-Score	Precision	Recall
XGBoost	0.965	0.965	0.983	0.947
Random Forest	0.947	0.948	0.957	0.940
Decision Tree	0.953	0.954	0.965	0.941
Logistic Regression	0.879	0.874	0.916	0.837
Naive Bayes	0.736	0.683	0.859	0.567

Table 5.
Predictive models results: (a) Precision, (b) Recall, (c) F1-Score, (d) Accuracy. In bold the best model, underlined *the second.*

where correct positive predictions are more critical than capturing all potential positive instances. In contrast, LR and NB present substantially lower cross-validation metrics. LR achieves an accuracy of 0.879 and an *F*1-Score of 0.874, reflecting its limited ability to capture the complexities in the data compared to ensemble methods. Similarly, NB records the lowest performance across the board, with an accuracy of 0.736 and an *F*1-Score of 0.683, indicating that its assumptions may not align well with the underlying data distribution. Overall, the cross-validation metrics emphasize the robustness of ensemble methods, particularly XGB and RF, in delivering consistent and reliable predictions across varying datasets.

The recommendations for stakeholders are to carefully monitor the incidence of variations in total costs and contract completion times. For policymakers, it is a matter of proposing regulatory corrections, but also of carefully monitoring the overall impact of variations on public expenditure. Again, the big data available in the ANAC database can help, as it can be used to model the general behavior of economic operators in proposing and executing tenders, and compare them specifically for the frequency of variation requests. Data analysts and machine learning tools applied to the big data of public contracts could detect economic operators that represent anomalies in proposing several variations in a recurring manner and, on the contrary, propose best practices and examples of virtuous behavior.

6. Recommendation systems

By filtering the database for a description of CPV codes related to "consultancy" tenders, we obtained 72 CPV codes. In particular, the CPV codes used for filtering the ANAC database are mainly from these divisions based on the first two digits: **Table 6** shows the list of CPV codes retrieved by using the recommendation system on the description of codes. Results show that there are 25 categories of CPV codes starting with the 71XXX000-Y division which are related to counseling.

6.1 Item retrieval and precision score

The recommendation system trained on the original ANAC database was used to obtain the top 10 tenders most similar to each of the "consultancy" tenders used as a query example.

For item retrieval, we used a Bert LaBSE model (Language-agnostic Bidirectional Transformer Sentence Embedding) [20]. Embedding [18] is a transformative

Divisions	Description of CPV code	Categories
71XXX000-Y	Architectural consulting services, Construction consulting services, Geological and geophysical consulting services, Construction consulting services	25
72XXX000-Y	Software consulting services, Software integration consulting services, Hardware integration consulting services	11
73XXX000-Y	Research and development-related consulting services, Consulting in the field of research and development	4
66XXX000-Y	Financial advisory services, Financial transaction management and clearing services	4
79XXX000-Y	Software copyright consulting services	21
85XXX000-Y	Counseling services provided by nursing staff, Guidance and counseling services	3
66XXX000-Y	Consulting services in the field of insurance	4
30XXX000-Y	Computer equipment	1
22XXX000-Y	Computer manuals	1
98XXX000-Y	Equal opportunity counseling services	1

Table 6.
CPV division codes related to counseling and their category, used to filter the ANAC database for tenders to train the recommendation system.

approach to natural language that has become popular with deep artificial neural networks trained on large volumes of documents. It is used to represent the semantic content of documents written in natural language. As it is the case of language-agnostic models, documents might be written even in many languages. Embeddings were employed to treat the short description of procurement provided with the tender subject field in the ANAC database. Embeddings of the tender subjects represent, in a concise yet quite general and powerful way, the topic referred to in the tender subject. Embeddings are numerical vector representations that capture the semantic essence of the data. Cosine similarity was later used to find similar items.

To retrieve tenders related to the users' interest from ANAC-approved tenders, a query in natural language can be submitted by the user and processed to retrieve the top k tenders more similar to the description provided by the query. For example, **Table 7** shows the top 10 most similar tenders related to the query "legal counseling".[13] Cosine similarity [35], a mathematical metric used to measure the similarity between two vectors in a multi-dimensional space, is then used to compare these embeddings. It involves calculating the cosine of the angle between the embeddings, providing a measure of how similar they are, based on orientation rather than magnitude. **Table 7** shows the results obtained by the user when a query is made. The system, when processed the user's query and transformed it into an embedding using the deep neural network of Bert LaBSE, uses cosine similarity to measure the relevance of tenders in its database to the query. This ensures that the most similar and relevant tenders are returned, enhancing the efficiency and effectiveness of the

[13] In the original database, the tender object was in Italian: "SERVIZI LEGALI" and "SERVIZI DI ASSISTENZA LEGALE".

Query	Cig	Top k Tenders subject	Code CPV	Accuracy
1	69665502ED	LEGAL SERVICES	79,111,000-5	TP
2	8,018,638,568	LEGAL SERVICES	79,111,000-5	TP
3	76317249DE	LEGAL SERVICES	79,111,000-5	TP
4	8,139,176,483	LEGAL ASSISTANCE SERVICES	79,110,000-8	TP
5	78756296A5	LEGAL ASSISTANCE SERVICES	79,110,000-8	TP
6	8139089CB5	LEGAL ASSISTANCE SERVICES	79,110,000-8	TP
7	7993481D2F	LEGAL ASSISTANCE SERVICES	79,110,000-8	TP
8	7,912,174,489	LEGAL ASSISTANCE SERVICES	79,110,000-8	TP
9	79122199AA	LEGAL ASSISTANCE SERVICES	79,110,000-8	TP
10	7856558CC0	LEGAL ASSISTANCE SERVICES	79,110,000-8	TP

Table 7.
Top k tenders retrieved by the recommendation system for the query "LEGAL SERVICES" with $k = 10$.

search. However, these results can be explained by looking at the texts of the notices taken into consideration. Clearly, for the example provided by the query "legal counseling" for the recommendation system, it is easy to recognize that the sets of tenders shown in **Table 7** whose descriptions are "LEGAL SERVICES" and "LEGAL ASSISTANCE SERVICES" are similar to the query and to each other. These are assigned a cosine similarity of 0.99 and the two calls appear to be, each other, among the top 10 of their neighbors. If we consider as true positives (TP) the neighbors who are also of the "consultancy" type, we can calculate the *precision@*10 using the following formula:

$$\text{Precision@10} = \frac{\text{Relevant tenders in } top \text{ 10 recommendations}}{10} = \frac{TP}{10} \quad (2)$$

We tested the recommendation system for 100 queries randomly selected from the database with CPV in **Table 6**. We also filled the database with irrelevant examples randomly selected from the rest of the ANAC database to give the system also examples of irrelevant cases for the query. Their number is equal to the number of cases with CPV in **Table 6**. The obtained results of the recommendation system are that *precision@*10 values are, on average, equal to 0.85 considering the list of the top 10 most similar results to the queries. Results indicate that *more than half* of the recommended tenders out of the top 10 are of the "consultancy" type, and are similar to the tender under investigation (query tender). **Table 8** and the side picture show the results of precision for the tender recommendation system for random queries with CPV in **Table 6**. It results that 74.15% of queries have an extremely high precision score (equal to 0.9) while there is almost 8% of queries whose recommended tenders were less similar (with the lowest precision scores, in the two ranges 0.20–0.40 and 0.40–0.60).

The results allow to make claims for stakeholders: they should spread the possibility of using machine learning tools and recommendation systems, making the search for cases more effective and speeding up the bidding and awarding processes. If contracting authorities had a complete collection of cases similar to their own at

Precision score range	Percentage
> 0.90	74.15
0.80–0.90	4.49
0.60–0.80	8.98
0.40–0.60	3.37
0.20–0.40	4.49
<0.20	4.49

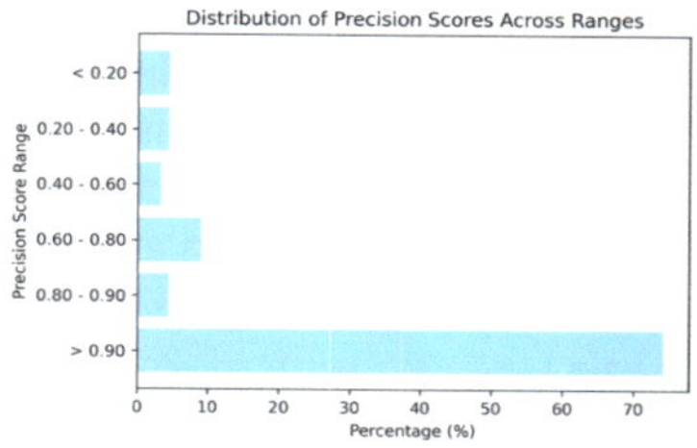

Table 8.
Distribution of precision scores for the tender recommendation system for random queries with CPV in ***Table 6****.*

the moment they were drawing up their tender, they could prepare their tender with the most appropriate constraints. As a result, we would expect to see a lower number of no bids. Similarly, if economic operators had a collection of similar cases to their own, they would propose more appropriate bids and see a higher success rate in their bidding, with a consequent reduction in effort and resources.

7. Conclusions

The case of tenders issued by public administrations in Italy in the field of consultancy over a period of 4 years is considered. A full analysis of the data in the ANAC database was carried out. A descriptive analysis of the data was applied in the form of a geographical heat map, which highlighted that Lazio was the Italian region with the highest number of tenders in consultancy.

Ensuring ethical and fair practices in public procurement is essential, particularly in light of regional economic disparities. The proposed study leverages ML models to assess fairness in the awarding of contracts. By applying fairness tests (independence, separation, and sufficiency), the discussed study shows that contracts tend to be awarded more frequently in northern regions compared to southern ones, despite similar economic conditions. This raises concerns about equity and fairness in the allocation of public funds, making it crucial to implement AI systems that promote fairness and reduce biases. The obtained results confirm the persistence of the historical southern question in Italy, the socio-economic consequences of which are inequality and unequal opportunities for the population throughout the Italian territory. Future procurement processes should consider these findings to ensure fair opportunities for all regions.

As regards the predictive task, the experiments successfully identified procurement cases with variants, highlighting their effects on budget distribution. When a variant causes an increase in the final price, it alters expenditure allocations, potentially depriving other activities of necessary funds. The predictive tasks highlight that XGBoost (accuracy 96.5%) outperformed all other models, making it ideal for predicting tender contract variations where both false positives and negatives are costly. RF (accuracy 94.7%) also showed strong performance, while Logistic Regression and Naive Bayes were less effective, with lower metrics indicating their unsuitability for complex datasets. For public authorities, implementing XGBoost or Random Forest models can help prevent delays and cost overruns by accurately predicting variations in bids. Policymakers should focus on integrating these AI tools to ensure fair and efficient public procurement processes. Contractors can use the insights from these models to better structure their bids.

Another discussed task is to train recommendation systems on the description of the tender topics. The recent technology of transformers (SBERT) was used, which is very successful in grouping texts with similar content. This type of recommendation service could be extremely useful to speed up the search for interesting cases in a large volume of examples, as well as to find similar situations or economic operators working in the same domain. The recommendation system boosts bidders' experience to access and design with more competitive techniques by providing insights into previous bidders and winners for similar tenders. The results obtained by the recommendation system trained on the same consultancy data show that the majority of the queries (74.15%) submitted to the system have a high precision score (higher than 0.90), which serves as an evaluation of the relevance of the answers within the top 10 results. If the remaining precision score ranges are considered (below 0.90) the percentage of queries drops to values similar to 4.49, this indicates that a very small number of queries resulted in less relevant outputs and shows that the performance of the system follows a skewed distribution, skewed toward the high precision scores. However, analyzing the characteristics of these lower-performing queries can reveal specific patterns or contexts where the system struggles.

The recommendation to stakeholders and policymakers is to enlarge and enforce the use of AI/ML tools to assist actors in the public contract bidding process and execution in order to effectively use the available big data and make the process more efficient in the use of resources. A recommendation system based on a Large Language Model (LLM) specifically trained on tenders and their related data (such as bid amount, successful bidders, and contracting authorities) can improve the tendering process for the various stakeholders in decision-making and improve the efficiency of the operations. It indicates the most relevant tenders by analyzing the supplier's or company's history and the expertise related to the area of interest. The LLM-based recommendation system can offer insights into risk assessment by keeping a track record of specific sectors of winning bidders and allowing the financial authorities to access the risk of investment and finances for specific companies. The future work is to employ the presented tools to discover anomalies, propose best practices, and recommend suitable actors in order to enlarge, especially in the Mezzogiorno, the economic operators' participation in the public tenders.

As Artificial Intelligence continues to transform delicate sectors of society, from healthcare to finance, it is crucial to ensure transparency, trust, and acceptance of AI technology [2]. Unfortunately, the complexity of many AI models often renders them "black boxes" with limited interpretability. Future works consider integrating Explainable AI (XAI) in predictive and recommendation models.

Acknowledgements

The authors thank the Department of Management for supporting this research with legal domain experts in public tenders, particularly Prof. Gabriella Margherita Racca and Dr. Francesco Gorgerino for contributing to understanding the procurement domain.

Conflict of interest

The authors declare no conflict of interest.

Appendices and addenda must be cited in the main text (example: See Appendix A). The section containing them must be titled accordingly ("Appendices", "Appendix A", "Addendum", "Nomenclature", etc). An example of appendix/addendum/nomenclature is given below:

Abbreviations

ANAC	National authority for anti-corruption
CPV	common procurement vocabulary
ISTAT	Italian statistical institute
PIL	gross domestic product

Author details

Ishrat Fatima*†, Roberto Nai† and Rosa Meo†
Computer Science Department, University of Turin, Torino, IT, Italy

*Address all correspondence to: ishrat.fatima@unito.it

†These authors contributed equally.

References

[1] ANAC. Catalog of Open Data ANAC. 2024. Available from: https://dati.anticorruzione.it/opendata [Accessed: August 10, 2024]

[2] Meo R, Nai R, Sulis E. Explainable, interpretable, trustworthy, responsible, ethical, fair, verifiable AI. What's next? In: Advances in Databases and Information Systems - 26th European Conference, ADBIS 2022; 5-8 September 2022; Turin, Italy. Lecture Notes in Computer Science. Vol. 13389. Heidelberg, DE: Springer; 2022. pp. 25-34. DOI: 10.1007/978-3-031-15740-0_3

[3] Barocas S, Hardt M, Narayanan A. Fairness and Machine Learning Limitations and Opportunities, 2018. Cambridge, MA: The MIT Press ebook; 19 December 2023. pp. 55-60. Available from: https://api.semanticscholar.org/CorpusID:113402716

[4] Nai R, Sulis E, Pasteris P, Giunta M, Meo R. Exploitation and merge of information sources for public procurement improvement. In: International Workshops of ECML PKDD 2022 Grenoble, France; 19-23 September 2022 Proceedings, Part I. Heidelberg, DE: Springer; 2023. pp. 89-102. DOI: 10.1007/978-3-031-23618-1_6

[5] Nai R, Sulis E, Genga L. Automated analysis with event log enrichment of the European public procurement processes. In: Sales TP, Guizzardi G, Araújo J, Borbinha J, Guizzardi G, editors. Advances in Conceptual Modeling: ER 2023 Workshops, CMLS, CMOMM4FAIR, EmpER, JUSMOD, OntoCom, QUAMES, and SmartFood; 6-9 November 2023; Lisbon, Portugal. Lecture Notes in Computer Science (LNCS). Vol. 14319. Heidelberg, DE: Springer; 2023. pp. 178-188. DOI: 10.1007/978-3-031-47112-4_17

[6] Goebel P, Reuter C, Pibernik R, Sichtmann C. The influence of ethical culture on supplier selection in the context of sustainable sourcing. International Journal of Production Economics. 2012;**140**(1):7-17. DOI: 10.1016/j.ijpe.2012.01.021

[7] Kim S, Colicchia C, Menachof D. Ethical sourcing: An analysis of the literature and implications for future research. Journal of Business Ethics. 2018;**152**(4):1033-1052. DOI: 10.1007/s10551-016-3369-4

[8] Hazen BT, Boone CA, Ezell JD, Jones-Farmer LA. Artificial intelligence and big data analytics for supply chain resilience: A systematic literature review. Annals of Operations Research. 2021;**299**(1):277-315. DOI: 10.1007/s10479-019-03472-8

[9] Belhadi A, Kamble S, Wamba SF, Gunasekaran A, Ndubisi NO, Venkatesh M. Artificial intelligence and big data analytics for supply chain resilience: A systematic literature review. Annals of Operations Research. 2021;**302**(1):1-52. DOI: 10.1007/s10479-020-03626-1

[10] Goodwin D, Bok B, Zhao F, Zhang P. A systematic literature review of research on social procurement in the construction and infrastructure sector: Barriers, enablers, and strategies. Sustainability. 2023;**15**(17):12964. DOI: 10.3390/su151712964

[11] Nai R, Sulis E, Meo R. Public procurement fraud detection and artificial intelligence techniques: A literature review. In: Symeonidou D,

Yu R, Ceolin D, Poveda-Villalón M, Audrito D, Caro LD, et al., editors. Companion Proceedings of the 23rd International Conference on Knowledge Engineering and Knowledge Management. Vol. 3256. Bozen-Bolzano, Italy: CEUR-WS.org, 2022. Available from: https://ceur-ws.org/Vol-3256/km4law4.pdf

[12] Nai R, Fatima I, Morina G, Sulis E, Genga L, Meo R, et al. AI applied to the analysis of the contracts of the Italian public administrations. In: Falchi F, Giannotti F, Monreale A, Boldrini C, Rinzivillo S, Colantonio S, editors. Proceedings of the Italia Intelligenza Artificiale - Thematic Workshops co-Located with the 3rd CINI National lab AIIS Conference on Artificial Intelligence (Ital IA 2023), Pisa, Italy, May 29-30, 2023, CEUR Workshop Proceedings. CEUR-WS.org. Vol. 3486. 2023. pp. 255-260. Available from: https://ceur-ws.org/Vol-3486/100.pdf

[13] Hoejmose SU, Adrien-Kirby PAJ. Socially and environmentally responsible procurement: A literature review and future research agenda of a managerial issue in the 21st century. Journal of Purchasing and Supply Management. 2012;**18**(4):232-242. DOI: 10.1016/j.pursup.2012.06.002

[14] Lozano R. A holistic perspective on corporate sustainability drivers. Corporate Social Responsibility and Environmental Management. 2015;**22**(1):32-44. DOI: 10.1002/csr.1325

[15] Dhanani J, Mehta R, Rana D. Legal document recommendation system: A cluster based pairwise similarity computation. Journal of Intelligent and Fuzzy Systems. 2021;**41**(5):5497-5509. DOI: 10.3233/JIFS-202576

[16] Nai R, Meo R, Morina G, Pasteris P. Public tenders, complaints, machine learning and recommender systems: A case study in public administration. Computer Law and Security Review. 2023;**51**:105887. DOI: 10.1016/j.clsr.2023.105887

[17] Reimers N, Gurevych I. Sentence-BERT: Sentence embeddings using Siamese BERT-networks. In: Proceedings of the 2019 Conference on Empirical Methods in Natural Language Processing and the 9th International Joint Conference on Natural Language Processing (EMNLP-IJCNLP); 3-7 November 2019; Hong Kong. 2019. pp. 3982-3992. DOI: 10.18653/v1/d19-1410

[18] Devlin J, Chang M-W, Lee K, Toutanova K. BERT: Pre-Training of Deep Bidirectional Transformers for Language Understanding. 2019. eprint: 1810.04805. arXiv, cs.CL. Available from: https://arxiv.org/abs/1810.04805

[19] SBERT.net. SentenceTransformers Documentation. GitHub; 2023. Available from: https://sbert.net/ [Accessed: August 10, 2024]

[20] Feng F, Yang Y, Cer D, Arivazhagan N, Wang W. Language-Agnostic BERT Sentence Embedding. 2022. eprint: 2007.01852. arXiv, cs.CL. Available from: https://arxiv.org/abs/2007.01852

[21] Nai R, Sulis E, Fatima I, Meo R. Large language models and recommendation systems: A proof-of-concept study on public procurements. In: Rapp A, Di Caro L, Meziane F, Sugumaran V, editors. Natural Language Processing and Information Systems. Switzerland, Cham: Springer Nature; 2024. pp. 280-290. DOI: 10.1007/978-3-031-70242-6_27

[22] van Dijk E, Wilke H. Differential interests, equity, and public good provision. Journal of Experimental Social Psychology. 1993. ISSN

0022-1031;**29**(1):1-16. DOI: 10.1006/jesp.1993.1001

[23] Decarolis F, Giorgiantonio C. Corruption red flags in public procurement: New evidence from Italian calls for tenders. EPJ Data Science. 2022;**11**(1):1-38. DOI: 10.1140/epjds/s13688-022-00325-x

[24] Caton S, Haas C. Fairness in machine learning: A survey. ACM Computing Surveys. 2024;**56**(7), Art. No.: 166:1-38. DOI: 10.1145/3616865

[25] Lombardini S. Modello macroeconomico previsionale per il PIL delle regioni italiane. Italy: CPT Ricerca and University of Genova; 2022. ISBN 9791280477170

[26] Khatun M, Siddiqui S. Testing pairs of continuous random variables for independence: A simple heuristic. Journal of Computational Mathematics and Data Science. 2021;**1**:100012. DOI: 10.1016/j.jcmds.2021.100012. ISSN 2772-4158

[27] Cox DR. The regression analysis of binary sequences. Journal of the Royal Statistical Society: Series B (Methodological). 1958;**20**(2):215-232. Wiley Online Library. DOI: 10.1111/j.2517-6161.1958.tb00292.x

[28] Breiman L, Friedman J, Stone CJ, Olshen RA. Classification and Regression Trees. Belmont, CA: CRC Press; 1984. DOI: 10.1201/9781315139470

[29] Breiman L. Random forests. Machine Learning. 2001;**45**(1):5-32. DOI: 10.1023/A:1010933404324

[30] Chen T, Guestrin C. XGBoost: A scalable tree boosting system. In: Proceedings of the 22nd ACM SIGKDD International Conference on Knowledge Discovery and Data Mining. New York, NY: ACM; 2016. pp. 785-794. DOI: 10.1145/2939672.2939785

[31] Domingos P, Pazzani M. On the optimality of the simple Bayesian classifier under zero-one loss. Machine Learning. 1997;**29**(2-3):103-130. DOI: 10.1023/A:1007413511361

[32] Géron A. Hands-on Machine Learning with Scikit-Learn, Keras, and TensorFlow: Concepts, Tools, and Techniques to Build Intelligent Systems. 2nd ed. Sebastopol, CA: O'Reilly Media; 2019. ISBN 978-1492032649. Available from: https://www.oreilly.com/library/view/hands-on-machine-learning/9781492032632/10.5555/3380750

[33] Kohavi R. A study of cross-validation and bootstrap for accuracy estimation and model selection. In: Proceedings of the 14th International Joint Conference on Artificial Intelligence (IJCAI). Vol. 2. 1995. pp. 1137-1145. DOI: 10.5555/1643031.1643047

[34] Powers DMW. Evaluation: From precision, recall and F-measure to ROC, informedness, markedness and correlation. Journal of Machine Learning Technologies. 2011;**2**(1):37-63

[35] Duarte GN. The Cosine Similarity and its Use in Recommendation Systems. Medium; 2023. Available from: https://naomy-gomes.medium.com/the-cosine-similarity-and-its-use-in-recommendation-systems-cb2ebd811ce1 [Accessed: August 10, 2024]